T H E
COMPLETE
ADOPTION
HANDBOOK

THE
COMPLETE
ADOPTION
HANDBOOK

KAY MARSHALL STROM
DOUGLAS R. DONNELLY

ZondervanPublishingHouse
Grand Rapids, Michigan

A Division of HarperCollinsPublishers

THE COMPLETE ADOPTION HANDBOOK
Copyright © 1985, 1992 by Kay Marshall Strom and Douglas R. Donnelly

Requests for information should be addressed to:
Zondervan Publishing House
Grand Rapids, Michigan 49530

Library of Congress Cataloging-in-Publication Data

Strom, Kay Marshall, 1943–
   The complete adoption handbook/ Kay Marshall Strom & Douglas R.
Donnelly.
     p. cm.
   Rev. and updated ed. of: Chosen families, 1985.
   ISBN 0-310-57461-7 (paper)
    1. Adoption—United States. 2. Adoption—Religious aspects—
Christianity. I. Strom, Kay Marshall, 1943– Chosen families.
Title.
HV875.55.S763   1992
362.7'34—dc20   92–12179
                                             CIP

Permission has been granted by the American Public Welfare Association
(APWA) to reproduce "Independent Adoption Laws and Policies," © 1987
by APWA. All rights reserved. Used by permission.

All Scripture verses, unless otherwise noted, are taken from the *Living Bible*,
copyright © 1971 by Tyndale House Publishers, Wheaton, Illinois 60187.
All rights reserved.

Edited by Becky Fish
Cover design by Foster Design Associates

Printed in the United States of America

92 93 94 95 96 97 /   / 10 9 8 7 6 5 4 3 2 1

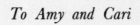

To Amy and Cari

CONTENTS

PREFACE

Homeless children. Caring adults. Drawn together by love and united by adoption, they can become families—real families in which each member is accepted and respected.

Some of you have already expanded your families with one or more adopted children. Congratulations! You have chosen to increase your family in the same way that God increases his. Others of you are just beginning to explore this possibility. It will be exciting to see what God has in store for you.

Before you read further in this book, we want to tell you something about ourselves.

KAY MARSHALL STROM

My husband, Larry, and I are the parents of two children. Lisa is petite, brown-haired, and golden-eyed and is interested in anything artistic or musical. Eric is a tall, slender blond, always intense and always on the go. They are nothing alike in appearance or personality, nor do they share the same interests or abilities. They are not much like their parents, either. But Lisa and Eric are not adopted. Both were born to Larry and me.

Not only am I not an adoptive parent, but I wasn't even an adopted child. So why am I writing this book? What right have I to speak on the subject? Actually, I'm speaking on the very best of authority—the experiences of almost fifty adoptive families.

In the chapters that follow you will be sharing in the lives and deeply emotional experiences of these adoptive families, so it is good for you to know something about them. They run the gamut from a retired couple in their late sixties to a couple in their early thirties who, after years of waiting, have recently welcomed a two-month-old baby into their home. Included among the families are a variety of national backgrounds and lifestyles: doctors and lawyers; secretaries and a librarian; construction workers, an artist, and a musician; teachers, homemakers, and engineers; business professionals, a pilot, and a farmer. Some families are well-to-do while others are struggling to make ends meet.

These families represent many different adoptive situations. Some adopted through agencies while others chose independent adoptions. Some adopted children from overseas. A few have chosen to accept hard-to-place children—those who are older or who have a physical, mental, or emotional handicap. Some, because of death or divorce, are adoptive stepparents. Two are single parents. Many have very happy or deeply moving experiences to relate, but there are a few who, through tears, share in this book the bitterness and pain that adoption has brought to them.

Despite their differences, the people I interviewed all have two things in common: Each is a Christian adoptive parent, and each has an important story to tell. Although their stories are unique, it is interesting to note the threads of similarity that run through them all.

As I interviewed these families and listened to their adoptive experiences, I was struck by the sharply differing points of reference. "Adoption is the only way to go!" announced one obviously satisfied father. "I don't think any family is really complete without an adopted child!" But another stated, "If we had it to do again, my wife and I would remain childless." One parent shook her head and sighed, "There are so many problems with an adopted child," while another happily claimed, "Problems? We haven't had any. If you want my opinion, people make their own problems."

Had any of these families chosen to write a book on adoption, it would almost certainly have been based on their own experiences and therefore would have reflected their own situations—perhaps overly negative, perhaps overly positive, perhaps just narrow in scope. It is only by basing a book on the combined experiences of many families that we can hope to achieve a relatively objective, overall picture of the adoptive experience. My hope and prayer is that this has been achieved in this book and that in the following pages many of you will find a source of help and encouragement. Perhaps you will even discover that special place in the adoptive circle into which you can fit.

I am gratefully indebted to each of the adoptive mothers and fathers who shared their experiences with me. Without them there would be no book. To each of them I say, "Thank you." I was fortunate as well to have had the help, advice, suggestions, and criticism of many professionals who are intimately acquainted with the tough realities of adoption today. In particular, I would like to thank Dr. Samuel McDill, licensed family counselor. His time, interest, and expertise were invaluable in the completion of this book.

DOUGLAS R. DONNELLY

My participation in this book was made possible by two very special young ladies: Amy, age thirteen, and Cari, age eleven. Amy is tall, slender, and has blond hair and green eyes. She is thoughtful, sensitive, kind, and intensely honest. Cari is of average height for her age, has brown hair and eyes, and is playful, outgoing, and bubbly. They are both my daughters, yet neither was delivered by my wife, Gail. Amy was adopted through an agency in California and came into our home when she was twelve days old. Cari was adopted in an independent adoption and was just three days old when we brought her home from the hospital where a brave and loving young woman had given birth to her.

When Gail and I adopted our first daughter, my law practice consisted primarily of real estate law. Following that adoption, friends, acquaintances, and total strangers began approaching me, asking questions about our adoption and requesting that I assist them with their efforts to adopt. In time, the adoption caseload grew to the point where, one day—much to my surprise—I discovered that I had become an adoption lawyer. For the past five years my practice has been limited to adoption law, and I have been involved in about one hundred adoptions each year. At present, I have handled over eight hundred cases.

Because my approach to adoptions is hands-on, I have become very close to many adoptive parents and birth parents over the years, including some of the families whose stories are related throughout this book. As a result, my exposure to the adoption field is broad enough to transcend my individual experience as an adoptive parent. My adoption experience has not only been overwhelmingly positive, but it has been the most rewarding experience of my life. My children are a never-ending source of joy, challenge, and satisfaction. So my perspective on adoption is both broad and positive.

In counseling adopting families, I have found that they almost always ask the same questions. They have the same fears, most of which are the same fears which troubled me when Gail and I began our adoption odyssey. For example, I was concerned that I might have difficulty in fully loving a child who was not genetically mine. Would it take time to develop that full love? How much time? In the pages that follow, we will address these and other frequently asked questions.

As you read this book, we ask that you do so prayerfully. Answer the questions at the end of each chapter thoughtfully. It is our earnest desire and prayer that you discover your own personal answer to the questions, "Is there, somewhere, a child for me?" and "How can I find my child?"

1.

Is There a Child for You?

"Shortly after our marriage, Patrick and I saw a television documentary on the plight of homeless children," said Laura Reid. "That started us thinking. We could either build our own family by bringing children into the world as our parents did, or we could choose to provide a loving Christian home for children who are already living. We decided on the latter. All of our children were to be adopted."

"After Ginger endured three miscarriages and an endless string of tests, the doctor broke the news to us that she would never be able to bear a child," said Bert Delgado. "We have discussed the possibility of adoption, but now it's time for us to check into it seriously. We need to see exactly what our options are."

"My husband and I have three natural children," said Corrine Borowitz, "but we want more. Both Stephen and I have always wanted lots of kids—at least five or six. Adoption seems the perfect way for us to complete our family."

Life is made up of a progression of decisions. We all have to make them. Like the Reids, the Delgados, and the Borowitzes, many of you have made or will be making a decision about the adoption of a child. You are not alone. There are approximately 2.5 million adoptees in the United States, and every one of them represents a similar decision made by their adoptive parents.

Unless you are just beginning to consider adoption, you have probably heard and read conflicting and discouraging reports about what can be expected. You may be feeling

15

frustrated, confused, or simply uninformed. Perhaps you have already adopted, but now you are faced with hard problems and difficult questions for which you feel unprepared. If you fit into either of these categories, this book will help you.

What is adoption? Very simply it means taking a child who was not born to you and making that child your own. It is a legal process governed by the particular laws of your specific state (see Appendix A). But there is more. Adoption is also an emotional process governed by your heart. This is how it is expressed in the Talmud:

> A mother is likened to a mountain spring that nourishes the tree at the root. But one who mothers another's child is likened unto a water that rises into a cloud and goes a long distance to nourish a lone tree in the desert.

It used to be that the emphasis in adoption was put on finding children for childless couples—almost always upper-middle income, well-educated, Anglo-Saxon families. Fortunately that has changed. Today the emphasis is on the children and what is best for them. All children have a right to loving parents, to the security of belonging, and to a permanent place in families of their own.

WHAT DO I HAVE TO OFFER?

So the place to start your consideration of adoption is with yourself. What do you have to offer children? We don't mean material things: money and clothes and toys and private schools. We mean the basic necessities such as love, understanding, guidance, acceptance, security, and the firm foundation that only comes from a well-grounded faith in God. It takes a strong, mature, secure person to be a good parent. Do you qualify? These questions might help you decide:

- Do my family and I want to make a lifelong commitment to children?
- Does my spouse want children as much as I do?

- Do I have a happy, stable marriage flexible enough to include children?
- Can I truly love and accept children who were not born to me? Can I allow them to be themselves, whatever that might be?
- Can I love children through the bad times as well as the good times?
- Can I be reasonable in my expectations for my children? Can I accept failures no matter how big and praise successes no matter how small?
- If I decide to accept older children, can I wait patiently for them to love and accept me? Do I understand that this may take quite a while?
- Can I talk honestly with my children about their adoptions?
- Will I be able to accept and honestly answer my children's questions about their biological parents without feeling threatened or defensive?

Now let us consider another list. These are some excellent reasons *not* to adopt any children:

- Do I feel that adopted children would be second best, not really like my own?
- Would I always be embarrassed about the fact that my children were adopted?
- Do I fear that my adopted children would repeat the mistakes and carry on the problems of their biological parents?
- Do I feel that adopting needy, homeless children is my moral duty? Do I see myself as a rescuer?
- Have I already decided who and what I want my children to be? Would I have trouble accepting children whose abilities and interests were different from my expectations?
- Do I feel that adopting a child might help to hold together my shaky marriage?

We must understand and accept the fact that no child

ever comes with a guarantee. Our precious baby may grow up to be lazy, stubborn, dull, rebellious, or ugly. This is true of biological children and it is true of adopted children. Somehow, though, birth parents seem to have less trouble adjusting to such unexpected traits than adoptive parents do. But the fact is, adoptive parenthood brings with it the very same ups and downs, joys and disappointments as biological parenthood. And there are extra challenges as well.

No one expects us to be perfect parents. There is no such thing, just as there is no such thing as a perfect child. Like children, parents are individuals. Every one of them has problems and personality flaws. The most important consideration is that the adoptive parents be able to meet the physical and emotional needs of their children.

Just what are the needs of children? Unfortunately there is no single right answer to the question, because needs vary from child to child. There are, however, some universals.

All infants' physical needs must be met. Infants are totally dependent on others for their survival and well-being.

Children need good examples on which to base their own actions. They are learning constantly, and what they learn depends on what they see.

Children need the love and care of an adult whom they can trust and who will give them security. Without this they will grow up severely handicapped when it comes time to form other relationships in life.

To develop to their full potential, children need to be raised in an atmosphere of acceptance. They need to be appreciated for who and what they are.

These needs are the same for all children, adopted or not. In fact, there are not nearly so many differences between the two groups as we might imagine. Birth families and adoptive families alike must endure the trials and tribulations of everyday life. Broken bones, temper tantrums, diaper rashes, spilled milk, crying and pouting, sibling rivalry, wet beds, bouts with the flu, disappointing report cards, piano lessons, joys, love, hate, hurts, laughter—they happen to all of us. They are a part of life. Every family has crises and problems, strengths and weaknesses, good times and bad.

Yet adoptive families do face pressures, problems, and questions that other families know nothing about. Even when adopted children grow up in a secure, loving family, they still need to gain some understanding of why they were placed for adoption in the first place. They, and their adoptive parents as well, need to recognize and accept both their birth background and their adoption as part of their identity.

Adopted children are certain to have questions about their birth parents (see chapter 11). At times they will feel different and wonder if they belong at all. This may cause you to think that you were a failure as a parent and that your children don't love you. That's not true. Their questions and anxieties are simply a part of growing up. Over the years your children have learned to trust you, and when they are in need of help and support it is to you that they will turn. After all, you are their parent.

When we think of adoption, we tend to think of childless couples who choose babies very similar in appearance to what their own biological children might be. If this is the only adoptive situation you will accept, you might have to wait a very long time. (This book, however, will help you find the ways most likely to keep your search within a reasonable length.) Today there are fewer healthy infants available for adoption than there were just a decade or two ago. But that doesn't mean there is a shortage of adoptive children. There isn't. Minority and mixed-race children are available (chapter 5). So are children with physical, mental, or emotional handicaps (chapter 6). There are older children, and there are siblings who must be placed together (chapter 7). Even if a newborn baby is not available to you or you are not interested in one, there may still be a child for you.

In the past it was next to impossible for an unmarried person to adopt a child. Today more and more children are being placed with single parents (chapter 10). As divorce and remarriage continue to increase, so also do the number of adoptions by stepparents (chapter 9).

If, after considering all the alternatives, you decide you really are not interested in adopting any child other than a healthy newborn, don't let anyone influence you differently. It is far better to run the risk of a long wait or of never getting a baby at all, than to adopt a child out of desperation. If you do that, you may never be able to really love and accept that child. So listen to yourself. You must do what is right for you.

"HOW CAN WE PREPARE?"

"We think we want to adopt," said a thirty-one-year-old wife of ten years, "but neither my husband nor I have had any experience with children. How can we best prepare ourselves to make a wise decision?"

This is a good question, one that many thoughtful couples ask. There are many child-oriented activities in which you can become involved—scouts, athletic coaching, Sunday school teaching, or church nursery volunteering—but these all offer limited exposure. An ideal approach is to become a foster parent for a child who needs temporary care (chapter 8). In most areas of the country there is a serious shortage of such homes.

Adoption can be a rewarding and challenging experience. What an opportunity to help children move toward the development of their particular abilities and unique personalities!

But parenting is never an easy job. Along with the wonderfully rewarding times come the times of questions and nagging doubts. Worst of all are the times when our only feeling is one of failure. Perhaps because they have gone through so much to become parents in the first place, adoptive parents seem to be especially vulnerable to the concerns and questions of parenting.

To provide some concrete help, advice, and comfort to Christian adoptive parents, we called together representatives from the two groups of people who have the most to offer them: trained professionals and parents who have been there. Ten couples met together with us and a Christian counselor,

Dr. Samuel R. McDill, to discuss some of the most common problems and concerns of adoptive parenthood. Portions of this open forum, presented in dialogue form, are included in many of the following chapters.

Dr. McDill is a family counselor with a private practice in Santa Barbara, California. Except for Dr. McDill's name and those of the authors, all the names used in this book are fictitious.

To further protect the privacy of the families who graciously shared their experiences with us, the accounts presented here are composites. All the situations are true experiences of the adoptive families, but no family will be able to point to a specific family in the book and say, "That's us." Parts of a situation are drawn from one family, other parts from another family.

This book will show that there are a number of adoptive options open to you. Read about the needs and rewards each option presents, but also consider the difficulties. If you decide to adopt, you must go into the relationship with your eyes open. Be prepared for love, fulfillment, and a great blessing. They will come. But also be prepared for problems and disappointments. They will also come. An adopted family is, in every sense of the term, a *real* family.

QUESTIONS FOR DISCUSSION

1. In your opinion is the shift in the emphasis of adoption from the needs of childless couples to the needs of the children good or bad? Why?
2. In making the decision whether or not to adopt a child, what should be the most important considerations?
3. In what ways are birth families and adoptive families alike? In what ways are they different?

2.
Adoption: Whose Choice?

It was the first day of school, and Mrs. Martin, the sixth-grade teacher, was getting acquainted with the students in her class. When Tom and Stephen Jamison introduced themselves as brothers, Mrs. Martin could scarcely hide her amazement. Stephen, tall and thin, had sandy-blond hair and a freckled face; Tom was short and husky with a full head of unruly black curls.

"Surely you boys aren't twins!" Mrs. Martin exclaimed.

"Oh, no," Stephen replied. "I'm five months older than Tom."

"Yeah," Tom agreed. Then he added, "One of us is adopted, but I forget which one."

The boys' casual attitude toward adoption made such an impression on their teacher that she decided to make it a point to meet their parents and see for herself what kind of family could foster such open-minded acceptance in their children.

When Mrs. Jamison visited her sons' classroom later that week, Mrs. Martin greeted her warmly. "I can't tell you how impressed I am with your boys!" she exclaimed. "It's wonderful to see a family in which adoption makes no difference at all."

"I'm afraid you don't understand," said Mrs. Jamison quickly. "Adoption makes a great deal of difference in our family. In fact, it has been a regular part of our conversation since our sons were toddlers. You see, we are all adopted— my husband and me, Tom and Stephen—all of us." Noticing the teacher's puzzled look, Mrs. Jamison explained, "We are

Christians. Each of us has been adopted by God into his family so that now we're all his children. It's God himself who is the model for our attitude toward adoption."

What understanding the Jamison family had! Not only was adoption an important fact of life for them, but it was a vital part of their religious faith as well. As his adopted sons and daughters, all Christians are truly the children of God. What a complete and perfect family relationship!

In his letter to the Galatians, the apostle Paul wrote: "But when the right time came, the time God decided on, he sent his Son, born of a woman, born as a Jew, to buy freedom for us who were slaves to the law so that he could adopt us as his very own sons. And because we are his sons God has sent the Spirit of his Son into our hearts, so now we can rightly speak of God as our dear Father" (Galatians 4:4–6).

Can there be a more perfect example for adoptive parents?

In God's eyes, every Christian is so completely a part of his family that each one shares equally in all its rights, privileges, and responsibilities. Paul adds, "Now we are no longer slaves, but God's own sons. And since we are his sons, everything he has belongs to us, for that is the way God planned" (Galatians 4:7). We share a wonderful legacy.

Can you imagine such a thing as a second-class member of God's family? Of course not! Every one of his children is equal in his sight. The same equality should be present in every Christian family, adoptive or not. It is inevitable that children will be influenced by the attitudes and prejudices of their parents. If adoptive parents feel that they have somehow failed by not being able to bring children into the world, why should they be surprised when their adopted children consider themselves second-best? It is hard to feel like a first-class person when your parents consider you a consolation prize.

Even when parents accept the idea of adoption from God's perspective, there are sure to be friends and relatives who do not understand. But with prayer, careful teaching, and a consistent example, these children will be able to withstand the thoughtlessness of others.

"Once when our boys were little," said Mrs. Jamison, "Stephen got a birthday present from my sister. On the card she had written, 'Happy birthday from your adopted Aunt Margaret.' After Stephen read it he said, 'I never knew that Aunt Margaret was adopted.'" Stephen was secure in his position as a worthy member of the family. He belonged and he knew it.

Is it realistic to expect to be able to love an adopted child in the same way we love a biological child? Consider how Mrs. Jamison expressed her relationship to her two sons:

> Tom was born to us, so he's our son. Stephen was born to another woman but we adopted him, so he's our son. The two boys entered our family in different ways, one physically and the other legally. Only a mother who has borne a child can fully understand the wonder of birth, and only one who has adopted can fully understand the miracle that makes an adopted child her own. How fortunate I am to have experienced both miracles and to know that they are really not so very different after all! The different ways in which our boys came into our family make no difference at all. They were both given to us by God, and we love them both the same.

Every child in the world is a separate little person—an individual with unique potential, problems, characteristics, and personality. We are told in the Bible that God has a perfect plan for each of his children and a reason for everything that happens in their lives. The psalmist said, "You saw me before I was born and scheduled each day of my life before I began to breathe. Every day was recorded in your Book!" (Psalm 139:16). And in Romans 8:28 we read, "And we know that all that happens to us is working for our good if we love God and are fitting into his plans."

How wonderful it is to know that God has personally chosen one very special child for one very special home and for very special reasons. There is no luck involved—no fate, no chance. The arrangements are all in the hands of God.

Although children are born with certain abilities, talents, and potential, there is no question but that they are greatly influenced by the way they are raised. What they learn at home goes a long way toward helping to determine who and what they will become. Potential—no matter how great—means nothing without the daily example of dedicated parents.

This is a great challenge to us as parents. We must help our children to realize and develop their own potential; we must help to direct them in such a way that when God needs them, they will be ready and willing to do his bidding. God alone knows what is possible with the perfect combination of your home and those specific lives he has entrusted to your care.

Do you feel inadequate for the task? Don't! God also sets us an example as the Ideal Parent. He is loving and kind, patient and just. When we do wrong, he chastises us in love. But he is also merciful and always willing to forgive. God promised that when he calls us to meet the needs of our children, his grace will be sufficient for us (2 Corinthians 12:9). He will enable us to do what he has called us to do.

TRIUMPHANT EXAMPLES IN THE BIBLE

Have you ever noticed how many stories there are in the Bible about children who were removed from the homes of their birth and raised by others? It is noteworthy that in most cases the story begins as a tragedy, but in the end stands as a triumphant example of God's sovereignty over all things. Let's look at a few of these displaced children and see how God in his great wisdom changed each tragedy into a life of victory.

Joseph was seventeen when he was sold by his jealous brothers and taken as a slave to the faraway country of Egypt. Surely this was the most bitter tragedy that could befall Joseph and his father, Jacob. Yet years later, Joseph, looking back on his long, often difficult life, said to his brothers, "As far as I am concerned, God turned into good what you meant for evil, for he brought me to this high position I have today so that I could save the lives of many people" (Genesis 50:20). And it was the descendants of Jacob, brought to Egypt by Joseph and so saved from sure starvation, who grew into the great nation of Israel. Had Joseph remained at home with his father, there would never have been an Israel through which Jesus, the Savior of the world, would come.

As the years passed, pharaohs who had never known Joseph ascended the throne of Egypt. Conditions grew worse and worse for God's people. Finally they were forced into cruel slavery, where they led a wretched and miserable existence. But there were so many Israelites that the Egyptians began to fear they would revolt and take over the land. So the pharaoh issued a decree that every male born to an Israelite woman was to be thrown into the Nile River to drown. It was at this time of crisis that Moses was born. As far as we know, only this baby—floating down the Nile in a little reed boat made by his mother—managed to survive the deadly decree. By the intervention of the all-powerful hand of God, Moses lived to become the greatest leader Israel ever knew, the person God chose to lead the Exodus of his people from Egyptian captivity.

Esther was a beautiful Jewish girl who lived with her cousin Mordecai. They were captives in the heathen land of Persia. Imagine her feelings when she was ordered to become one of the wives of the vain, powerful, and sometimes brutal Persian king! Some time later a terrible death plot was laid for the Jewish population of Persia. Queen Esther alone was in a position to intervene with the king on behalf of the Jews, knowing that if she were to do so, her own life would be in danger. As she struggled with this momentous decision, Mordecai sent this message to her: "Who can say but that God has brought you into the palace for just such a time as this?" (Esther 4:14). Esther had her answer: "I will go in to see the king; and if I perish, I perish." You remember what happened. Esther was graciously received by the king, and because of her brave action, the Jews in Persia were saved from genocide.

Perhaps you are saying, "But my adopted child will never be a Joseph or a Moses or an Esther." You are probably right. God chooses few people for such history-changing assignments. Yet you can be certain that God has chosen your child for unique service to him. Your child is being prepared in your home to meet whatever challenges God may bring. In God's perfect opinion, no one can raise that child as well as you, the parents he has selected for the task. Remember, parenting does not mean simply conceiving a child; it also means raising one. It is a singular privilege. It is a singular responsibility.

EXAMINE YOUR MOTIVES

A word of warning is necessary. If you are a Christian who is considering adoption you must prayerfully, in complete honesty, examine your reasons for wanting to take a child into your home and heart. This is a crucial decision for you and the child, and you dare not enter into it lightly.

"I want a baby of my own more than I've ever wanted anything in my life," said the thirty-year-old wife of a successful banker. "Yet after ten years of marriage there still is no baby. My husband and I have been to specialist after specialist, but they haven't been able to help us. One doctor did tell me that when a couple adopts a baby it often happens that they soon have one of their own. I can't understand how this would work, but after ten years of waiting, I'm willing to try anything."

A twenty-six-year-old secretary, married for five years, nervously related, "I hate to admit it, but my marriage is on pretty shaky ground. Lately I've been thinking about adopting a baby because I'm sure a baby would draw my husband and me back together. It would give us a common interest. With a new baby, maybe we would have a chance to be a real family after all."

"Whenever I read a story about a family who adopts little children no one else wants, I get a warm feeling inside," said a twenty-two-year-old wife of three years. "I think it would be fun to adopt. What I have in mind is two little girls, one blond with blue eyes and the other a brunette with big brown eyes. I can almost see them now—all dressed up in pretty ruffled dresses, their long curls tied up in ribbons. My husband laughs at me, but I know he will agree. He's always saying I need something to keep me busy."

Do these reasons for wanting to adopt sound incredible? Unfortunately, they aren't uncommon. It is surprising how many people seem to forget that babies are not dolls; they are real, live, human beings who get dirty and cry and grow into stubborn children who stomp their feet and yell, "I hate you!" Any couple who decides to take a child in order to satisfy a romantic idea of having a real live doll to cuddle and dress up and show off is being terribly unfair to all concerned. Inevitably those who adopt in the hopes either of increasing their chances of having "their own" baby or of saving a troubled marriage will soon find that parenthood is not the magic solution they had thought it would be. (Furthermore, the belief that if you adopt you will immediately become pregnant is a myth. Statistical studies have found that of those families who have been told by their doctors that they are infertile and cannot have a child, eight percent will prove the doctors wrong and give birth to a child anyway. The same and other studies have found that among adopting families, about eight percent will give birth to a child. Obviously, we are talking about the same eight percent chance of proving the doctors wrong. Adoption has nothing to do with fertility.)

Take the time to consider carefully. Discuss your motives openly with your spouse. Pray together. Do you automatically assume that children are a necessity for a married couple? Do you want a son to carry on your family name? Do you have to talk a reluctant spouse into agreeing to the adoption? Do you want a child to take the place of one who died? None of these is an adequate reason for adopting. Only when a couple has a true, God-given desire to take a child into their home and to make that child their very own—to provide that child with a warm, secure, understanding, loving, and nurturing family—can an adoption be successful.

Adopted children, like any other children, must be loved and wanted and appreciated for themselves, not for what they can do for their parents.

"My husband and I love each other very much," said an energetic mother of two adopted daughters. "In a way the two of us were already a complete family, but we so wanted children with whom we could share our love. Together we prayed that God would either give us the baby we wanted so badly, or else take away our great desire to be parents. Instead of fading, our deep longing for a child continued to grow, so we were convinced that this desire was truly from the Lord." Then, her eyes sparkling, she gazed out the window into the backyard where her two preschoolers were playing in the sandbox. "Do you want proof of God's faithfulness?" she asked. "Just look at the two wonderful, healthy, bright little girls he gave us!"

THE UNIQUENESS OF CHRISTIAN ADOPTION

A Christian view of adoption, then, is unique in several ways. It is a concept authored by God and demonstrated by him in its most perfect and complete sense by his adoption of all Christian believers into his own family. It is the providential choosing of a very special child selected above all other children to be placed in a very special family for a very special purpose. It is a calling—a divine appointment—from the Lord God himself.

Seen in this light, it is clear that adoption is a function of God's grace, and to be successful as adoptive parents, we must mirror his grace to our adopted children. We cannot be adopted into God's family through any merit or virtue of our own, nor because of our works or accomplishments. Likewise, adoptive parents must accept a child into their family as an act of grace. This is not to say that there is no expectation of a warm, fulfilling, and rewarding parent and child relationship. Viewed from the eyes of the adoptive parent, however, adoption is more about giving—the giving of love and companionship and the provision of one's material posses-sions—than it is about receiving.

Through grace, the birth mother makes a painful but heroic decision and is granted the strength to see the decision through. Also through grace, the adoptive parents accept a child into their home as their own, and bestow on the child their name, their material possessions, and the fullest measure of their love and affection. A special bond exists between birth mothers and adoptive parents. Through teamwork of a most magnificent kind, they have created a human being with a soul and personality. Neither could have accomplished this without the other. There is no greater human example of grace.

"I have a poem by Fleur Conkling Heylinger that I claim as my own," said Mrs. Jamison, the mother of Tom and Stephen. "It's special to me because it expresses so well what I have always felt in my heart. It could have been written by me. Will you please share it with other adoptive parents?" Here is the poem:

To an Adopted Child

Not flesh of my flesh,
Nor bone of my bone,
But still miraculously my own.
Never forget for a single minute,
You didn't grow under my heart,
You grew in it!

—Fleur Conkling Heylinger

QUESTIONS FOR DISCUSSION

1. The analogy drawn between God's adoption of his children and the Christian's adoption of earthly children is sound. However, as in all analogies, there are differences. In what ways is human adoption different from divine adoption?
2. To what extent do you feel you can and should expect God to choose a specific child for your family?

3.   *The Classic Story*

"All along, Dan and I had planned for the day when we would have a family," said Ellen O'Brien. A slender, soft-spoken woman of thirty-three, Ellen paused for a moment, silently remembering. "We were young and idealistic then. We had our whole lives planned out. I was going to teach for two years while Dan finished graduate school. By then I would be pregnant, and—according to our plan—by the time the baby was born Dan would be set up in his own accounting office and I would have retired from teaching. Two years later there would be a second baby and two years after that we would complete our family with a third. It all seemed so perfect.

"But God had plans of his own. After five years I still had not conceived. Together we went to see a doctor who specialized in fertility problems. After endless tests and weeks of waiting, he broke the news to us. I would never be able to have a baby. What a terrible shock! All our plans and dreams and hopes—gone in a minute! I cried all the way home.

"Dan was terribly shaken too. In fact, he refused to believe it. 'Our God is a God of miracles,' he said. 'We will take this matter up with him.' So we prayed and prayed and prayed. We carefully pointed out to God our excellent qualifications for parenthood. We promised to dedicate the baby to him. Again and again we reminded God of his promise to give us the desires of our heart. Sometimes I felt certain that God was going to answer us and give us a baby, and we repeatedly claimed the promise of Psalm 113:9: 'He honors the childless wife in her home; he makes her happy by giving her children. Praise the Lord!' At other times I wondered in despair if he even heard us. Those were horribly frustrating days for both of us.

"After two long years of tearful praying and pleading with God, Dan and I began to think about the possibility of adopting. The more we discussed it, the more certain we became that this was the way God would answer our prayers. He was going to give us our baby, all right, but it was to be according to his plan, not ours.

"Together Dan and I filled out an application at our local adoption agency and, with great excitement and anticipation, we turned it in. Although we were certain of our guidance from God, the agency apparently was not. We received a long, official letter from them. What it really said was: 'Don't call us, we'll call you—in about two years!' "

Dan and Ellen O'Brien had gone to the agency knowing exactly what they wanted: a healthy, white infant. They were not interested in any child who did not fit this description. Most couples have the same expectations as the O'Briens, so the demand for these babies is much greater than the supply. It is estimated that for every baby available for adoption, there are forty infertile couples looking to adopt. The couple who desires to adopt a healthy Caucasian newborn must be prepared either to wait a very long time or to pursue adoption very aggressively.

"Just nine months after we talked to the lady at the adoption agency, we got a call," Ellen continued. "They already had a baby for us! I was so excited that I spent the next two days on the phone making our happy announcement to relatives and friends. We chose names—Jessica Hope for a girl, Jeremy Sean for a boy. That weekend we papered and painted the nursery, and I ordered furniture for it. Then I went shopping and bought piles of baby clothes and a fuzzy bear that played Brahms' 'Lullaby' when it was wound up. There would be no hand-me-downs for our little Jessica or Jeremy. We were going first-class all the way.

"Then came the shattering blow. The baby was born right on time, a perfect little boy. But when we arrived at the hospital to get him, he was gone. His biological grandmother had suddenly appeared out of nowhere and claimed him as her own. There was nothing we could do about it. We had no rights; she was a blood relative. It was as if our baby, born strong and healthy, had suddenly died. My heart was broken.

"For the first time, Dan and I realized that if there was ever going to be an O'Brien baby, it would have to be because God had given it to us. This was a hard thing for us to admit. We had always believed that the two of us together could solve any problems that might come into our lives. We prided ourselves on our own sufficiency. Everything that was important to us—education, a new home, a nice savings account—we had worked hard for and achieved. But now we were faced with a situation over which we had absolutely no control, a situation in which we had to depend on God in a totally new way. He had put this desire in our hearts for a baby; we knew that he, in his own time and in his own way, would satisfy it.

"And do you know what? Just six months later we got Heather." Ellen's eyes sparkled with pride as she spoke of her little daughter. "What an answer God gave us! I surely am glad that he didn't listen to my advice."

Ellen and Dan's story could be echoed with only minor variations by the majority of adoptive parents across the United States. In general they are educated, financially secure people. Unable to have children, they decided to adopt. The child each couple wanted was a newborn baby who looked as much like them as possible. Because people who live closely together tend to pick up each other's habits and mannerisms, these parents and the children they adopted often have a remarkable family resemblance. They walk and talk alike, their expressions and gestures are alike, they even think and act alike. To all appearances, these families are no different from any other families.

Suppose a couple has thoughtfully and prayerfully made the decision to adopt. What is the next step? Dan and Ellen O'Brien made application through a state-licensed adoption agency, but in all but a few states it is also possible to arrange an independent adoption (see Appendix A). Which option is better? There is no simple answer because there are advantages and disadvantages to each approach.

AGENCY ADOPTIONS

Historically most adoptions in the United States were arranged by adoption agencies. In an agency adoption, the biological parents relinquish to the agency all rights to their child and trust the agency to find the best possible home for their little one. The agency then selects a prospective adoptive family and places the child with them. Because the baby is surrendered and the agency makes all the necessary arrangements, it is possible for the identity of the biological parents to be kept confidential. After a trial placement period of six to twelve months, the agency surrenders to the adoptive family all legal rights to the child, and the court approves the adoption.

There are two kinds of adoption agencies. "Public agencies" are operated by governmental departments such as a state or county department of social services. "Private agencies" are organizations licensed by the state to process adoptions but owned by a private individual or corporation. In some states, only a non-profit corporation can be licensed as a private adoption agency, but many states still allow "for profit" adoption agencies. In most states, a public agency can arrange an adoption for substantially less cost than can a private agency, but the wait tends to be much longer in a public agency, especially for a healthy Caucasian newborn.

In the recent past, the only role an agency might allow the birth mother to play in the selection process was to specify a religious preference for the home into which her child was to be placed. Unfortunately, many social workers are not very sophisticated in theological matters. One birth mother asked the agency's social worker to promise that her child would be placed in a Christian home. "No problem," the social worker replied. "We have many Christian couples available right now." The social worker then described prospective adopting couples who were members of various cults. The birth mother, convinced that not all groups who call themselves Christian deserve the title, chose not to place her child through that agency.

Some agencies have begun to allow birth mothers to have much more input into the selection of a family. Regardless of how much the birth mother is allowed to contribute, however, it is the agency which ultimately selects the adoptive family.

Couples or single people who have an application accepted at an adoption agency are assigned to a social worker who will serve them throughout the entire procedure. Because social workers have had training in psychology, human development, and counseling, they can provide more than just information about the legal process of adoption. They are also able to offer support and guidance. If the social worker feels that a couple is not ready to adopt or wants to adopt for the wrong reasons, a child will not be placed in that home.

In their anxiety about the possibility of being turned down, many prospective parents make a big mistake. They try to guess what the social worker wants to hear and then adjust their answers accordingly. It is absolutely essential that prospective parents be open and honest. Remember, the social worker's only concern is the benefit of the child.

Yet much does depend on the social worker's impressions. How can prospective parents deal in the best way with this very important person? The following suggestions come from several social workers who have had a great deal of experience with adoptive parents.

- Relax! Don't be afraid. The social worker is not trying to trap you.
- Be as honest as you can. If you have strong feelings about something, say so.
- If you are confused, ask for clarification. If you have a question, ask it.
- Don't try to convince the social worker that you are a

perfect person or that you would be a perfect parent. There is no such thing, and the social worker knows it.

- If you have doubts, don't hide them. Let the social worker help you work them out.
- Feel free to disagree with the social worker, but do so in a kind, pleasant way. Explain your point of view. It may be that you're right.
- Insist on being given all the information available concerning any child placed in your home. The time will come when you will be glad you have it.
- If your application is turned down, ask for an explanation. It may be that you really are not ready to take this step at this time.

To spare families the anguish that Dan and Ellen O'Brien suffered when their baby was claimed by his grandmother, agencies make a practice of placing newborn infants in foster care until all questions regarding their legal relinquishment are cleared up. It may take several months to find the right home for the baby. Many people object to a baby's spending these very important first weeks and months of life in a foster home.

In response to these concerns, many agencies today are making "direct placements," that is, newborns are placed directly into the home of the adopting family. Direct placement has the distinct advantage of allowing the adoptive family to experience each stage of the child's infancy. However, in a direct placement the adoptive family must remember that there are many legal obstacles to adoption which can arise early on, and that if something does happen, they run the risk of having the child taken from their home.

There are many families who are not able to adopt through an agency because of the strict rules and regulations. Certainly these rules are based on concern for the welfare of the children in their care, yet many feel that most agencies are unfairly restrictive. Are all people over a certain age too old to meet a child's needs? Are no single people or women employed outside the home able to be good parents to infants?

Most agencies will not place a newborn with a family where either prospective adoptive parent is over the age of forty; some will not place a child with a family if the parents' combined ages exceed eighty years. Other agencies will not place a child with a family of a particular denomination, or in a particular geographic area, or in a family in which a spouse has been married previously, or where the couple has been married less than three years. It is our firm belief that each family has a right to be evaluated on its own merits. An agency is often unable to grant that right.

Any couple who gets far enough with an agency to be seriously considered for a child must undergo a home study.

"We were both given complete physicals," said Ellen O'Brien, "and we were fingerprinted to assure that neither of us had a criminal record. Then our home was visited. After that we were required to see a psychologist twice a week for five months. We talked about everything—budgets, child discipline, our goals personally and as a couple, education, relationships with our friends and with our families, our relationship as a couple, how we fight and how we make up— everything! This was not a Christian agency, but they were very interested in how our Christianity affects our everyday lives. That agency knows everything there is to know about us."

Some people greatly resent the home study. They consider many of the questions to be overly intrusive and an invasion of privacy. But others, like Ellen and Dan, appreciate the questions.

"The counseling we got was fantastic!" Dan O'Brien said. "Ellen and I learned to really communicate with each other. Even if we had never gotten a baby, the counseling would have been worth all the time and tears we spent. As a couple we will never be the same."

The agency with which the O'Briens worked received almost two thousand applications in one year. Nearly 650 were accepted. Ellen and Dan were one of only twenty-four families who received babies. That means there were approximately 1,976 disappointed families at just that one agency in that single year. Brad and Lenore Lombardi were one of the disappointed couples.

"We filled out an application, but the agency wouldn't even interview us," Lenore said with a trace of bitterness. "I called and tried to talk to someone by phone, but the woman who answered would only say, 'I'm sorry, but we do not interview rejections.' I cannot tell you the shock and confusion I felt. My husband and I were both in our early thirties, so surely we weren't too old. We had been happily married for seven years. Our lovely, spacious home had a very small mortgage and we have no other debts. Brad owns his own construction business, which is very successful, so we could easily support a child. What was wrong with us? We've asked ourselves this question a thousand times." Shaking her head she said softly, "We never did find out."

Brad and Lenore's case is not unusual. Most agencies are reluctant to discuss their reasons for rejecting a couple. Often the reason is that the agency already has such a long waiting list that it doesn't feel it's fair to add another name. Sometimes, with there being so few babies available, a family is automatically eliminated from consideration because it already has a child. But because no explanation is given, the family assumes there is something terribly wrong with them. It is our position that every rejected family is entitled to an explanation, no matter what the situation is.

INDEPENDENT ADOPTIONS

An independent adoption is the other option open to families who want to adopt. Independent adoptions are legal in all but a few states (see Appendix A). In these arrangements the biological mother does not surrender her baby to be placed at the discretion of someone else. Instead, she agrees to place the child with a family she selects. A mediator, often a lawyer, gathers all the information available about a number of families who might be suitable parents for this specific baby. This information is then given to the birth parent or parents, who are free to ask questions and request any additional information they need to make a selection.

Independent adoptions are met with varying degrees of acceptance throughout the United States. In California, for example, independent adoption accounts for 86 percent of all adoptions of newborns, according to that state's Department of Social Services. In a number of states, independent adoption represents the norm and agency adoptions are the exception. Yet in Michigan, attempting to arrange an independent adoption is still considered a felony. In Maryland, Minnesota, and North Dakota, a birth parent may arrange an independent adoption only if the adoptive parent is a member of the birth parent's family.

At one time, most independent adoptions were anonymous, or closed, adoptions. Today a large majority are "open adoptions," one in which the birth mother not only selects the adopting family, but also meets them and develops a relationship with them. Many adoptive families are very nervous about meeting a birth mother. They are afraid that if the birth mother knows who they are and where they live, she might someday come back and interfere.

"I was terrified at the prospect of meeting a birth mother," recalls Steve Wilkinson. "What if she didn't like us? Or what was to keep her from showing up on our doorstep three years after the adoption was final? I told our attorney about my concerns, and he asked me what I would do if I were giving away a cherished puppy. I told him I would want to talk to the person first to make sure he knew how to care for the dog. I love animals, and in order to have peace of mind I probably would insist on seeing the person's yard to make sure it was a fit place to raise a puppy. 'You have just described the feelings of most birth mothers,' the attorney told me. When I pointed out that you can't compare giving away a puppy with placing a child for adoption, the attorney smiled and said, 'That's precisely my point. A birth mother's feelings are far stronger and more profound, but the basic emotion is the same.' It helped me to realize that a birth mother is probably more like me than I realized."

Steve Wilkinson and his wife, Marianne, are now the proud parents of two-year-old Jason. "We not only got to know, respect, and befriend our son's birth mother," related Marianne, "she even asked me to be in the delivery room when our son was born. She asked Steve to cut the umbilical cord."

Many birth mothers want to visit the prospective adoptive family's home so they can have the peace of mind that comes from knowing what kind of a home environment the family will provide and so they can picture the child's living conditions. Other birth mothers, concerned about the church the adoptive parents intend to raise the child in, ask to visit their church with them on a Sunday.

It's very common for adoptive parents to worry that if the birth mother knows where they live, she might someday appear at their door and interrupt their family. Actually this seldom happens. One respected organization of adoption attorneys surveyed its members and found that of more than twenty thousand adoptions handled by the members, not a single attorney was aware of a birth mother who had appeared uninvited at the door at the adoptive parents' home.

Unfortunately, the media continue to portray the interfering birth mother as a common occurrence. The isolated cases we have found in which birth mothers have appeared uninvited at the adoptive parents' door have been *closed* adoptions. In fact, most adoption workers theorize that what drives some birth mothers to find and visit the adoptive family is the "curiosity factor." The ultimate goal in open adoption is to eliminate this curiosity factor by providing the birth mother with as much information as she needs to feel at peace with her decision. It is common in open adoption for the adoptive parents to send her pictures periodically so that she can see what the child looks like. Advocates of open adoption argue that this kind of information actually gives the birth mother the freedom to stay *away* from the door of the adopting family.

"When we got nothing but discouragement from the adoption agency, Brad and I decided to take matters into our own hands," said Lenore Lombardi. "We knew that there were babies who needed homes, and we knew that we would be good parents. I decided to write letters to hundreds of doctors throughout the state telling them all about Brad and me and our great desire to adopt a baby. I even sent along several pictures of us. Any doctors who knew of possible babies for us were asked to contact our lawyer, a specialist in independent adoptions. It wasn't long before we began to get replies, some of them very encouraging. We were told that many mothers keep their babies simply because they can't bear to blindly give them up with no idea of the kind of homes into which they would be placed.

"Several possibilities developed over the next few months, but each time something happened. Brad always said, 'When it's the right one, it will all work out. We'll just have to be patient.' He was right. Early one morning our lawyer called and said, 'Mrs. Lombardi, I have a girl here who looks enough like you to be your sister. She's interested in you and your husband as possible parents for her baby.' That has to have been the most wonderful day of my entire life!"

The Lombardis were impressed by the genuine concern the young woman showed for her unborn child. "She was Roman Catholic, and it was very important to her that the baby be placed in a Christian home," Lenore said. "She had many questions. How did we feel about infant baptism? What did we think it meant to be a Christian? If the baby were a girl, what would we teach her about abortion? What methods of discipline would we use? The list went on and on."

When questions such as these arise, some adoption professionals suggest that the adults involved meet together to talk them over in person. Neither the Lombardis nor the teenage girl and her boyfriend wanted to do that. Yet Lenore found it almost impossible to communicate these personal

Christian values through a non-Christian lawyer. Her solution was to write a long letter to the girl.

"I can tell how very much you love this baby," Lenore began. "And already I love it, too. I want you to know that this thing that has been such a tragedy in your life is the greatest thing that could possibly have happened for my husband and me. We see your child as a special gift from the Lord." Then, in as much detail as possible, she wrote about Brad and herself—their home, their hobbies, everything she could think of. She did her best to answer every question that the girl had asked as honestly and as fully as she could. In conclusion she wrote, "My husband and I want you to know that from the beginning we will teach our baby to know the Lord as Savior and Friend. Already we are praying that God in his tender love and mercy will bring our child to himself. And most of all we must all remember that the One to whom this child really belongs is God."

The girl was satisfied. "We were called as soon as our little son was born," Lenore said. "From that moment on, we had all the privileges of any other parents. Three days after his birth, Garrett was released from the hospital directly to us. No foster homes, no delays—he was ours!"

A quick placement like this is one of the main advantages of an independent adoption. There is, however, a negative side. In most states a birth mother has the right to change her mind for a period of time after delivery, and if she does, she has the right to reclaim her child. The adoptive parents have no choice but to return the child to her. The length of this time can be as short as a few days (Texas or Oregon) or as long as one year (Colorado). Fortunately, it is quite rare for a birth mother to change her mind, but it is always a risk which the prospective adoptive parent should bear in mind.

Another possible disadvantage of an independent adoption is the cost. Typically it is more costly than an adoption arranged by a public adoption agency, but the cost is usually comparable to or less than the cost of an adoption arranged by a private adoption agency. Not only are the adoptive parents typically responsible for all the birth mother's medical bills—including any unexpected complications such as a Caesarean section—but they also must cover all the attorney's fees. This can easily amount to several thousand dollars. (Making extra payments to the birth mother is *never* legal. It is considered baby selling and is a serious crime.)

Through an independent adoption, many qualified couples who would never be considered by an agency are the proud parents of happy, well-adjusted children. "No agency would even take an application from us," said Shirley Carson. "They didn't beat around the bush, either. They came right out and said we were too old."

Stan Carson was forty-nine and the father of three grown sons by his first wife when he married Shirley. Shirley, forty-five, had a married daughter and one in college. Two years later they wanted a family they could raise together. From the start they knew their ages would be against them, but even so they were sure they had a lot to offer a child. They were financially secure and owned a beautiful home, and they had a great deal of time and love to invest in a child.

"We had been told about a lawyer who did a lot of independent adoptions, so we made an appointment and flew across the country to see him. In less than a year he found a baby for us. The mother was an unmarried fourteen-year-old who specifically requested an older couple. She had been raised in poverty and neglect, so it was important to her that her baby be placed with a family who not only had money, but also had plenty of time and interest to spend on the baby. She selected us, and we became the parents of Leanne, the sweetest baby girl any couple could ever hope for.

"That was fifteen years and two more children ago. Looking back, Stan and I are convinced that our age has really been an advantage. We have certainly been better parents to Leanne and her brother and sister than we ever were to our first families." Laughing, she added, "Us, old? Not at all! Our second family has kept us young."

At the same time, some people are wary of independent adoptions. Rumors persist of black market dealings where children are sold for great amounts of money, although these rumors are seldom found to have any basis in reality. As the supply of healthy infants decreases, the possibilities for such abuse increases. Yet the buying and selling of babies is a very serious crime. Adoptive parents are forbidden by law to pay any money to the birth parents for the privilege of adopting their babies. Furthermore, most lawyers who work with adoptions charge an hourly rate rather than a flat fee so that it will be abundantly clear that they are acting as attorneys and not as baby brokers.

SELECTING AN ADOPTION PROFESSIONAL

Because of the sensitivity of the adoption field and because the laws vary so widely from state to state, it is important that you use utmost care when selecting a lawyer to act on your behalf. The lawyer must be reputable and trustworthy, someone in whom you have great confidence. Your lawyer must also be capable of seeing the entire adoption process through in a way that meets all the legal requirements in every state that is in any way involved with the adoption. Otherwise you could well be faced with legal problems when the adoption is brought to court to be finalized.

It is absolutely critical to consult with expert legal counsel in an independent adoption. Some people try to save money by retaining a lawyer who is a friend or neighbor or a general practitioner to help them with their adoption. This often backfires. Expert legal advice usually pays for itself by preventing missteps and wasted time and effort, not to mention the heartache which accompanies the failure of an adoption. Adoption law is a very demanding field, full of traps for the unwary. For example, under North Carolina law it is illegal for an adoptive parent to pay any expense of the birth mother whatsoever—even giving her an aspirin would be a technical violation of the law. Yet most other states allow the adoptive family to pay medical bills, counseling bills, legal bills, and pregnancy-related living expenses of the birth mother.

You wouldn't hire a doctor who was a general practitioner to perform neurosurgery. Neither should you hire a general practitioner lawyer to arrange an independent adoption. Properly handled, an independent adoption can be a joyful experience with few risks. Improperly handled, it can be a source of unending heartache and enormous financial loss. Because most of the legal assistance required can be handled through the mail or over the telephone, it is less important that the attorney be nearby than it is that the attorney be knowledgeable, ethical, and conscientious.

The largest organization of adoption attorneys in the United States is the American Academy of Adoption Attorneys. It has members in over forty states. Although the Academy is not an accrediting organization and membership in the organization is not a guarantee that an attorney is knowledgeable and ethical, it is helpful to know that an attorney has sufficient interest in the field of adoption law to join an organization dedicated to the furtherance of ethical adoption. To obtain a list of members in your state, write to:

American Academy of Adoption Attorneys
P.O. Box 33053
Washington, D.C. 20033-0053

Another reputable professional organization of attorneys with a special interest in the welfare of children (although not necessarily adoption) is:

National Association of Counsel For Children
1205 Oneida
Denver, CO 80220

Not all professionals in the adoption field are attorneys. There are many psychologists, licensed clinical social workers, pastors, and physicians who are very active in assisting those who wish to adopt. Many of these do a very creditable job of assisting with the sensitive arrangements required in an independent adoption. Others, although well intentioned, may undermine the adoption's prospects for a happy conclusion.

One alarming recent development is the increasing number of "adoption consultants." An adoption consultant is an unlicensed individual or organization which assists persons seeking to adopt, usually in exchange for a substantial fee paid in advance. Because no license is required, anyone can open an office as an adoption consultant and can charge whatever fees the market will bear. Several of these organizations are flourishing on an interstate basis, and they often refer to themselves by the euphemistic title of a "center" for adoption or an adoption "counseling organization."

Unfortunately, these adoption consultants are accountable to no one. If a licensed attorney or psychologist commits a negligent or dishonest act, there is a licensing authority to whom that person can be reported and there is a license which may be revoked or suspended. On the other hand, if an adoption consultant commits a negligent or dishonest act, the injured adoptive parent has no recourse except to sue the offender, which most people are financially or emotionally unable to do after the devastation of a failed adoption. Before you pay an adoption consultant's advance fee (which can be as high as $7,500), understand exactly what you are going to get for your money. If all you will receive are leads to a birth mother and counseling for her, look elsewhere.

FINDING A BIRTH MOTHER

In any independent adoption, the central task is to locate a suitable birth mother. There are four main methods used to find such a person. The Lombardis used the first method. They mailed a "birth mother letter" to professionals likely to come into contact with a potential birth mother. These letters are usually one page long and include a photograph of the family.

When this approach first began to be used back in the fifties, it was spectacularly successful, mainly because it was so unusual. Increasingly, at least on the West Coast, adoption professionals are coming to the conclusion that this method is not as cost effective as it used to be because the novelty is long gone. Most doctors receive dozens of these birth mother letters each week. Because such letters haven't been as widely used in the Midwest and the East, they may still be cost-effective in those parts of the country.

A second common method used to find a birth mother is to advertise. This is illegal in many states, so don't try this until you are sure you're not inadvertently breaking the law. In states where such ads are legal, they are generally published in the personals columns of local newspapers. The advantage of this approach is that it allows one to reach the largest possible audience of prospective birth mothers.

There are several distinct disadvantages to advertising for a birth mother. First, it is very expensive to advertise in a large enough geographic area for the ad to be widely read. Second, even the proponents of advertising for birth mothers acknowledge that about 95 percent of the calls received in response to ads will be from persons who are mentally unbalanced or are demanding money for a child or they will be abusive or obscene calls. Third, it is impossible to tell for certain which calls are legitimate and which are fraudulent.

"After we placed our first ad, we received several calls very early in the morning from women claiming to be pregnant and in urgent need of financial assistance," related Steve Wilkinson, shaking his head in dismay. "I remember one in particular—she told me that finding our ad had been the answer to her prayers, because she was about to be evicted from her apartment for nonpayment of rent. She wanted us to immediately wire her five hundred dollars. She sounded so sincere that we were in a quandary: Should we insist on checking her out before sending any money and risk losing her, or should we just send the money and risk being defrauded? We called our attorney. He found out that the girl, who was not even pregnant, had been supporting herself for over two years by taking advantage of desperate adoptive families."

The third method commonly used to locate a birth mother is through word of mouth and personal contacts. The general rule of thumb applied for this approach is the "first name rule": If you are on a first name basis with someone, that person ought to be made aware that you are aggressively seeking a child to adopt. If you are not on a first name basis with someone, then sharing your adoption desire with that person may be too personal. This approach has none of the disadvantages of the others, and it is extremely cost-effective when it works. Advocates of this approach point out that although it may result in reaching a smaller audience, it is a more select audience and one that is largely "self-screening," thereby minimizing the number of false leads and disappointments.

The fourth common method used to find a birth mother is to work with an adoption professional who can provide leads. Most adoption attorneys have prospective adopting families prepare an adoption "résumé" or "profile" summarizing the family's qualifications and their desire to adopt. Then when a birth mother is referred to the attorney or other professional, she is shown the résumés of prospective adopting families in the hope that one of the families will be to her liking. In fact, most adoption attorneys employ this approach in combination with one or more of the other approaches so that the adopting couple's desire to adopt is exposed to as many possible birth parents as possible.

OPEN ADOPTION AND COOPERATIVE ADOPTION

It used to be that adoption records were sealed and confidential; they were "closed," we were told. That's where we got the term "closed adoption." In traditional closed adoptions, a birth mother relinquished her child to an agency, and the agency placed the child with an appropriate adoptive family. Neither the adoptive parents nor the birth mother was told much about the other.

This traditional approach to adoption has developed into

a decidedly mixed legacy: While many children have been placed into wonderful and loving homes, critics charge that the closed adoption system treated the birth mother as a non-person and was insensitive to the needs of many adoptees to know "Who am I, really?"

It was in response to these concerns that open adoption developed. An open adoption is defined as one in which there is a relationship between the adoptive parents and the birth mother. In most open adoptions, the birth parent(s) select and meet the adoptive parents. From then on, both before and after the birth of the child and the completion of the adoption, there can be widely varying degrees of interaction. For example, it is not uncommon for an adoptive family to agree to send the birth mother pictures of the child once or twice a year.

The term "cooperative adoption" refers to an adoption in which the birth mother has an ongoing relationship with the child after the adoption is final. The distinction between "open" and "cooperative" adoption is this: With whom does the birth mother have a relationship? If her relationship is with the adoptive parents only, it is an open adoption. If her relationship is with the child as well, then it is a cooperative adoption. The critical distinguishing feature of cooperative adoption is that the birth parent(s) have the right to visit with the child after the adoption is final. Most people mistakenly confuse these two separate and distinct concepts and refer to both as open adoption.

Cooperative adoption is extremely controversial, and its critics have suggested that it amounts to co-parenting, a charge its proponents deny. The mental health professions have been particularly critical of cooperative adoption, pointing out that childhood is confusing enough for a toddler who has one mother and one father with whom to bond and one set of standards to uphold. Adding a second mother and/or father and a second set of standards can create far more confusion than a child can deal with effectively. A further problem of cooperative adoption is that it may interfere with the adoptive parents' ability to bond to the child. They can end up feeling that they are merely long-term baby-sitters rather than real parents. Advocates of cooperative adoption suggest that these problems are vastly exaggerated and that reasonable people of good will can work out the problems.

THE SOVEREIGNTY OF GOD

It is easy, and tempting, to become so focused on the how-to aspects of adoption that we forget that adoption is part of God's plan, subject to his control and timing.

Heather O'Brien is now an active four-year-old with bright red curls and big brown eyes. At seven, Garrett Lombardi looks and acts just like his dad. Leanne Carson is a fifteen-year-old high school student who is planning to pursue a career as a social worker. All three were adopted as newborn infants. Here is what their parents observed as they looked back on their experiences with adoption:

"God is indeed sovereign," said Ellen O'Brien. "Had he allowed me to have children the way I wanted to, Dan and I would never have been Heather's parents. Even if by some miracle I were able to conceive and have a baby, Heather would never lose her special place in my heart. She is the one who changed my life."

"How we prayed for our son!" said Lenore Lombardi. "No one could ever have wanted a child more than we did. And I'm sure that there is no child who is more loved. Garrett may have been born to another woman, but God made him for us. We are truly, truly blessed."

Stan and Shirley Carson's feelings are just as strong, but for them there is more to the story. At the time they adopted Leanne, neither of them knew the Lord. Today they attribute their coming to him to Leanne's entrance into their home.

"It was when we got Leanne that I first became interested in knowing God," Shirley says. "From the very first I realized she was a special gift from God. There is no other way we could have gotten such a wonderful, healthy baby—not at our age. Neither my first family nor my husband's was a great success. This time I was determined that we would give our child a firm foundation on which to build her life. So I got involved in a Bible study. It was there that I accepted Christ. Two years and many prayers later, Stan came to know him too. Then when Leanne was seven years old, she made the decision to ask Jesus to be her Lord and Savior. Our other two have just recently taken this step. Because of Leanne, our very special gift from heaven, we are truly a chosen family."

"We cannot know everything that God knows," says Brad Lombardi thoughtfully. "If we did, we would always say, 'Go ahead, Lord. Do whatever you want to do; it's fine with me.' My favorite verse is Ephesians 3:20: 'Now glory be to God who by his mighty power at work within us is able to do far more than we would ever dare to ask or even dream of—infinitely beyond our highest prayers, desires, thoughts, or hopes.' Even though I cannot know all God knows, I am satisfied that he does have a master plan with every single one of the details already drawn in."

OPEN FORUM

Victoria Meyers: Ben and I got our first child two months ago. Before he was placed with us, our son spent an entire month in a foster home. I really resent that lost time. A friend suggested that the next time we adopt we could eliminate the foster home by going through a lawyer instead of an agency. Is this true?

Mr. Donnelly: In a traditional agency adoption, the agency won't place an infant in an adoptive home until the final relinquishment documents have been signed. The reason for this is very simple: They don't want to run the risk of having to remove the child if the mother should change her mind and want the baby back. The completion of these documents takes, on average, from two to six weeks. Until then the mother has all rights to the baby and the infant is kept in a foster home. In independent adoptions, foster homes aren't used except in a couple of states where they are required by law. But adoptive parents who receive their infant immediately after birth must realize that they are running a risk. If the birth mother should change her mind, the adoptive parents have absolutely no legal rights to the child. Fortunately it's not likely to happen, but it is a risk.

Victoria Meyers: Why does the final relinquishment take so long?

Mr. Donnelly: Just getting the necessary documents prepared takes time. The signed release papers—which in many states must be signed in the presence of a judge or a licensed social worker employed by a licensed agency—must be accompanied by a certified copy of the baby's birth certificate. But the most important reason for the delay is that the birth mother must be given time to be certain that she truly does want to place her baby.

Ben Meyers: Are independent adoptions completely legal and aboveboard?

Mr. Donnelly: There are only a few states in which such adoptions aren't legal. The idea that independent adoptions are somehow under-the-table affairs is totally false. In California, for example, there was a recent survey taken of the judges whose specific job it is to hear all the state's adoption cases. When asked if they had ever encountered abuses involving independent adoptions, every one of the judges answered no. Some adoption workers resent independent adoptions, however, because they see them as unfair competition. In a recent year, one local agency reported that they received six thousand inquiries, yet were able to place only forty-two children. With statistics like that, there certainly seems to be room for everyone!

Lenore Lombardi: Why was it necessary for us to hire a second lawyer in the state where our son was born?

Mr. Donnelly: In an interstate adoption, it is necessary to comply with the laws of both states and to have the adoption approved by both states through a bureaucracy called the "Interstate Compact on the Placement of Children." This involves a great deal of paperwork, and it is helpful to have counsel in each state to assure compliance with all of the laws of every state involved. Also, in most states it is considered unethical for one lawyer to represent both the birth mother and the adoptive family in the same adoption. California currently has a statute allowing this, and a few other states have court rulings to the effect that it is not necessarily a conflict of interest for the lawyer to represent everyone if proper disclosure has been made and a written waiver obtained from all concerned. If both you and the birth mother lived in a state where one lawyer was not allowed to represent everyone, then it might have been necessary to hire a second lawyer to represent and advise the birth mother, even if it were not an interstate adoption.

Dan O'Brien: Isn't independent adoption quite a bit more expensive than agency adoption?

Mr. Donnelly: Not necessarily. You have to distinguish between public adoption agencies, which are an arm of the state or local government, and private agencies, which are privately controlled but licensed by the state. Since the budget of a public adoption agency is largely underwritten by the taxpayers, the fees they charge are typically a fraction of the fees charged in either private agency adoptions or independent adoption. Most people are surprised to hear that an independent adoption usually costs about the same as or even somewhat less than an adoption through a private adoption agency.

Bert Delgado: One agency I spoke to told me that if we wanted to adopt a healthy newborn, we should expect to wait about five years. The problem is that by then, I will be over forty years old, and the agency will not place a newborn with a parent over forty. What is the average wait for a baby in independent adoption?

Mr. Donnelly: There is no average wait. In independent adoption, the birth parent, usually the mother, selects the adoptive family herself and selection is not made on a first-come, first-served basis. As a result, some couples are selected immediately, and some are never selected at all, while some couples are selected only after a long wait comparable to what they could expect through an agency. Our record is three hours, but that is a record I do not expect to see broken any time soon!

Lenore Lombardi: That raises an interesting question: Just what is a birth mother looking for in an adoptive family?

Mr. Donnelly: I wish I knew the answer to that question, but the reality is that each birth mother is looking for something different, and usually she herself doesn't know what it is until she encounters it. We have had birth mothers select a family because she liked the breed of dog they had as their family pet, or because the family hobby was model railroading. That stated, there are some generalizations which can be made. Birth mothers are usually looking, first and foremost, for a stable marriage. If you ask a birth mother why she chose to place her child for adoption, usually the first reason she will give you is that she wants her child to be raised by both a mommy and a daddy, and she recognizes that she cannot provide the child with a daddy. Therefore, her greatest fear may be that the family she selects to adopt her child will later divorce and that the child will be deprived of the father figure the birth mother has sacrificed so much for the child to have. Second, virtually all birth mothers are looking for a family which is financially stable.

Lenore Lombardi: Don't birth mothers simply look for the wealthiest family?

Mr. Donnelly: On rare occasions, perhaps, but generally no. In fact, I have seen some excellent and very wealthy adoptive families passed over by a birth mother because she felt that they were too wealthy, and there is a widespread assumption that wealthy people are all "jet setters" and make lousy parents.

Dan O'Brien: I'm not sure I would feel comfortable meeting a birth mother, and I am sure that I could not handle being at the hospital when the baby was born. Isn't that awfully awkward?

Mr. Donnelly: Yes, it can be awkward, but it doesn't need to be. I carry with me a letter I received from a nurse at a hospital who witnessed an open adoption, and I would like to read it to you. Although it is a bit long, I will read it in its entirety because it does such an excellent job of presenting the emotions of the people involved. I will change the names of the author and the participants to protect their privacy.

Dear Mr. Donnelly:

It is 3:00 A.M. and all is quiet. I have just checked Susan, the birth mother, and she is doing well. I feel I must share with you one of the most bitter-sweet experiences that labor and delivery nurses see—the plight of the unwed mother. Susan's baby was born at 11:17 P.M., a beautiful and extremely handsome boy. She was exhausted by pushing for three hours, the doctor was busy sewing up a large episiotomy, and Susan's sister was quiet. Ann, the adoptive mother, just glowed as she watched Susan hold her son, and you could feel the love she felt for both—it was apparent in her touch on Susan's hand—the holding back from touching the baby and letting Susan have her moment of joy.

After I cleaned the room and Susan, I let her parents in. They looked at the baby and Susan, talked briefly, and came out of the room. Her mother dissolved in tears and quiet sobs. I held her for five minutes and let her cry—it was her grandson that was being given away. They left. Susan's sister left a few minutes later, but Ann stayed with Susan. I gave some pain and sleeping pills to Susan, and still Ann stayed. She stayed until Susan was asleep—holding her hand, telling her what a good job she did and how beautiful the baby is. What love, what care. I feel so certain that this baby will be in a wonderful home.

Finally, both Ann and Paul, her husband, spent about forty-five minutes in a quiet room with Timothy Andrew, their new son. I came in and they were both sitting on the bed, crying just watching the baby suck on his hand. I told them that they could pick him up—he was theirs. Paul expressed concern that it might cause the baby to cry. Ann could only say, "What a beautiful gift Susan has given to us."

They had a beautiful bouquet of flowers for Susan, and Ann came back to her room to see her again. Susan was asleep, and she has slept since.

Mr. Donnelly, you see the people involved in an office setting—the paperwork and all. I just felt you should know the drama, and the love shown tonight—it was beautiful—and sad.

And I cried while washing up the instruments. No one could see me or hear me—my heart aches too.

Karen Patton, RN

QUESTIONS FOR DISCUSSION

1. What are the main differences between an agency adoption and an independent adoption?
2. Under what circumstances would it be preferable to go through an agency?
3. When would an independent adoption be better?
4. If you pursued an independent adoption, what approach would be best in your efforts to locate a birth mother?
5. What degree of "openness" would best suit your needs and desires?

4.   *Yes, But ... A Realistic Picture*

Soon it will be Julia's fifth birthday. She wants to celebrate by taking cupcakes to her kindergarten class, but her foster mother says she will probably be moved to a different home before then. Because she has a major hearing loss, Julia needs more time and special care than this foster mother is able to give.

It's an old story for Julia. This artistic, intelligent little girl with big brown eyes, curly black hair, and a turned-up pug nose has spent her short life shuffled from one foster home to another. What she really needs is a family who will adopt her. But because she is older and handicapped, it is doubtful that this will ever happen.

The great majority of families who express interest in adopting a child want a cuddly, alert infant or perhaps a cute little toddler. But many of the families who request such babies will have to wait for years to get one. Some never will.

The fact is that there simply are not enough healthy, white infants to meet the current demand. Even though the birth rate of illegitimate children has risen at an alarming rate, fewer and fewer of them are available for adoption. The main reason for this is that many unwed mothers are now choosing to keep their infants. This trend, along with the prevalence of birth control, the availability of abortion, and the widespread popularity of adoption, has resulted in a shortage of adoptable white infants. The babies who do become available are quickly placed in the most ideal adoptive homes, usually with families who have been waiting for years or who have retained the most well-connected attorneys.

The American culture is currently in a period of adjusting values. It's too bad that this is occurring only because healthy white babies have become scarce. Today families wanting a healthy white infant may be disappointed. There are, however, many little children already legally freed for adoption who remain in desperate need of permanent homes. Like Julia, they grow up bounced from one foster home to another. Many of them have been waiting for years to find families that will welcome them into their homes and their hearts. Most will wait a lifetime.

Who are these unwanted little ones? They are older, handicapped, racially mixed, or minority children. They are siblings who must be placed together. Like any other children, they come in all shapes and sizes. Some are outgoing and some are shy, some extremely bright and others slow. They come from various ethnic, cultural, and religious backgrounds. Each one has unique potential, personality, talents, and limitations. And like any other child, each of these children has a driving need to be special and important to someone. They need a family to care about them, to care for them, and to love them.

A CHANGE IN ATTITUDES

In recent years there has been a major shift in the emphasis of many adoption agencies around the country. Increasingly, healthy newborns are being placed through independent adoptions, therefore agencies have begun to concentrate on finding adoptive homes for hard-to-place children. In an effort to find families for them, the agencies are becoming more flexible in their requirements.

It is difficult to talk in a general way about adoption policies nationwide because state laws vary. Even within the same local area, policies differ from agency to agency. In 1978 the U.S. Congress finally passed the country's first federal legislation on adoption. This law, called the Adoption

Opportunities Act, provides for a National Resource Exchange that lists waiting children and waiting parents with a computerized system that keeps track of children in foster care. To find a group in your area that deals with the adoption of hard-to-place children, write:

> National Adoption Informational Exchange
> of the Child Welfare League
> 67 Irving Place
> New York, NY 10003

Again, the first concern of any responsible adoption agency is to ensure to the best of its ability that every child it places will be raised in a secure, loving, and nurturing home. But by reviewing requirements, application procedures, and the selection of adoptive parents, many agencies have begun to concentrate more on screening in than on screening out prospective families. Only applicants who are considered to be incapable of providing good care and a warm, loving home to a needy child are ruled out by every adoption agency.

In serving hard-to-place children, agencies tend to ease their rules and regulations. Most agencies are willing to consider each case individually and to waive some of their requirements—and even their fees—when it seems appropriate. Two couples who have benefitted from this trend are the Allens and the Powells.

Hindered by a poor credit rating and a modest savings account, Fred and Suzanne Allen had been discouraged from filling out an application for adoption. But they persisted in their determination to have a child. Two years ago, on the basis of Fred's steady income, the Allens were able to adopt a deaf, three-year-old boy.

Under the old requirements, Tony and Joy Powell could never have adopted because they don't own a house. Fortunately, the agency with which they worked recognized that the ability to provide a secure home with an atmosphere of love and patient understanding is more important to a child than having parents who are homeowners. Last year the way was cleared for the Powells to adopt a brother and sister who had been abandoned by their parents.

These changes have brought hope to many families whose applications for adoption would have been quickly turned down a few years ago. As a result, many homes are being enriched by the presence of much-wanted, much-loved children. Working mothers, older couples, lower-income families, families with other children, and single persons are being recognized as people who can be excellent parents. Suddenly there are many more potential adoptive families around than anyone had imagined. And somewhere along the way, adoption agencies have made an interesting discovery: Some of the qualities that have always been considered essential to the nurture of well-adjusted children are not really all that important after all.

And what about the children? If it has been difficult for a family seeking to adopt, just imagine what it has been like for the children waiting for adoption. To be considered acceptable to the "perfect family," children also had to be perfect. They had to be completely healthy and had to have been born of healthy parents. Even children with such minor or correctable defects as crossed eyes or a harelip were considered unadoptable. What a tragedy! The basic needs of a child with a physical, mental, or emotional handicap are just as great as the needs of any other child. And who among us would dare to question God's equal and unconditional love for every single one of these little ones?

As agencies began to try to place formerly unadoptable children, they made another discovery. Many of the couples who had requested a "normal" child responded with love and sensitive understanding to the needs of hard-to-place children. They came forward, anxious to become parents to these little ones and expressing a readiness to cope with problems of all kinds.

For little Julia, there is as yet no happy ending. For many other children there is. The desire to love and provide a home for a very special child occurs in different ways and for different reasons. Probably the most common is the one told by Frank and Helen Smithson, an active couple in their early forties.

"We knew there was little chance of having a baby placed with us," said Helen. "Our age was against us. And to tell the truth, I'm not at all sure I have the energy to keep up with an active two-year-old. So for us, adopting an older child really made sense.

"Cindy was eight years old when we adopted her. She immediately became the center of our lives. Being an only child was good for her because she was in such need emotionally. She was like a little sponge, ready to soak up all the love and attention we could pour on. And how she responded!

"God made us for each other, we know that. What Cindy so desperately needed to receive, Frank and I needed to give."

FILLING THE EMPTY PLACE

But difficulties in qualifying for a healthy newborn are by no means the only reason for choosing a hard-to-place child. Jerry Woods and his wife, parents of two healthy boys, chose to adopt from the most unwanted group of all—the mentally retarded.

"My youngest brother, Phillip, suffered from Down's syndrome," Jerry said in a quiet voice. "You can't imagine what a blow it was to our family when he was born. But before long we began to see him for what he really was—a very special gift that God in his great wisdom had entrusted to our family. And that's just how he was treated.

"Phillip died of heart failure two weeks before his seventeenth birthday. We all cried for the empty place he left in our hearts. My brother had that pure joy, that unconditional love and trust that is reserved for the very young and the very innocent. From him we learned the vital lessons of tolerance for all people, however God made them.

"Although no parents would ever want their child to be

born with such a handicap, I truly wished that my children could have had the chance to grow up loving, caring for, and learning from their Uncle Phillip.

"When our boys were five and seven, my wife and I read a newspaper account of a Down's syndrome baby who had been deserted at birth. After discussing it with our sons, we decided to inquire about the possibility of adopting that baby.

"As it turned out, that baby wasn't available, but in less than two months we were given Tyler, a sweet, brown-haired baby with the same disability. That was seven years ago and I can honestly say that Tyler is every bit as precious to us as Phillip was to me. The agency says that Tyler would have had little chance of ever becoming a part of a family had it not been for us. That may be true, but I don't think they realize how much we have gained. Without a doubt we are a better family because of Tyler."

Dennis and Sue Hardy chose to adopt Nancy, a red-haired, freckle-faced eight-year-old. Nancy suffers from cerebral palsy (C.P.) and is confined to a wheelchair.

"Our birth daughter, Allison, also has cerebral palsy," said Sue, "so we knew exactly what was involved in caring for a child with this handicap. We also were keenly aware of just how badly such children need the love and support of a caring family. Because of her disability, Allison has always felt isolated. She attends a special school and has never had playmates in the neighborhood.

"Actually it was Allison who first talked about wanting a sister who was like her. After a few months of such talk, my husband and I began to think seriously about adopting a little girl with C.P. We applied, and within months we were introduced to Nancy. She won our hearts on her first visit. Just one year younger than nine-year-old Allison, she was also confined to a wheelchair. The girls loved each other from the start.

"In many ways Allison and Nancy are just like any other sisters. They play together, laugh together, and cry together. Sometimes they argue and sometimes they pout. But in other ways they are closer than most sisters. Because they have the same handicap, they depend on each other a great deal. They are each other's only real friend. They help and encourage each other. There's no doubt: As a family of four, we are a resounding success."

Some people have a seemingly limitless capacity to love children and a willingness always to make room for "just one more." God has blessed these special people with the patience, understanding, and acceptance needed to expand and adapt their homes to meet the varied needs of many different little ones. Not many have this God-given gift, but Wes and Peggy Mendez do.

"When the youngest of our five children was ten, our seventeen-year-old said, 'Isn't it time we got some more little kids around here?' That was exactly what I had been thinking!" laughed Peggy, a forty-two-year-old grandmother. "With our oldest daughter married and one of our sons away at college, we had plenty of room.

"I asked the placement agency if they had a child who was in special need. Instead of one they told me about the plight of three children: two brothers, aged four and five, and their seven-year-old sister. They had been living in an overcrowded foster home and were to be moved just as soon as a satisfactory place could be found. Although they were legally available for adoption, such a permanent placement was unlikely because they had to be kept together. That night after a family discussion, we decided to invite the children to spend the weekend with us. They have been here ever since.

"It would be less than honest to say that the adoption has been problem-free. Of course there have been problems. And there have been adjustments for every one of us. But I know that I'm speaking for the entire family when I say that we don't regret our decision to adopt the children. We gave them the home they needed, and they have repaid us a hundredfold by filling our home with the joyous noise and clutter that only comes from happy children.

"There were two more than we had planned on. But really, three are not so much more trouble than one!"

Some families seek out a large adopted family as a form

of ministry. Dennis and Cindy Garland had all the things most people in our culture prize: Dennis was a highly respected and successful doctor and Cindy was a nurse. After giving birth to two handsome sons, they adopted a little girl and announced to their friends that their family was complete. They lived in a large house with ample garage space for Dennis's collection of classic cars. "One day our Bible study group was going through the book of Matthew," related Dennis, "and I was asked to read aloud chapter 25, verses 35–40, where Jesus was speaking of the forthcoming judgment and said: 'For I was hungry and you fed me; I was thirsty and you gave me water; I was a stranger and you invited me into your homes; naked and you clothed me; sick and in prison, and you visited me. . . . And I, the King, will tell them, "When you did it to these my brothers you were doing it to me!"'

"That set me to thinking of how blessed we had been materially and of the empty bedrooms in our home. That night, Cindy and I prayed together, and the next day we called our local county adoption agency to inquire about adopting a sibling group. A few months later three children, two boys and their sister, came to our home, and the adoption was final six months after that. I do not think of myself as a 'rescuer,' and I will not judge others who may disagree. But in my view, adopting those kids and sharing the material resources, time, attention, and love which the Lord had so generously provided was an act of obedience."

SOMETIMES IT JUST HAPPENS

For some families, adoption isn't planned. It just seems to happen. That's how it was for Matt and Charlene Dunham.

"With three daughters of our own we were already a good-sized family," said Matt, a middle-aged elementary schoolteacher. "My salary is not great, and Charlene has been working part time ever since the girls were little just to make ends meet. Adopting a child had never entered our minds.

"Then Maggie came to my fifth-grade class. She was a sweet child and smart, but she was terribly withdrawn and depressed. Just months before, Maggie's parents and older sister had been killed in an automobile accident. Maggie herself had spent weeks in the hospital. When she was released she went to a foster home because she had no relatives. My heart went out to that sad, silent, lonely little girl.

"When Maggie's foster parents wanted to go away without the children for a weekend, I offered to have Maggie spend the two days with our family. It was amazing to see how perfectly she fit in. She seemed to belong with us. Before the visit was over, Maggie was laughing and playing like any other ten-year-old.

"After that weekend our family started to talk about the possibility of adopting Maggie. Before school was over for the year, we had a fourth daughter and Maggie had a family."

Should your family decide to adopt a hard-to-place child, you must realize that he or she does not come with a guarantee. Expect a challenge. That way you won't be caught off guard when difficulties arise.

"Three-quarters of the children we have available are boys over seven," one social worker reported. "Most of them come with emotional scars from abandonment, abuse, and neglect. At first I was hesitant to place special-needs children in adoptive homes because I knew there would be problems. I am wiser now. With few exceptions, the parents who chose to adopt these children have found a very special reward for loving and accepting them.

"But we neither need nor want 'do-gooders' or 'rescuers,'" the social worker emphasized. "We just want average families who are happy and secure and want a child or children to share their family life. Families or single parents who feel that they can make the commitment to a child with special needs are now given priority in our adoption agency and in many others as well. We welcome the chance to explore with them whether adoption is right for them and, if so, what child would best fit into their home and lifestyle."

Any adoption gives the adoptive parents the great privilege and the awesome responsibility of becoming the most important people in the entire world to a special little person. At the same time the adopted child becomes a special part of a new family. As this family grows together in love, the parents will find that they are giving a great deal of themselves to their new child. But they must do it willingly and lovingly, appreciating whatever their child is able to give in return and demanding no more.

"There was a time when we only wanted a healthy, white baby girl," said one woman who is still awaiting word on the application for adoption she and her husband submitted two years ago. "But our ideas have changed. We've grown older and more mature. Today we would have no reservations about adopting a racially mixed child or one with a mild physical or mental handicap."

In the chapters that follow we will take a closer look at some of the options available in adoption. Maybe you will see your own situation and will be helped and encouraged. Or perhaps you will see a need that you can meet especially well because of the particular circumstances in which God has placed you. Surely Jesus was thinking of children like Cindy and Tyler and Nancy and Julia when he said, "Any of you who welcomes a little child like this because you are mine, is welcoming me and caring for me" (Matthew 18:5).

QUESTIONS FOR DISCUSSION

1. What are the options available in adoption today?
2. We have all heard, read, and seen on television the emotional, inspiring stories of wonderfully successful adoptions of problem children. How can a family best prepare for the realities of adoption?

5.   *Love Comes in*
               Many Colors

Lisa is an active nine-year-old, the youngest of Gary and Joyce Barber's four children. Like her older brothers, she is on the local swimming team. Like her older sister, she plays violin in the school orchestra. Unlike her brothers and sister, Lisa is adopted.

"When the children were young, they were always being asked why their baby sister didn't look like them," Joyce Barber said. "They would answer, 'She isn't supposed to look like us. She's supposed to look like her!'"

Lisa Barber was one of the thousands of children fathered by American GI's in Vietnam. These children were despised by the Vietnamese people because of their mixed race and rejected by the United States government, which refused to take any responsibility for them. So multitudes of them were put into filthy, fly-infested, crowded orphanages in Vietnam. They received minimal care and attention. Hundreds died from malnutrition or commonplace diseases such as the measles. Lisa was one of the fortunate ones who survived.

"Gary and I had always thought that someday we would adopt a child," Joyce said. "When our three children were two, four, and six, we saw a television program sponsored by a Christian organization that depicted the tragic plight of the Vietnamese orphans. It told of one case in which an agency in Vietnam had sixty children eligible and ready for adoption, but before their paperwork could be completed, fifty-two of them had died. We knew immediately what the Lord wanted us to do.

"Because of the great emotional outpouring of concern for these orphans, the agencies had to screen the applicants very carefully. Many would-be parents had not really thought through all the ramifications of such an adoption, and after considering the problems that could lie ahead, many of them changed their minds. Although there were more than twenty couples in our first preadoption session, we were the only ones to complete the procedure and finally, ten months later, get a baby."

One problem that must be faced by any family considering interracial adoption is the burden of prejudice imposed by our society. The reactions vary greatly, both within the community and within the couple's own family. According to one adoption director, the problem is not a matter of educating the public as a whole, so much as it is the need to foster a sense of understanding and acceptance in individual neighbors, friends, and relatives.

When a family chooses to adopt across racial lines, a new family is being created in which children of different races or nationalities become brothers and sisters. Because the other children of the family will be very much affected by the adoption, it is only fair to discuss the matter thoroughly with them. Their feelings must be taken into account because any adoption is a commitment for the entire family. Each member must be determined to make it a success.

These considerations caused no problem for the Barber family. For one thing, they adopted Lisa at a time when there was a nationwide outpouring of concern over the welfare of mixed-race children in Vietnam. Many of Gary and Joyce's friends and neighbors were also discussing the possibility of such an adoption. Then, too, the Barbers' own families were encouraging. Gary's aunt and uncle had adopted three Chinese orphans while they were serving as missionaries in Thailand. Now in their twenties, these Chinese "aunties" are favorites of the Barber children.

"Lisa came from Vietnam on a special plane chartered by a group of adoptive parents," Gary said. "Everyone wanted to come along with us to meet the plane—relatives, neighbors, friends, people from our church—but on the recommendation of the social worker, we went alone. We were determined to keep our first meeting with Lisa a very special, private time just for the three of us.

"When we got to the airport two hours before the flight was due in from Saigon, other couples were already there waiting," Joyce continued. "We were so excited, we just couldn't sit still. We spent the time swapping stories with other 'expectant' parents. We met a heart surgeon and his wife who were adopting a little boy with a congenital heart defect. They had requested him because they felt they were better equipped to handle a problem like his than most other people.

"When the plane's arrival was announced over the speaker, everyone started to cheer. We all rushed to the window and watched as the plane landed. Then one mother called out, 'Here come the babies!' All around us were cries of greeting, hugs and kisses, cameras flashing, while we waited for what seemed like an eternity. Finally our name was called.

"I can't begin to describe my feelings when the escort placed that tiny bundle in my arms. Gary and I unwrapped her blanket and examined our new daughter from head to toe. From that moment on, she was our baby.

"We couldn't help but think of the host of possible problems about which we had been warned. We were told that, because of the differences in the temperaments and practices of the two cultures and because of the severe emotional strain, many of these babies become disoriented and upset—some even seriously ill. Many are unable to respond to all the loving they receive. We were also warned about the possibility of physical or mental problems that might not show up until later.

"Lisa's amazingly easy adjustment was a pleasant surprise. We congratulated ourselves on our expert parenting. Our baby never cried at all. But then she never smiled or laughed, either. In fact, she seemed almost totally emotionless. Her little face always wore the same serious expression. Although she was six months old, she couldn't sit

69

alone or roll over. She could hardly even hold her head up. When we held something out to her, she just stared instead of reaching for it. But it had been a long time since I had a six-month-old and I had forgotten what a baby of that age should be doing. So I didn't worry.

"When I took Lisa for her first checkup, the blow came. The doctor examined her carefully and told me that there was a real possibility that our baby was mentally retarded. I was shocked! But by then Lisa was our daughter just as surely as if she had been born to us, and we would keep her no matter what.

"The first thing Gary and I did was to have a long talk with the Lord. We acknowledged the fact that Lisa was his little girl, only loaned to us. We committed her to his sovereign will and promised to love and care for her whatever her condition.

"Next we planned our strategy. Gary took a month's vacation and we spent hours and hours playing with Lisa, holding her, stimulating her in any way possible. The results were amazing! In three weeks she had caught up to where a six-month-old should be. She was alert, active, sitting well, even starting to crawl. The doctor was astounded at her progress. He said it was nothing short of a miracle. We agree. A miracle is exactly what it was."

Gary and Joyce Barber are good examples of the kind of people who successfully adopt children from a different racial background. They are mature, strong, flexible people. They are able to unconditionally accept a child who is different from themselves. They don't follow the tendency to attribute superior qualities to people who are like them and inferior qualities to anyone who is different. With the decision to adopt a child of a different race they demonstrated a willingness to meet, with God's help, any problems that came along, never letting those problems affect their love and acceptance of their child. Although they certainly realized their child's need for a secure home life, they did not see themselves primarily as "rescuers," nor were they interested in making a social statement. Instead, they recognized and appreciated their daughter for who she was: a special and satisfying addition to their family.

A family who adopts a child of another race is no longer a single-race family. Both the child and family will have to contend with whatever stereotypes and racial prejudices exist in their community. Also, by adopting, the parents are accepting an obligation to share in their child's heritage. It is a mistake to try to make a child give up his or her racial heritage to better assimilate with the family. If family members are not ready to be proud of a child's unique identity, they have no business adopting in the first place.

"In her hand-drawn pictures, Lisa had always shown people with big round faces and little round eyes," said Joyce Barber. "Then one day when she was in kindergarten, Lisa drew a different kind of picture. She started out by drawing the usual big round face, but on this one she put small, almond-shaped eyes. 'That's me!' she announced proudly. For the first time Lisa seemed to see herself as she was, not as she saw us. We want to encourage that individuality and also a real pride in her heritage."

Not all interracial adoptions are as smooth as Lisa's. Like the Barbers, Burt and Carolyn Rhoades were deeply moved by the tragic plight of the Indochinese orphans. They opened their home to four children who had escaped from Vietnam with their mother and an uncle.

"The children have been with us for almost two years now," Burt said, "and believe me, these years haven't been easy. When the children first came to us, they were totally engulfed in fear. They would cringe and cover their heads with their arms at any sudden move. The younger ones have pretty much overcome this fear, but ten-year-old Hoa is still a real problem. At the first sign of any kind of trouble he rounds up his eight-year-old brother and his two sisters, five and four, and hides them in the hall closet. His whole attitude is one of 'us against the world.'

"When you consider his background, Hoa's actions are understandable. In his ten short years he has been through

71

more tragedy and despair than anyone should have to experience in a lifetime.

"In Vietnam, Hoa's father was dragged out of his hut and shot by Communist soldiers. In terror, his mother paid her life savings to have the family smuggled out of the country aboard a jam-packed fishing boat. During a violent storm, Hoa's uncle and one sister were swept overboard and lost at sea. Two days later the youngest child was born. The rickety fishing boat finally made it to the Philippine Islands, and the family spent a year in a refugee camp there before they were allowed into the United States.

"Just when things were beginning to look up for the family, a deranged man—also a refugee from Vietnam—broke into their apartment and killed their mother while the children looked on in horror. The authorities picked up the four children and placed them in separate foster homes. They didn't see each other again until they were reunited at our house."

Carolyn picked up the story. "The little girls have adjusted beautifully. They are too young to really remember much of what happened. The younger boy isn't a problem, either. He tries awfully hard to fit into the family. But poor Hoa. He sees himself as a survivor and everyone around him—including us—as the enemy. We want so badly to help him, but where do we begin? At this point we can only trust the Lord."

COPING WITH RACIAL FACTORS

Some people question the wisdom of going outside the United States to adopt children when there are so many needy ones in our own country. Although welfare agencies see to it that homeless children have their physical needs met in institutions or foster homes, the children often grow up starved for the love and security that only a caring family can provide. Many of them are minority or biracial children, and while any child raised without a family faces a life of uncertainty, children who discover that they were rejected for adoption simply because of their racial background can hardly help but be hurt and bitter.

It would be ideal for all children to be placed with families of their own racial or national backgrounds. Unfortunately that is not always possible. In the United States the pattern of demand for children does not match the racial makeup of those who are available. There are many more white applicants than there are adoptable white babies, and there are not nearly as many adoptive minority applicants as there are minority babies.

Chuck and Sandy Judson live in an area with a large Mexican population. Their two children, now twenty and twenty-two, were adopted as infants.

"When we decided to adopt, many of the available babies and young children were part Mexican," said Sandy. "But very few Mexican families applied to adopt, and because of the ethnic prejudices in our area, few white couples were interested in taking them. Because the child's nationality didn't make any difference to us, we chose children of Mexican descent. Nick was our first child; he was a small, gentle, sensitive boy. Two years later we got Monica, a real fireball. By the time Monica was two, she already ruled the roost. At five she was taller and stronger than her big brother. She played basketball and softball and ran track in high school. With very little effort she got all A's and B's in school. When Monica was growing up, our house was always filled with kids and noise and fun and laughter.

"But it was different for Nick. He was too small to excel in sports, and academics never came easily for him. He was shy and quiet, and while he was always included in whatever Monica and her friends were doing, Nick felt more comfortable on the sidelines. His two great loves were his music—he plays piano, clarinet, and drums—and Buddy, his beautiful Labrador retriever."

"Monica has traveled through her growing-up years relatively problem-free," said Chuck. "Now twenty, she is a university junior majoring in business and is engaged to a seminary student. But things have been much harder for

Nick. A lot of the problem, I suppose, was the contrast between him and his athletic, outgoing, popular younger sister—a common situation even among biological siblings. But I also think that his adoption by an Anglo family was a contributing factor.

"In our area most Mexicans occupy a pretty low social status. Nick has Latin features, but because of his name and his family, people didn't think of him as being of Mexican descent. Without realizing what they were doing, other kids would make racial slurs or uncomplimentary remarks about Mexicans in his presence. That certainly did nothing to help foster a sense of pride in his own heritage.

"Since his preteen years, Nick has had to battle low self-esteem. If I had it to do again, I would make a conscious effort from day one to build up our son's sense of self-worth and to encourage pride in who he is. This is important for any child, but for one who is adopted and physically different from his family, it is especially crucial."

PROTECTION FROM INTOLERANCE

There is much controversy surrounding interracial adoptions. Many people wonder if Caucasian parents can properly prepare a minority child for life in a prejudiced world. There are even those who go so far as to say that minority children should remain under foster care and in institutions rather than be placed in the homes of willing white families. What a tragic point of view!

In the 1980s, a national association of black social workers passed a resolution that black children should not be adopted by non-black families because to allow a black child to grow up in a home of a different race was "cultural genocide." Some states, including California, have also passed laws which require that, if at all possible, children must be placed in an adoptive home of the same race. This would be logical and appropriate if there were enough minority adoptive and foster homes, but there aren't. The tragic consequence is that minority children have languished in foster care even though there were adoptive homes available. It is difficult to understand how anyone could maintain that it is better for a child to have no family than to have a family of a different race. One has to wonder about the motivations of those who would gladly sacrifice the children of their race in order to further their social agenda.

The sad truth is that in today's American society, children of minority heritage are likely to face prejudice no matter who raises them. But with parents and a loving, understanding, stable Christian home, these children should be able to face life secure in the knowledge that they are truly loved and wanted. Such a foundation is the only real protection any minority child has against intolerance in society. Parents who see themselves and their children not as white or black or brown or any other color, but rather as children created in the image of God, will succeed in making minority children part of their family. They can help these children develop a sense of personal worth and value that will equip them to overcome the problems of life rather than be overcome by them.

JUST A PLAIN KID

It is much easier to adopt transracially if the family lives in a racially mixed community. No child likes to be different. Being the only oriental or black child in a school isn't easy. A child whose racial background is shared by friends, neighbors, teachers, and classmates can be just a plain kid instead of "the adopted black child."

Larry and Janelle Kingman are the parents of two sons by birth and of Katie, a ten-year-old black girl they adopted as a baby. Even though they live in a predominantly white neighborhood, the Kingmans have experienced few race-related problems. Katie is a bright girl who is at the top of her class scholastically. She is a natural leader and always has many friends. Only recently has she begun to speak about her hidden conflicts and concerns.

"Once I went to Los Angeles on a field trip with my

school class," Katie said thoughtfully. "I saw buses full of kids who looked just like me. I kept wondering if any of them were my real brothers or sisters." Katie paused, then added, "You know what I really hate? I hate it when people ask me why I'm different from my family. I don't want to be different!"

Katie Kingman's parents have tried to help her come to terms with these conflicts and develop a true sense of pride in who she is.

"Last year we decided to transfer Katie to a different school," Janelle said. "The school in our neighborhood is all white. The new one, just a few miles away, has a fair percentage of black students. Now in addition to her neighborhood friends, Katie has black friends with whom she can more easily identify. Also, at the suggestion of her teacher, we are helping Katie with a project that has to do with tracing her roots. It has really been interesting for all of us."

"There is one question we're asked all the time," Larry interjected. "People always say, 'How would you feel if your sons decided to marry black girls?' Well, Janelle and I have talked about it and I can honestly say it wouldn't matter at all. In fact, our oldest son is now dating a black girl. As for Katie's choice of a lifetime partner—white, black, or any other color—it makes no difference to us."

After a pause Larry continued, "I must tell you, though, that we're not really as open-minded as you may think. There is one area in which we are very prejudiced. We would be very distressed if any of our children were to marry a non-Christian."

UNEXPECTED BLESSINGS

The problems, concerns, and considerations of interracial adoptions are certainly greater than those of classic adoptions. Still, every family interviewed who had been involved in such an adoption emphasized the very special—

and often unexpected—blessings that their adopted child had brought to their home.

If you are interested in finding out more about the possibilities for interracial adoption where you live, contact your local adoption agency. Names and addresses of American agencies that specialize in foreign adoptions can be obtained by writing to:

> The Children's Bureau of the United States
> Department of Health and Human Services
> P.O. Box 1182
> Washington, D.C. 20013

Ask for the National Directory of Intercountry Adoption Services.

"I feel sorry for the people who tell me how wonderful we are for having adopted Katie," said Janelle Kingman. "It's sad that they can't understand that we are the lucky ones. By giving her to us, God has blessed our family more than I can ever tell."

OPEN FORUM

Ken Randle: Our son is of another nationality, one not held in very high esteem in the area where we live. I think I made a mistake in how I handled him. I was guilty of not being aware of his conflicts and feelings of being different and inferior.

Dr. McDill: If you had it to do again, what would you do differently?

Ken Randle: I would take my role of fathering more seriously. I would keep in close touch with him and work hard at keeping the lines of communication open. Then I could guide him along and help him to come to terms with who he is.

Dr. McDill: That's important for every parent—especially for fathers, who often fail to realize just how important their parenting role really is.

QUESTIONS FOR DISCUSSION

1. What were the elements that made the Barbers' adoption of Lisa so much easier than the Rhoades' adoption of the Vietnamese children?
2. What might the Rhoades do to help Hoa adjust?
3. The problem of self-esteem is of concern to many people today. What practical steps would you take to help your child develop healthy self-esteem? (There is more about this in chapter 12.)

6. God's Special Children

Throughout history people have placed great value on physical and mental strength. In primitive times the problem of imperfect babies was usually solved simply and quickly. The child died.

In our enlightened age and sophisticated society, imperfect children whose birth parents cannot or will not care for them are usually placed in a system of foster care or institutional living. Only occasionally are they adopted. While many people are moved by feelings of sympathy and pity, not many have an understanding love strong enough to cause them to want to take one of these children as their own.

In the past, children with handicaps were not considered adoptable. It never occurred to social workers that there might be some families who would welcome and value these children in their homes. But times are changing. More and more families are now choosing to lovingly raise children with special needs.

WHY A PROBLEM CHILD?

What motivates families to adopt problem children when healthy children are available? What do they get in return for the extraordinary care and responsibility these children require? Consider Mike and Fran Nelson's experience.

When their church began a ministry at a local home for mentally retarded children, the Nelsons—both teachers— volunteered to help out on a regular basis. It was there that they first met Keith, a tiny four-year-old abandoned by his parents at birth. He had been diagnosed as autistic.

"Keith lived in a strange world of his own," said Fran, a woman in her middle forties. "He didn't show the slightest response to anyone or anything around him. I worked and played with many of the other children, but I just couldn't keep my eyes off that little boy. He sat in silence, playing unknown games with his fingers or gently knocking his head against the wall. I was really intrigued. What could be going on in that little mind of his?

"To the workers at the home, Keith was little more than an accessory to the room's furniture. Each morning he was carried in and set down in his corner, and there he stayed until someone carried him to his bed at night. He never talked, he never smiled, and he never cried."

"I really wanted to work with Keith," Mike said, "even though the nurse told me that it would be a waste of time. I couldn't get over the feeling that there was a lot of potential locked up inside him. Maybe we just needed to find the right key. The children Fran and I were assigned to work with had very limited mental abilities. The most we could hope for was that they would eventually be able to feed and dress themselves. But with Keith, no one really knew. Anything was possible."

Because of their interest in Keith, Fran and Mike spent more and more time at the home. Whenever possible they would talk to Keith, sing to him, play with him—anything to try to get his attention. But weeks and months passed with no change. The situation seemed hopeless. Keith never gave the slightest indication that he knew or cared that they were there. After six months, the Nelsons, disappointed and discouraged, were ready to admit defeat.

"We were so sure God was going to accomplish a miraculous healing right before our eyes," Fran admitted. "But it just wasn't happening. We decided it would be best for everyone if we stayed away from the home for a while.

"Two weeks later we got a telephone call from the nurse at the children's home. She said that Keith seemed to be looking for us! For several days he had been less interested in his finger games and, for the first time in his life, he was looking around. We were back that afternoon."

"After six more disappointing months with Keith," Mike said, "I read an article about two researchers at a university near our home who had developed a very successful program for working with autistic children. I called them and described Keith, and they agreed to see him right away. But when I asked the home for permission to take him to the university, my request was denied. Rules and regulations, you know. I was frustrated and angry. Fran and I had grown to really care about that little guy. We felt as if we were fighting for *our* child.

"After a lot of prayer, discussion, and counsel, Fran and I decided to ask permission to adopt Keith. We had seen his full medical evaluation and report, so we were well aware of the uphill battle we would face. The medical prognosis wasn't good. Still, we were convinced that the Lord had already brought us together in a very special way, and we wanted to be sure that Keith would have every possible opportunity. We wanted him with us.

"The pile of red tape we faced was monumental, but finally Keith was released to our care. Amid dire warnings and reminders that we could always return him before the adoption became final, we took our little son home."

"The program in which Keith was enrolled was a rigid, difficult, sometimes seemingly heartless one," Fran said. "Many, many nights I fell into bed exhausted and cried myself to sleep. Each morning before even attempting to get out of bed, I prayed, 'Show me just one little victory today and I'll be satisfied.' And that's exactly what God did. It was those little victories that carried us through.

"What a little trooper Keith was! He was the most single-minded, determined little fellow I've ever seen. You might call him just plain stubborn. But it was that trait that kept pushing him on.

"Keith is now nineteen years old. If you're expecting me to say that he has grown into a perfectly normal young man, you'll be disappointed. He hasn't. But when you consider what he was and what he would have been had he remained in that institution, our son is perfect.

"This year Keith graduated from a vocational high school. The first three rows of the auditorium were filled with friends and relatives who had shared in his long struggle toward this day. When he was handed his diploma, there wasn't a dry eye among us. Our graduation gifts to him were a new watch and—at his request—a construction-worker lunch box to take to work.

"Keith had a job waiting for him on an assembly line, a job he had found himself. The next month he moved into a house with six other young men who have similar disabilities. A live-in couple act as house parents. Keith rides the city bus to and from work and anywhere else he wants to go. His Sundays are spent with us."

"We're proud of our son," Mike said. "He's a happy, self-sufficient, Christian young man who is determined to be a contributing member of society. I hate to think of how close he came to spending his life sitting in a corner of that institution, doing nothing but playing with his fingers and hitting his head against the wall. It makes me wonder, how many other children are there out there like Keith?"

There are many. Thousands of the children awaiting homes have physical and mental disabilities. Their problems range from short-term, relatively unimportant disorders to life-threatening illnesses.

WHAT REASONS ARE GOOD ENOUGH?

Any family interested in adopting a special-needs child must consider the matter carefully and prayerfully. Feelings of pity and guilt are not good-enough reasons for such an adoption. Nor is an emotional or romantic idea of the miracles God will perform for that child. It is vitally important to approach the adoption realistically. Sometimes God chooses to work a miracle, but more often he does not.

An adoptive family must be prepared to accept his answer either way.

It is one thing to read about a child with a handicap. Living with the problem day after day and year after year is quite another. Well-meaning new parents can easily become overwhelmed by the realities of daily life, by the lack of resources and understanding available, and often by the lack of knowledge on the part of the very professionals on whom they depend for help, guidance, and solutions.

A unique kind of family is needed for such an adoption to be successful. Parents must have extra patience and love for children with special needs. They must find satisfaction in small, slow gains, and they must be able to rejoice in gradual improvements. They must be able to look upon a child like Keith and see what can be accomplished, not focus on what can't be done.

The task requires people who can genuinely value such children and appreciate their individual potential. Like Mike and Fran Nelson, the families must emphasize giving to the children rather than receiving. They should be able to see something of great value in their children, to accept with pride whatever they can achieve, and to demand no more. After all, not everyone has to become a doctor or a lawyer or a schoolteacher to be successful. Most of all, these families need a deep faith in God so that they will have his strength and guidance supporting them daily.

Families who decide to adopt children with special needs must be willing to accept the fact that their children will be more dependent on them than is usual. Yet they must also encourage their children to become as independent as possible. It is vitally important that the children never be viewed as a second choice, accepted as the most convenient alternative to what the parents really wanted. Children with disabilities, like any other children, have the right to be loved because of their own personal worth as human beings created in the great wisdom of God.

When Don and Emily Owens adopted Curt they had no intentions of choosing a child with special needs. To all appearances their newborn son was perfect in every way. It wasn't until Curt was six months old that Emily began to suspect something was wrong. After a special battery of tests, Curt was diagnosed as suffering from muscular dystrophy, a degenerative genetic disease for which there is no known cure. His disease was expected to progress to the point where he would need a wheelchair, perhaps even be confined to bed.

"When Curt's condition was discovered, the adoption had not yet been finalized," Emily related. "Everyone—our families, our friends, even our adoption case worker—advised us to return him to the agency and wait for a healthy child. We prayerfully and painfully considered our options.

"Don pointed out that we had originally wanted to have a child born to us. Had this happened, there's no guarantee that our baby would have been perfect. And then we remembered the months we spent awaiting Curt's arrival. We had specifically prayed, 'Lord, you have a child picked out for us. Make him or her exactly the way you want our baby to be.' Now here Curt was, just the way God had made him, and God doesn't make mistakes. Our answer was obvious. How could we even have considered trading our baby in for a new, improved model?"

"God promised not to give us any job to do without also providing us with the resources necessary to get the job done," Don added. "We determined that we wouldn't stand around wringing our hands saying, 'Why us?' Instead we would press on saying, 'Lord, what now?' God can perform miracles. He *can* heal Curt. This we firmly believe. But we don't demand it. If God says no, if Curt's condition continues to deteriorate, it won't affect our love. Curt is now and he will always be our child."

At ten, Curt Owens is a bright, outgoing, well-adjusted boy. The effects of the disease are relatively mild. Sometimes he must use a wheelchair, but usually he does well on crutches.

"We have pointed out to Curt that most parts of him are like everyone else," added Emily. "He has the ability to love and to be loved, to learn and to accomplish, to know God and to become his child. The characteristics that make Curt different are the very things that make him special and unique."

Curt had something to say too. "My mother and father really love me. They didn't have to keep me—they wanted to. That's how I know they really love me."

APTITUDES AND LIMITATIONS

Children with handicaps, like all children, have certain aptitudes and limitations. They can achieve in some areas even though they cannot achieve in others. It's important for all parents to encourage their children to develop skills according to their natural abilities. Children with special problems need guidance from their parents to help them form a realistic view of themselves so that they will be able to establish goals that they can achieve.

It is especially important to match the right adoptive family with the right child when special needs are involved. In some families a child's epilepsy would only be a manageable inconvenience, while in other households it would be a constant source of concern and embarrassment. Remember, in adoption you *do* have a choice. Even if you are willing to adopt a child with special needs, it's unrealistic to think you will feel the same about every handicap. Take a close look at your educational expectations, your lifestyle, your personal prejudices (which we all have), and your family's finances.

A family's financial situation is important in certain special-needs cases. Problems like Curt's and Keith's can cause a financial drain on any family. In many cases governmental subsidies may provide the help the family needs. To make the adoption of hard-to-place children feasible, most states have some programs available (see Appendix A). The amount of the financial aid and the requirements for qualifying vary widely. Some states also allow special tax credits or deductions for the expenses incurred in adopting a special-needs child, including agency and attorney fees. Because laws can be changed at any time, it is wise to check with your attorney or tax consultant about the amount of aid to which you may be entitled.

LEARNING BY EXPERIENCE

Foster parents who accept children with special problems on a temporary basis sometimes become so lovingly attached to the children that they want to keep them permanently. These parents have a real advantage. They have already learned how much time and energy a child requires day by day. This was the experience of Bill and Marilyn Schultz.

"We love children and always wanted our own," said Marilyn, a soft-spoken woman of thirty. "When we turned in our application at the adoption agency we were told to expect a wait of several years. To fill the time, and also to prepare ourselves for parenthood, Bill and I decided to become foster parents. Three little ones were placed in our home in the first year. Each of them stayed just long enough for us to get attached, then they were taken away. Every time I had to say good-by, I cried for days. Just when I had decided that foster care was not for me, we got the call about Anna.

"Anna had been born to a married couple with four other children, all boys. Her parents had really wanted a girl and they were ecstatic—until they found out about her problem. Anna had been born with an abnormality of the esophagus that caused her to stop breathing several times a day. Her parents, feeling they couldn't cope with such a deformity, left her at the hospital. The social worker who called us said it was just as well. If Anna's parents had taken her home, it's doubtful that she would have lived more than a few days.

"Bill and I agreed to take Anna until another home could be found for her. We were taught to care for her, to feed her, and to revive her when she stopped breathing. A warning alarm was attached to her crib, but whenever she was out of her crib she had to be watched constantly.

"The doctor told us that if Anna could be kept alive, she

would almost certainly outgrow her condition. But as we soon learned, that was a very big 'if.' That very night she stopped breathing, and we couldn't revive her. We had to call an ambulance. After that we lived constantly on the edge of panic."

"I wasn't in favor of taking Anna," said Bill. "I had seen how brokenhearted Marilyn got each time one of the other kids was taken away. What would happen to her if this baby should die? That was a real possibility, you know. But I finally agreed, and after we had Anna for a few days I found that I was the one who was getting emotionally involved. There's something inexplicably engaging about a baby who literally depends on you for her very breath.

"By the time Anna was six months old she had become a part of us. We knew that we couldn't let her go, so we asked about adopting her. At first her natural parents wouldn't release her, but later they changed their minds and signed the papers.

"Everyone told us we were foolish to adopt a baby who could die at any minute. I guess in a way we were, but we just couldn't stand the thought of Anna being taken away from us. Anyway, we were so used to her condition by then that it hardly seemed abnormal any more."

"Anna is now six years old, a first-grader who would make any mother proud," beamed Marilyn as she passed around a picture of her brown-haired, green-eyed daughter with deep dimples and no front teeth. "It's been over a year since she's had a serious breathing attack, although we still have to watch her when she eats. She's scheduled for surgery on her esophagus, and the doctor says that afterward her problem will be a thing of the past. Anna will be as normal and as healthy as any other little girl."

"I'm really glad we weren't given one of those perfect babies," added Bill emphatically. "They all got good homes. But our Anna probably wouldn't even be alive today without us."

Simply loving and accepting a special child into your home is not enough, however. Parents must also instill in their child a sense of identity and self-worth. Most children with handicaps are convinced they were given up by their mothers because they weren't good enough. In some cases, like Anna's, it's true. In any case children with special needs must be told and reassured that they, like every other human being on earth, were created in the image of God. God does not call us to understand his reasons for everything he does. But he does instruct us to trust in his perfect wisdom.

The really fortunate families of special-needs children have neighbors, friends, and relatives who are warm and understanding toward their children. These people are ready to open their hearts to them and to judge them only for the values they have, not for the skills they lack. But some people are shy, uncertain, and embarrassed in the presence of such children; they must learn to become comfortable with them. Occasionally there are those who never will be able to accept them. It may help to remember that they—not the children or their parents—are the real losers. It is essential that parents help their children deal with the possibility of rejection.

HELP FROM OUTSIDE

Prejudice and rejection added to the difficulties caused by the handicap itself take their toll on both the adoptive parents and the child. Sooner or later the time comes when outside help, comfort, and encouragement are needed. A valuable source of supportive help can be found in other parents who have gone through or are now experiencing the same problem. Others who can help are psychiatrists, psychologists, pastors, and social workers. If you find it necessary to search out support people, don't ever consider it a sign of weakness. It isn't. You are simply showing a mature realization that none of us is meant to exist alone. We need each other.

An important consideration that is often overlooked is the need for relaxation and time alone for the parents of special-needs children. A good arrangement is to find a friend or relative who is willing to assume responsibility for the child during such an absence.

"For over a year we never let Anna out of our sight," said Marilyn. "Then one Sunday an acquaintance at church, a registered nurse, asked if she could watch Anna for us one day a month so that we could have a little time to ourselves. We reluctantly agreed. The first time, we stayed away barely two hours and worried the whole time. But the next time was easier and we stayed away a little longer. Soon we were taking the whole day and enjoying every minute of it. We even found we enjoyed Anna more after our monthly breaks."

Some people think that taking time away from their child means they aren't good parents. This just isn't true. What it does mean is that all parents are human and have a normal need for rest and relaxation.

The most important of all considerations for families thinking about adopting children with special needs are the children themselves. They are the ones who so badly need to love and be loved. Whatever problems these children have will almost certainly make some aspects of their lives more difficult for them and their adoptive families, but these needs do not affect who the children are.

Can you give the time, the care, the patience, and the understanding it takes to raise a child with a handicap? For those whom God calls on to raise his special children, there are great satisfactions and rewards, although not necessarily our traditionally accepted ones. But who's to say that our traditional values are true in this case? Perhaps our values would be much different if we could see through the truly wise, loving eyes of the Creator. God says, "For I know the plans I have for you. . . . They are plans for good and not for evil, to give you a future and a hope" (Jeremiah 29:11).

QUESTIONS FOR DISCUSSION

1. What are the important qualifications for adopting a special-needs child? Which ones do or do not fit your situation?

2. Again it must be emphasized: In adoption there are no guarantees. This is especially true when children with handicaps are involved. The Nelsons, the Owenses, and the Schultzes could just as well have seen their children's conditions degenerate instead of improve. Do you think they were prepared for this possibility?

7.   No Longer Babies

"Even before we were married, Gordon and I agreed on the type of family we wanted," said Janet Van Dyke, an elegant woman of thirty-five. "We wanted children, but we did not want babies.

"Again and again my mother complained that I was denying her the pleasures of having a grandbaby of her own. According to her, I was just too selfish to let a baby interfere with my career.

"I'll admit that my job as purchasing manager for a large department store was—and is—a very important part of my life, but that wasn't my reason for not wanting to have a baby. It's just that I never was baby-oriented. Both Gordon and I felt that we would be better parents to an older child.

"When we took our request for a school-age child to the county adoption agency, we were welcomed enthusiastically. Any child over the age of four, it seems, is considered a geriatric loser in adoption circles. Still, the social worker to whom we were assigned wanted to be very sure we knew exactly what we would be getting into. She covered the potential problems so thoroughly that we began to suspect she might actually be trying to scare us off. Again and again she reminded us that many, many adjustments would be necessary."

The social worker was right. An adoption involving an older child entails many adjustments for both the parents and the child. In many ways the arrangement is more like a marriage than an adoption. There must be a spirit of acceptance on both sides and a genuine willingness to give as well as to take. For this kind of adoption to be successful, both the child and the new parents must agree to live together as a family, and both sides must be willing to make concessions for the sake of harmony.

Since they come with their personality already formed, older children will not easily be molded into the likeness of their new parents. They come with a past, with their own memories and established tastes, with their own pattern of life. Older children have usually been in foster care for several years and have been shifted from home to home. They have learned how risky it is to trust, how dangerous to love. Some have suffered physical and emotional damage.

It takes time for love to grow between adopted children and their new parents. Though the children desperately want to be part of a loving family, they may act in ways that serve only to drive others away. There will be moments when you will wonder how you ever got yourself into this relationship, and there will be moments when you will wonder why you waited so long. In between there will be challenges, victories, and some losses.

"Six months after we were approved as adoptive parents," Janet related, "Eric, a seven-year-old blond with huge brown eyes and freckles on his nose, came to visit our home. He and his ten-year-old brother, Craig, had been living with a couple who were in the process of adopting them. But when that couple filed for divorce, the brothers were returned to the agency. It was decided that the boys' only hope of ever being adopted was to split them up and make them available to separate families.

"When Eric arrived to stay with us, I took a six-month leave of absence from my job. I thought that by spending time together we could really get to know each other. But Eric was a quiet, withdrawn boy who seldom spoke. When he did talk, it was always about the good times he had had in his foster homes and how much he missed his brother. I knew for a fact that Craig had bullied Eric unmercifully, but to hear the boy talk you would have thought his brother had been a saint. I began to wonder if Eric would ever love and accept Gordon and me as his family."

Though confusing and frustrating to his new parents, Eric's reactions were completely normal. He was experiencing a deep sense of separation, and he needed time to grieve over his loss. Fortunately, his new parents were ready and able to give him the support he needed to resolve his feelings of sorrow and conflicting loyalties.

"Gordon was very good to Eric during this difficult time," Janet continued. "He spent hours with him and in very special ways demonstrated that he truly valued him for who he was—a good boy, worthy of our love. Gordon felt that Eric must understand that he was in no way responsible for anything that had happened in the past. My husband's excellent fathering deserves a great deal of credit for our son's relatively easy adjustment.

"That's not to say that the adoption was problem-free. Eric went through a time of testing us, but we dealt with his misbehavior immediately and firmly. We made it perfectly clear that we expected him to make an effort to adjust, but we also let him know that we were willing to do the same. In the end we were able to reach a happy medium and come to a mutual understanding. Eric was accepted for who he was; we did not try to make him over to be like us. In really important areas we were definite and strict, but in areas that didn't matter so much we were relaxed and flexible. It wasn't long before Eric developed a true appreciation for his new home and a real love for us. Never once did he say that he wanted to leave."

Three years after Eric's adoption, Gordon Van Dyke was killed in an automobile accident. His death was a terrible blow to the little boy who had spent his whole life struggling for security and a sense of permanence.

"Gordon's tragic death was the most terrible thing that has ever happened to me," Janet said. "But it was even worse for Eric. He and his father had become extremely close. At first Eric was angry. He felt that his father had deserted him just as everyone else had done before. But that anger soon gave way to overwhelming sadness. Through our shared sorrow Eric and I were drawn closer to each other. The morning after Gordon's funeral, Eric came and climbed into bed with me. With tears in his eyes he said, 'We'll stick together, Mom. You take care of me and I'll take care of you.'

"Soon after Gordon's death, Eric's insecurities began to resurface. Even though he was ten years old, he did not want me out of his sight. Everywhere I went, he went. He even took to sleeping in a sleeping bag on my bedroom floor. After three months of this, a business situation came up which called for me to be out of town for a weekend. I considered taking Eric along, but it just wasn't practical. When Gordon's sister offered to keep him, I agreed. It was awfully hard on Eric, but it was just what he needed. He had to learn that I could go away and always be depended upon to come back. Gradually he began to get over his terror of losing me.

"Gordon's relatives and my own here in town have been a great help. My sister-in-law and her husband have a boy just older and a girl just younger than Eric, and they all get along together very well. Even my parents, who at first were so opposed to the adoption, have grown to love Eric. He and my dad have developed an especially close relationship.

"Eric is very open about his adoption," Janet continued. "Most of his questions concern Gordon's and my national background and our family histories. Everything he hears from me and his other relatives is incorporated into himself, and it all becomes a part of who he is.

"So far Eric has shown almost no interest in his birth family, though his history would be quite easy to trace. His brother, Craig, remembers a lot and has many of the family's records. When Eric came to us, he brought a book containing his baby pictures, pictures of his mother and brother, and pictures of his different foster families. He enjoys having me add to the book. The other day he asked me to put my picture on top of the picture of his birth mother. When I asked him why, he said, 'Because I don't even know that woman. You're my real mother.'"

Eric's relatively painless adjustment is a testimony to his

parents' patient acceptance and sensitive handling, especially the excellent fathering he received from Gordon. The Van Dykes possessed those characteristics important for a couple interested in adopting an older child. They were warm, mature, flexible, understanding, and accepting.

ARE YOU READY?

Families who are considering such an adoption should ask themselves these questions:

- Can we open our arms to a child who, because of unhappy experiences, may not be able to reach out to us?
- Can we accept the fact that the child has a past of which we will never really be a part?
- Will our new child receive our highest priority?
- Can we accept the whirlwind of activity that the child may bring to our home?
- If it is needed, are we willing to ask for and heed professional counsel?
- Can we accept the possibility that it may take time to gain the child's love?
- Can we be flexible in our lives and our expectations?

Flexibility is probably the most important characteristic of all. No matter how smooth the adoption, one thing is certain: There will be drastic changes in the household. The new parents had better be ready for them.

Ted and Jean Howard approached the adoption agency specifically asking for an older boy.

"My father was born in Georgia," Jean said in a soft southern drawl. "He lived in an orphanage until he was adopted by a farm couple at the age of ten. I remember hearing him tell about how the farmer came to the orphanage and looked all the older boys over. He tested their strength and asked endless questions about their behavior. Because my dad was large for his age and was quiet and cooperative, he was chosen.

"But it wasn't a son the farmer and his wife wanted. It was a farmhand: cheap labor. They provided Dad with food and clothes, but love and affection were never included in their business deal. After Dad left the farm at the age of twenty-two, he never saw his 'parents' again. When they died, in accordance with their will the farm went to an uncle.

"Dad never expressed any bitterness or resentment toward the couple. He seemed to accept the adoption as a legitimate business deal that provided him with a better life than he would have had in the orphanage. Perhaps he's right, but it's always bothered me.

"I was amazed when I found out that my father-in-law had been raised in a similar situation. Early in our marriage, Ted and I decided that someday we too would make room for a homeless boy in our family. But our boy would not be raised like his grandfathers were. He would be loved. He would be a real son.

"When our own children were twelve and nine, we adopted Christopher, an eleven-year-old who had spent his life in a series of foster homes—twelve in two years! Like my own father he was big for his age, several inches taller than his new older brother. He was a troubled, insecure boy. What Chris had seen and endured in his short life we can only guess.

"Chris's reputation as a troublemaker preceded him, but I had always believed that enough love could win over any child, no matter what his problems. Our first several weeks together certainly seemed to prove my point. Chris was polite, helpful, cooperative, and responsive—everything we could hope for. Then one night after Chris had been in our home for six weeks Ted reprimanded him for teasing the dog. To our utter amazement, he completely blew up. He stomped his feet and threw things, slammed doors, and cursed. Then, looking straight at Ted, he yelled, 'You're not my real father! You can't tell me what to do!' I couldn't believe what was happening. How could my motherly love have failed so miserably?"

Christopher was not turning into a juvenile delinquent,

and the Howards were not the failures they thought they were. They were experiencing the end of what is often called the "honeymoon period." For six weeks Chris had been on his best behavior, as had Ted and Jean and their biological children. But such a guarded life is artificial, and in time it has to come to an end.

"It was obviously time for me to take action," said Ted, a six-four, former college linebacker. "I decided that if Chris was to be a member of our family, he must be treated like one. I told him to go up to his room. When he refused to obey me, I picked him up and carried him out. Later on when he had calmed down, we talked about his behavior and agreed on a punishment: The next afternoon he was to clean up the patio. The job was completed without complaint."

Ted was wise to deal immediately and firmly—while not being overly strict—with Christopher's misbehavior. Chris continued to defy and test his father's authority, but Ted had been warned this would happen and he was prepared. Armed with resilience, determination, and plenty of energy, he pressed on without compromise throughout the entire period of adjustment.

"I understood Chris's need to test and retest me," Ted explained, "but in order for our home to be a pleasant and secure place for all of us, he needed to adjust—and he needed to do it quickly. My plan of attack was to set firm and consistent limits for him just as I did for my other kids. My end goal was for him to learn to set those controls for himself. This was the first time Chris had ever had consistent discipline, but I knew that if Jean and I were to be his parents he would have to learn what we expected of our children. We didn't expect overnight success. Short-term goals, for Chris and for us, were enough of a challenge at first. We had to prove to him that when we made a deal, we could be depended upon to hold up our end."

No matter how much an older child is loved and wanted by his adoptive family, there will certainly be some rough times. The child is struggling to make a big adjustment. Bed-wetting, offensive language, lying, stealing, whining, tan-

THE COMPLETE ADOPTION HANDBOOK

trums, and disruptive behavior are common. Some children demand expensive clothes and more spending money as proof of their parents' love. Some will criticize and rebel against their new parents' way of doing things. Some will try to divide the family by setting one parent against the other. Just how long this difficult period lasts depends a lot on the child's age, personality, past experiences, and to some extent on the adoptive parents. When the child finally feels secure in the adoptive parents' love and acceptance, the testing will come to an end.

"We endured six months of Chris's awful behavior," said Jean with a sigh. "The strain was evident in our family. But we were certain that we were doing the right thing and were determined to make the adoption work, not in our own strength—that was long gone—but in the strength of the Lord.

"The hardest thing to accept was that all the love and attention I showered on Chris seemed wasted. He just didn't love me back. I couldn't figure out what I was doing wrong. At the suggestion of our counselor, Ted and I joined a support group made up of five other couples who had also adopted older children.

"We gained an entirely different perspective through that group. We discovered that our problems with Chris were not unique. Everyone there had gone through the same thing. We were encouraged to try to see things from Chris's point of view. As for his loving us, he simply wasn't ready to make himself vulnerable to another set of parents who, he felt, probably wouldn't keep him anyway. He had been hurt and rejected so many times that he wasn't about to let himself be hurt again. It was up to Ted and me to prove ourselves to him. We had to love him and love him and love him some more, even though we received little in return.

"And do you know what? It really worked! As Chris was consistently cared for, understood, and loved by us, he gradually began to love and trust us in return. His trying behavior was his way of asking, 'Will you love me even if I act terrible?' While we certainly could not condone his behavior, we needed to be flexible and willing and able to cope with it. We had to be sensitive to Christopher's emotional needs, to try to understand why he did what he did. We talked to him about his attitudes, his feelings, his fears, and his expectations. And we shared our ideas with him."

KEEPING THEM TOGETHER

With older children so hard to place, imagine the problems an agency encounters in attempting to find homes for siblings who must be kept together. For most of them, the venture is doomed from the start.

"If people had ever suggested that my husband and I would adopt four kids at once, I would have said they were crazy!" laughed Paula Moreno, a jovial woman of forty-five. "Our home is licensed for foster care. One day a social worker called and begged me to take some kids for a couple of days. I figured, why not? Even in our tiny house we could make do for that short a time. About an hour later the dirtiest, the most bedraggled, forlorn-looking little things I've ever seen were herded into our living room. Tony, the senior member of the group, was ten. Scott was seven and the twins, Jenny and Jill, were four. What a motley bunch they were!

"Abandoned by their mother, their alcoholic father had left these little ones pretty much to their own devices for close to three years. The kids' predicament was discovered when the boys were picked up for starting a fire in a vacant lot.

"Fortunately my husband, Alex, and I have an easygoing household. I don't get upset about too much. The kids didn't feel too threatened here. Alex fell in love with them immediately, and they were his kids from the start. For me it was harder. You can imagine how my workload increased! To be honest, there were days when I would have gladly let them go.

"The kids had never been in a foster home before," Paula continued. "They came to us thinking that they'd be our children forever. Jenny and Jill called us 'Mommy' and 'Daddy' from the first day. Weeks passed, then months, and still the kids stayed on. There just was no place for them to go. Very few foster homes are set up to take in four kids at once.

"Tony, the oldest, was surprisingly mature and responsible. He and Alex became very close. And the twins and I took to each other right away. I was the only mother those little girls had ever known. Scott was our problem. As the middle child he easily got lost in the crowd, except when he was in trouble. Maybe that's why he always seemed to be in trouble. We were willing to work at our relationship, though, and to allow for differences. Alex and I both began to concentrate our efforts on Scott, and gradually he began to come around.

"The relationships among the kids were really perplexing to me. They alternated between protecting and teasing each other, between defending and tattling on each other. They actually seemed to enjoy getting each other punished. Jenny and Jill, those sweet little girls, were the worst of all."

"I could see what they were doing," interjected Alex Moreno. "Each one was trying to prove that he or she was our favorite child. They loved each other, but each one seemed to have an insatiable need to be loved the most. Paula and I refused to play that game. We were determined to love them all the same. And that included Scott."

"By the time the children had been with us for three years," Paula said, "we all felt that we truly belonged together. The big adjustments had been made and we were like a real family. Then it suddenly occurred to me, what if the kids were to be taken away from us someday? Alex and I decided the logical solution would be for us to adopt them. We asked the kids, and every one of them was in favor of it. In fact, Jenny and Jill thought they already were adopted. Next I wrote a letter to their father; he responded that we were right, the children should be with us. The only problem was the mother whom the kids had not seen since she deserted the family six years before. She didn't want them back; she just didn't want them to be adopted. She even showed up in court to protest. But the kids didn't recognize her, and the judge ruled in our favor."

"From the very beginning we were warned that we couldn't expect to remold the personalities of children as old as ours," Alex said. "We didn't even try. But we did teach them, by our words and more importantly by our actions. The kids have been with us for seven years now, and all of them have changed radically in their personalities as well as in their general views of life. That includes seventeen-year-old Tony, who came to us half-grown. It also includes Scott, who endured many emotional problems. Why the great change? I'm convinced that it's due to the Lord's working in their lives. What a testimony to the power of God! He can change anyone or anything, even the personality of a troubled child."

"It's hard to believe that there was a time when Tony, Scott, Jenny, and Jill were strangers to us and that things happened to them before I knew them," said Paula Moreno. "It's hard to believe I once wondered if we would ever be able to really love each other. It's hard to believe there was ever a time when we weren't a family." Grinning, she added, "I'm so glad those days are gone."

OPEN FORUM

Paul Conway: If there's one thing I can't stand, it's dishonesty. But no matter what Margaret and I do, we can't seem to break our daughter of lying and stealing. She was seven when we adopted her and now, two years later, she's as bad as ever.

Pamela Friedman: That surely sounds familiar. Our son, adopted at the age of six, was just the same. The support group we belong to was a real help. Lying isn't unusual behavior, you know.

Paul Conway: But what can we do?

Pamela Friedman: First of all, it helps to understand why she's doing it. She has probably never learned to trust adults. Some kids will try to lie their way out of everything to keep from getting into trouble. This lying can become an automatic response, especially when the child figures that if you punish her it means you are rejecting her.

Margaret Conway: Sometimes it seems as if our daughter actually tries to get herself into trouble. Whatever happens, she seems to try to work it around so that she will end up being the "victim."

Cliff Friedman: Maybe she's learned that the only way to get attention is to get into trouble. After all, negative attention is better than no attention at all. We had to make a real concentrated effort to give our son lots of positive attention. It took a lot of time, but it really did help.

Pamela Friedman: These older kids usually come to us with well-entrenched problems and responses. Over and over our support group stressed the importance of consistency, firm guidelines, and a great deal of praise and support.

QUESTIONS FOR DISCUSSION

1. According to Janet Van Dyke, her husband, Gordon, was the one most responsible for Eric's relatively easy adjustment. What do you consider to be the father's role in parenting? How important is it?
2. Jean and Ted Howard spoke of the great help they received from the support group. This idea was emphasized by the Friedmans in the open forum. In what ways can such a group be helpful? How might a person locate such a group? (See chapter 12.)

8.   *Sometimes Parents*

When Stacy and Christine's mother suffered a nervous breakdown, their father found he could not take care of his young daughters alone. The girls were placed in a foster home until their mother was well enough to care for them again. . . .

Two-year-old Joseph was found sitting on the courthouse steps. Pinned to his shirt was a note that read, "Please take care of Joseph. I have no money to buy him food or clothes, and no place to live." Joseph, too, was placed under foster care. If his mother did not return within one year, he would be considered abandoned and would be free for adoption. . . .

Mary Beth was born without a left arm or foot. Her mother could not accept a child with such a severe handicap, and early the next morning she walked out of the hospital, leaving her newborn daughter behind. Mary Beth was placed in a foster home to await adoption. . . .

Bobby's mother is a drug addict, and his father is in prison. As a baby, Bobby was left alone for hours at a time. He was two years old when concerned neighbors finally called the police. The neglected little boy was taken to a foster home. Bobby has spent six years in foster care. During this time his mother has visited him only five times. Though still on drugs and unable to care for her son, she adamantly refuses to release him for adoption. . . .

. . . Stacy and Christine's mother made a rapid recovery. After spending less than two months in foster care, the girls were able to return home.

. . . Joseph's mother never came back to claim her son, and he has now been legally freed for adoption. But three years have passed and, at the age of five, Joseph is considered a hard-to-place older child.

... Although Mary Beth has adapted well to her artificial limbs, her chances for adoption are even lower than Joseph's. Few families want a handicapped child.

Mary Beth and Joseph will probably join Bobby and the hundreds of thousands of other children for whom foster care has become a way of life—the children often referred to as "orphans of the living."

A STATE OF LIMBO

Social agencies generally agree that foster care should be a temporary situation during which permanent plans are made for children. It is hoped that they can either return home or, if this is not possible, be adopted. In reality, however, foster care is temporary for less than a third of the children who come under the system. For some, there is just no adoptive family available, especially for a handicapped child like Mary Beth or an older child like Joseph. In a case like Bobby's, where the child's parents show even a passing interest in him or flatly refuse to release him, there can be no adoption. Such children will remain locked into this "temporary" state of limbo until they are grown.

It is a sad fact that there are not enough good foster homes for all the children who need them. In many places out of pure desperation the screening process for foster families is minimal. The demand is so great that agencies are often willing to look the other way in questionable home situations.

"Even though our home is small and is licensed for only one child," Marie Kauffman said, "it's not unusual for a caseworker to plead with us to take two, three, or even four children 'just for a little while.' They know it's not the best arrangement, but the children have to go somewhere."

Marie Kauffman and her husband, Joe, a custodian at an elementary school, are in their mid-fifties. They have cared for foster children for more than twenty years.

"When our own children were little, Joe just wasn't

earning enough money for us to live on," Marie said. "I didn't want to go out and get a job because I needed to be home with the children. Anyway, being a homemaker and mother were all I knew how to do. Our solution was to take in a foster child. Not only did it give us a little extra income, but the child had a chance to live in a loving Christian home.

"I can't even count all the children we've had since that first little girl arrived twenty-three years ago. There have been newborn babies, teenage runaways, handicapped children, even a little three-year-old boy who had a heart attack and died in my arms. One time we had three mentally retarded teenage girls who were in some kind of job training together. We almost didn't take them, but I'm so glad we did. They were a real inspiration to us.

"Some of our children left our home because they were adopted. Some went back to their parents. Some reached that magic age of eighteen, and they graduated from foster care. Some were moved on to other foster homes.

"The very first day a child comes into our home," Marie continued, "we start a special book for him. In addition to medical records and school papers, I write down anecdotes about the child: his cute sayings and funny experiences. Joe takes pictures—lots and lots of them. When the child leaves us, we give him the book to keep. We hope that these books help to give some sort of continuity to the children's lives."

"Before any of our children leave our home," interjected Joe Kauffman, "Marie and I take him aside—away from the other kids—and pray with him about the new place to which he'll be going, whether it's back home to his parents or to an adoptive home or wherever. I think this has really helped the children. Not long ago a lady who had adopted one of our little ones called Marie to say thank you. She said, 'I'm not sure what you did to prepare her, but our daughter has had an unbelievably easy adjustment.' Marie told her she wasn't surprised: The Lord has simply answered our prayers.

"To my way of thinking, Marie and I are missionaries as much as anything else," Joe continued thoughtfully. "Most of these children come from very sad situations. They have never had any kind of security in their lives at all. In our home, even if it's only for a short time, they have a chance to be part of a solid, secure Christian family. We take them to Sunday school and to church. They participate in our family's regular Bible reading and prayer times. A lot of these kids have come to know the Lord while they were here."

"Never once have we said no when we were asked to take a child," Marie said. "Joe and I feel that the Lord brings to us those children who can best benefit from our home. This is what the Lord has called us to do: provide a Christian refuge for homeless children."

The Kauffmans' home might be considered an ideal foster home. But even in the best of foster homes children know they don't really belong. Their foster parents may love them and treat them kindly, but foster parents are not truly the children's parents and they know it. There is no assurance the children will still be with their foster parents next year, or even next week. There is no permanence, no commitment in the relationship.

Children are fed and sheltered in foster homes, but food and shelter alone aren't enough. All children have basic needs that must be met for them to grow into healthy, well-adjusted, productive adults. Family loving is crucial in the early years when children's personalities are being formed. If they are not consistently loved, children do not learn how to love—not even how to love themselves. Above all, children must belong to someone they can depend on and trust, someone they know will not leave them. Children without parents of their own enter life with a serious handicap. Most suffer emotional damage. Few ever achieve their full potential. But there is little else to offer these children. For most, foster care is the best option available.

FROM TEMPORARY TO PERMANENT

Sometimes foster parents become so deeply attached to the children in their care that they want to adopt them. If children have been freed for adoption, many agencies are making it possible for that to happen. Ned and Beth Simon, biological parents of two daughters, have adopted two of their foster children.

"Neither Tamara nor Jonathan had been released for adoption when they were placed in our home," Beth said. "Jonathan was one of our very first children. He came to us as a terrified, tearful, tantrum-prone baby. Our social worker told us he had been removed from his home because his mother had abused him so badly. By the time he had been with us for a year he had developed into a fun-loving, emotionally healthy first-grader. We were astounded at the change in him.

"During that entire first year, Jonathan never once heard from his mother, not even on his birthday or at Christmas. But still she refused to release him for adoption. Unless his mother could be persuaded to relinquish her parental rights or unless those rights were taken away from her by court order, Jonathan was doomed to grow up under foster care.

"During the next two years we became more and more attached to Jonathan, and he to us. Finally one day his mother did drop by—totally unannounced, of course—but he flatly refused to see her. He hid under his bed the entire time she was here. After she left, Jonathan emerged from his refuge and announced, 'I don't want that woman to come to my house anymore. She just wants to hit me!'

"We talked the situation over with Jonathan's caseworker. She encouraged us to go to court and charge his mother with abandonment to get Jonathan legally freed for adoption. We did. His mother didn't even take the trouble to appear. One year later, Jonathan was ours.

"Tamara was three years old when she was brought to us. She had been found wandering alone on a rainy night, dressed only in her underwear. Her mother had not been home for two days. At first Tamara's mother came to visit quite often. She really seemed to care about that little girl. She told us she was only fourteen when her baby was born and that she had felt pressured into keeping her. 'But how can I raise a kid?' she asked us. 'Look at me! I'm just a kid myself!' Through tears, she literally begged us to adopt Tamara and give her a good home. 'Maybe then she'll have a chance for a decent life,' she said. The mother never came to visit again."

"Both Beth and I wanted to adopt Tamara," Ned Simon said, "but I was concerned about our finances. I'm a carpenter by trade, and there are times when I can't get much work. We already had three children, and if we were to adopt Tamara, we would lose not only the money we received monthly for her support, but also the medical coverage that was paying for her costly allergy treatments. I didn't want money to stand in the way of her adoption, but for everyone's sake I felt that I had to be practical."

"I could certainly understand Ned's concern," Beth said, "but I felt that if the adoption were the Lord's will, he would surely work out the financial details. Still, I didn't want to push. If it were the thing to do, it would have to come from Ned.

"One evening when the kids were all sleeping, Ned surprised me by suddenly saying, 'Let's go through with Tamara's adoption. She belongs here with us. We'll just have to trust God to provide.' Well, we did go through with it and God did provide. Through a program called Aid to Adoptive Parents, the county offered to continue to pay for Tamara's support until she is eighteen. We had never even heard of this program before the social worker suggested it to us. If that isn't proof of the Lord's leading, I don't know what is!"

"For us, foster care seems to be the first step toward adoption," Ned laughed. "And do you know what? We have just accepted another foster child."

Anne and Bruce Riley are also foster parents, but unlike the children placed with the Simons and the Kauffmans, their little ones are all newborn. The Rileys care for infants from birth until they are legally relinquished by their birth mothers and are placed in adoptive homes. This process can take anywhere from two weeks to two months.

"We have had fourteen foster babies so far," said Anne,

a thirty-two-year-old mother of three little girls. "Since they are here for such a short time, we really don't have time to get too attached to them. But it's amazing how different each baby is. From the very beginning they have their own individual personalities. Some are a lot harder to give up than others.

"We often hear complaints about the impersonal, disinterested care babies receive in foster homes. But that just isn't true, at least not in our home. Each baby gets a lot of personal attention and a lot of holding and cuddling from both Bruce and me. No bottle is ever propped up on a pillow for our babies. We try to treat each little one with as much loving care as we do our own girls.

"Mickey was our most recent baby," Anne continued. "Though we had him less than two weeks, we will never forget him. You see, Mickey was adopted by our best friends. It was a providential placement from the very beginning. Mickey's teenage, unmarried mother was a Christian, and she specifically requested Christian parents for her child. She wrote a really neat letter in which she stated her definition of a born-again Christian. It was read to the entire board of the adoption agency. What a witness!

"When our friends saw Mickey at our house, it was love at first sight. For five years their name had been on the adoption agency's waiting list, and they had just about given up hope of ever getting a baby. We all knew, of course, that it was impossible for Mickey to be placed in their home. First of all, he was born locally, and according to agency regulations he had to be placed in another city. Secondly, our caseworker knew we were friends and had already told us that no baby from our home would be placed with them. But the word 'impossible' doesn't seem to be in God's vocabulary. He obviously had different ideas. Through an incredible set of circumstances, within days Mickey was their son."

"Our caseworker is also a Christian," Bruce said. "When we met at the agency to deliver Mickey to his new parents, all five of us took time to sit together in her office and pray for this new family. Now that is my definition of a truly chosen family."

Children who live in foster homes for long periods of time almost always suffer emotionally from feelings of rejection and impermanence, and many adoptive parents worry about the long-term effects. Ned Simon does not share their worry.

"Beth and I know that Jonathan and Tamara may have memories of their early lives," he says. "And there is a good chance they will run into some of their birth relatives here in town. In fact it's already happened. We have even discussed how we would feel if, as adults, they should decide to return to their birth families. I don't think there's much chance of that happening, but I suppose it could. The way I see it, no one has any guarantees about the future. It's in the hands of the Lord. But whatever happens, we know that for now our kids are exactly where God wants them: right here in our home. Our lives have certainly been a lot happier and more fulfilled because of Jonathan and Tamara."

There are many children without families of their own. Some, especially the babies, will be adopted right away. Others will wait and wait, and eventually the right family will claim them. But what about the rest? They will spend their entire childhood in a system of foster care. They will be shifted from family to family, from home to home. They will never know the deep love, the security, the warmth, and the permanence that real parents and a real family can offer. What will become of them?

FOST-ADOPT PROGRAMS

It is not always a coincidence when a foster parent winds up adopting a foster child. Often this happens by design and careful planning. Due to the shortages of both adoptable infants and foster homes, many agencies are now offering something called a "fost-adopt program." As its name implies, it is a mix of foster care and adoption.

Often when children enter the agency's custody, it seems fairly certain that in time they will become available for adoption. This is especially common with public adoption agencies which deal with children who have been removed from the custody of abusive or neglectful parents. At the same time, there are many families who dream of adopting a child and are willing to serve as foster parents as a way of fulfilling that dream. A fost-adopt program can bring about a happy ending for everyone.

When a family is accepted into a fost-adopt program, the agency performs a home study and determines the suitability of the family. If the agency receives a child for foster care who is likely to become available for adoption, the agency places the child in foster care with that family. When the child is freed for adoption, the foster/adoptive family has first priority to adopt that child. In some states, after a child has been in a foster home for four months, the child must be offered for adoption first to that family unless there is some reason to suspect the family is unfit.

In a fost-adopt program, the agency can never guarantee that the child will become available for adoption. Being accepted into such a program and receiving a foster child does not necessarily mean the family will be able to adopt that child. For any one of a number of reasons, the child might be returned to the birth parents.

Also, during the foster care stage of a fost-adopt program, the foster parents are, in effect, employees of the adoption agency and are supervised by the caseworker. Some caseworkers are quite demanding about the lifestyles and values which they are willing to allow in a foster home. It's not uncommon for the foster parents to be asked to sign an agreement with the agency that under no circumstances will they spank the child or use other forms of physical punishment. In one instance, a family was rejected from a fost-adopt program because they did not own a television. The social worker insisted the agency would not place a child in foster care with them because the child would be, in her words, "culturally deprived."

Although a fost-adopt program is not without emotional risks, it also offers substantial benefits. A fost-adopt program allows the family a trial period during which everyone concerned gets an opportunity to determine if the placement is likely to work. It also allows a prospective adoptive family to actually "leap-frog" ahead of other would-be adoptive families who may have been waiting much longer for an adoptable child.

OPEN FORUM

Greg Swanson: We thought we wanted children, but we had so little prior experience with them that we didn't feel right about making a positive commitment. Our social worker suggested foster care as a training ground.

Victoria Meyers: Is it really the same?

Lorraine Swanson: Not exactly, but it gives you an idea of all that is involved in the daily care of a child.

Ben Meyers: I thought most foster children weren't free to be adopted.

Lorraine Swanson: They aren't. The social worker warned us not to accept a foster child with the idea of adopting him or her. Only occasionally does that work out. It was just a way for us to see if we really wanted to be parents and, if so, what kind of child we would be willing to take.

Greg Swanson: Our first two children were older. We got along all right with both of them, but we would never have wanted to adopt either one. The third had a medical problem which we could easily live with.

Lorraine Swanson: Experience in foster care is especially important for someone who is considering adopting a child with a handicap.

QUESTIONS FOR DISCUSSION

1. What characteristics are important in a foster parent?
2. In what ways can foster care help you make your decision concerning adoption?

9.   *My Brother's Keeper*

"It was a rainy Sunday in November when my mother called to tell us that Danny had been freed for adoption," said Rita Zimmerman, a woman of forty. "Danny was the three-year-old son of my sister-in-law's cousin, Sharon.

"In the small town where I was raised, Sharon was considered the black sheep in a family of—shall I say—questionable reputation. She and her husband, both on drugs, were married at fifteen. Danny was born a month later. That poor boy spent his first three years in an awful home situation. One day he ended up in the hospital, and his father was placed in jail on charges of child abuse. But in Sharon's eyes all the problems were 'that bratty little kid's fault,' and she wanted Danny out of her life for good.

"Since my husband, Norm, and I had been married for almost ten years and we still had no children, my mother suggested that day that we might consider adopting Danny. We had exactly one week to make up our minds. Norm and I left that night to drive the nine hundred miles to my mother's house.

"When we got to the hospital and met Danny, it was love at first sight. Despite his black eye and the cast on his arm, he was a feisty little guy just bursting with energy. Norm spent hours playing and laughing with him. My husband was the very picture of a proud papa. We didn't need a week to decide. We wanted Danny to be our son.

"I was every bit as thrilled at becoming a mother as Norm was at becoming a father," Rita continued. "But the thrill ended abruptly on our way back home. That trip was pure torture. Danny wouldn't have a thing to do with me. He cried when I looked at him, and he screamed when I touched him. Norm was the one he liked. Finally in embarrassment and exasperation I told Norm to pull over to the side of the road. I drove the rest of the way home while Norm played Mommy."

"When we got home, however, Danny adjusted to us very quickly," Norm added. "The problem was his overprotectiveness. When my mother came for a weekend visit, he refused to let her step into his room. Nor would he let her touch either Rita or me. Fortunately that didn't last too long."

"Although he seems to have no recollection of those first three years, Danny has always known that he was adopted," Rita said. "It would have been foolish to try to keep it from him. He also knows who his birth parents are and why they couldn't keep him. He hasn't met them yet, but I'm sure it's just a matter of time until their paths cross.

"Danny's biological grandmother has been our biggest problem," Rita added with a sigh. "Danny stays with her for two weeks every summer, and she spends the entire time telling him how much she wishes he lived with her. According to Grandma, she begged to adopt him herself but wasn't allowed to because she was too sickly. She moans about how lonely she is and how she just lives for those two weeks each year when Danny is with her. By the time he gets back home, he's suffering terribly from depression and a deep sense of guilt.

"But Danny's grandmother's version of the story is less than accurate, to put it charitably. The truth is that several times during those first three years Sharon begged her mother to take Danny. But Grandma wasn't interested. She suggested that her grandson be put into a foster home; she wasn't about to let that little boy cramp her style.

"Last summer, when Danny was seven, he came home from his yearly visit talking endlessly about how much his grandmother loves him and how badly she wanted to keep him. The more he talked, the more irritated I became. Later that day, when I scolded him about something, he yelled, 'Grandma never treats me like you do! I should've stayed with her!' Without thinking I snapped back, 'If you think you would be so much happier with your grandmother, why don't you go back?' I immediately regretted saying that, but I get so angry with his grandmother that I can't think straight. Maybe I should just tell Danny the truth about her.''

"I can certainly understand Rita's frustration," said Norm, "but I don't think she should talk to Danny about his grandmother. For one thing, he probably wouldn't believe a thing Rita said. I think we should approach the problem by going directly to his grandmother. If she won't cooperate, we should simply put an end to the visits. I don't think Danny really cares that much about going anyway. There's very little for him to do there, and he always comes home so upset. At any rate, he's bound to learn the truth about her eventually. It's common knowledge among the relatives."

Special problems such as the Zimmermans were experiencing arise when the adopted child is a family member. John and Ruth Cornelius, who adopted their six-year-old grandson, Ricky, eight years ago, have the added problem of regular contact between Ricky and his birth mother, their daughter.

"Our daughter was a rebellious girl," Ruth said. "She was only fifteen when Ricky was born. Soon afterward, against our advice, she married her child's father and they both dropped out of school. They couldn't find jobs, so they lived on welfare, which suited them just fine. They partied all night and slept all day. Ricky was terribly neglected. John and I did all we could, but it was awfully hard. Our daughter was always accusing us of trying to run her life. After four years her husband moved out, and he hasn't been seen or heard from since.

"Ricky had been with us off and on since he was a baby. By the time he was five he was here more than he was with his mother. When the time came for him to start school, I talked my daughter into letting him live with us permanently. We adopted him the following year.

"Our daughter is around now and then," Ruth continued. "She tells Ricky that she's his real mother. That just seems to add to his feelings of abandonment and rejection. She tells him she loves him, and then she disappears for months at a time. She tells him he's always in her thoughts, but she has yet to remember him on his birthday or at Christmas. She says she cares about him, but she's never once taken care of him when he was sick. She tells him she's a Christian and she wants him to be a Christian, too, but she lives like the devil."

Ruth paused to wipe away a tear. "She's my daughter and I will always love her, but I would rather never see her again than to have her around hurting Ricky. So why can't I bring myself to throw her out?"

"At first I wasn't too happy about having Ricky with us on a permanent basis," said John Cornelius. "Ruth and I worked hard at raising our own children. Ricky was our daughter's problem. I felt too old and too tired to start over again with another little one. But now I can't imagine life without that boy. He has made me young again. And I'm good for Ricky too. I'm older and much wiser now. How can I help but be a better parent?"

SOMETIMES IT DOESN'T WORK OUT

Despite the difficulties, the Zimmermans and the Corneliuses are optimistic about their chances of successfully integrating Danny and Ricky into their families. But Tim and Ingrid Wolff are not so sure.

"Brian and Kara are my sister's children," Ingrid explained. "I had never met them because they lived in another state. But even my sister admitted they had real emotional problems. When her off-again, on-again marriage finally ended, my sister asked me to take her children. The judge at their custody hearing ruled that neither she nor her husband was a fit parent and that the children would have to be put into foster homes unless Tim and I agreed to take them. Under the circumstances, how could we refuse?

"From the very beginning it was a difficult situation. Brian was fourteen and Kara was eleven, exactly the ages of our own children. Our two considered their cousins a disruptive intrusion into our happy home. Having never experienced normal family life, Brian and Kara had no idea how to react to us or how to start trying to fit in. Because of their neglected upbringing, they had never developed healthy personalities or a sense of self-worth. But we tried. To the best of our ability, we truly did try."

"I felt sorry for Ingrid," Tim said. "She was always walking a tightrope between 'them' and 'us,' trying hard to please everyone. But that was an impossible undertaking. No matter how much she did for Brian and Kara, they demanded more. Because she wanted them to feel as if they belonged, she gave in to them more than she should have. Then our own children began to act up. They demanded to know why their mother preferred their cousins over them. It was a no-win situation."

"When Brian and Kara had been with us for fifteen stormy months," Ingrid continued, "my sister called to say she and her ex-husband both felt that Tim and I were giving their children a better life than either of them could ever provide. In tears, she begged us to adopt them. I was so shocked I couldn't think straight. I put her off by saying I'd have to talk it over with Tim and our children. Well, we did talk it over. The unanimous consensus was that, considering the shakiness of our temporary arrangement, it would be foolish to go ahead with a permanent commitment.

"That was a year ago. Brian and Kara are still with us. Although there are still a lot of unresolved problems, they have settled in a bit more comfortably and we feel more as if they are a part of our family. Gradually we have come to understand that no matter how rough things are, they can get better. Nothing that happens is truly fatal. There are solutions, and we can find them."

STEPFAMILY ADOPTIONS

According to recent statistics, two of every ten children will be affected by a divorce in their family. Because 85 percent of divorcees remarry within five years, the number of stepparents in our society is increasing rapidly. This condition has brought a whole new set of adoptive circumstances. Many Christian parents and stepparents are anxious to gain permanent custody of their children so they can be raised in a Christian home.

"I was still unmarried at the age of thirty-six," said Diane Cruz. "I had accepted the fact that God had called me to a single life. Then I met Luis. He had just moved to town with his two children, and he was visiting our singles group at church. I was attracted to him immediately. He seemed gentle and warm, and I could see that his relationship with the Lord was an important part of his life. But I never dreamed he would notice me."

"How could I help but notice her?" Luis Cruz laughed. "Diane was the only person in that class who wasn't trying to impress everyone else with her great wisdom and insights. I knew right away that I wanted to get to know her better."

"We got to know each other better, all right," Diane laughed. "After dating for a year we had a lovely Christmas wedding. Luis's children, six-year-old Denise and nine-year-old Todd, were in our wedding party.

"Todd and Denise's mother had made no effort to see them for over three years. I wanted to adopt the children right away because I was concerned about their welfare should anything happen to Luis. The problem was to find their mother and get her approval. When we were finally able to locate her, she offered no resistance.

"The children were outspoken about their desire to be with us, and we felt like a family from the very beginning. Many people have asked me how Todd and Denise were able to make such a quick and painless adjustment. I've given it a lot of thought and have decided that there were three important factors. First, instead of suddenly springing the idea of our marriage on the children, Luis and I included them in our relationship from the very beginning. Second, at the ages of six and nine the children were still young enough to be fairly adaptable. Third and most important, the foundation and controlling base of our family is God's providential love and care for all of us.

"When we had been married for three years," Diane continued, "God blessed us with a new baby. Though I loved Todd and Denise dearly, I worried throughout my pregnancy that I would love this new baby more. I'm pleased to say that my fears were groundless. The baby is no more my real child than the other two are. But my family can't quite understand this. The first Mother's Day after the baby was born I got a card from my sister. On it she had written, "For your first Mother's Day as a real mother." After looking at it for a minute, Todd tossed the card aside and snorted, "Aunt Janine doesn't know what a real mother is!"

As Diane herself acknowledged, the Cruz family had a lot going for it. Most blended families are not so fortunate.

When a child leaves his old family life behind and begins a new one, he cannot help but bring along his old habits, behavior, and ways of doing things. The adults involved will do the same. The problem is that one person's way of doing things won't be the same as someone else's. Everyone is bringing his own memories, his own confusion, his own fears and scars into this new family. It will take time for them to blend together into one cohesive group.

Children who are shifted from one parent to another or from one relationship to another have to face some monumental questions and fears. Whether by death or divorce, these children have experienced a breakup in their family. There is risk in letting themselves become attached to a new person: Will this stepparent also leave? This new stepparent has different expectations. Can the children ever hope to please everyone? To whom should they be loyal anyway—to their birth parent or their stepparent?

When problems appear in stepchildren—whether distrust, indifference, withdrawal, hostility, or rebellion—it's important to remember that they are in a very difficult situation not of their own making. It is hardly surprising that as innocent, helpless victims, they would protest in any way they can.

And what about stepparents? Even though they may really want to see a feeling of love and belonging develop between themselves and their stepchildren, they may discover that it's not all that easy to accomplish. Though stepparents want their stepchildren to adapt, too often they are not willing to do the same. Compromise is essential, and it's a two-way street. It is neither realistic nor fair to expect children to conform completely to their stepparent's expectations.

What can a stepparent do to help the family achieve a smooth, happy adjustment? There are no sure answers to this question, but there are some factors that will make it easier for everyone.

- Be sure that the children are prepared for the marriage and the adjustments that will be necessary. Assure them that you will all work together to find solutions for any problems that arise.
- It is important that you settle some matters with your spouse before the wedding so that you can present a united and consistent front. It is vital that you agree on such things as priorities, expectations, and approaches to discipline. Be willing to compromise; it's essential.
- Don't attempt to make any major changes right away. You must first allow time for everyone to get used to the new arrangement.
- Resist the temptation to denigrate the missing parent. Don't try to compete with him or her. Instead, point out the importance of appreciating the uniqueness that can be found in every person.
- Above all, be patient with your stepchildren. Cinderella, Hansel and Gretel, Sleeping Beauty, and a host

of others have taught them that it's dangerous to trust a stepparent. It's up to you to prove them wrong.

LOVE MUST BE EARNED

Love doesn't just happen. It cannot be legislated or demanded. It has to be earned through time and lots of hard work.

When Ed and Donna Jackson were married, it was the second time for both. Donna had three daughters and Ed had three sons. Neither Ed nor Donna was a Christian.

"I was married at sixteen and divorced at twenty-one," Donna related. "Four years later I married Ed. My daughters—Sarah, Ashley, and Christy—were eight, six, and four. Ed's sons were older: Paul was twelve, Jason was nine, and Nicholas was seven. The boys lived with their mother thirty miles away."

"Donna and I had been married for two years when a friend invited us to a weekend couples conference at a Christian campground," Ed Jackson said. "We had no idea what to expect, but since it was free we agreed to go. That weekend we both came to know Jesus Christ as our Savior. We immediately got involved in a great church and a group Bible study.

"As I grew in the Lord, I began to feel worse and worse about my boys growing up devoid of any Christian influence. What chance would they ever have to know the Lord? I was suddenly consumed with a great desire to have my boys with me. But that seemed impossible. I'd never be able to talk my ex-wife into giving them up. Together Donna and I sought the Lord's wisdom and guidance.

"It was Donna who suggested that we try to 'conquer with kindness.' You should have seen us! We went out of our way to be considerate and cooperative toward my former wife. Whenever she wanted to drop the boys off for a day or a weekend—which was often—we were ready to take them, even though it usually meant upsetting our own plans. After a while they were here more than they were with her. One day my ex-wife called and said, 'I hate to admit it, Ed, but you're a better father than I am a mother. I really think you love those boys more than I do. Maybe they'd be better off with you.' That's all there was to it. How's that for an answer to prayer?"

"After the boys came to live with us, people started calling us 'The Brady Bunch,'" Donna said. "But believe me, our problems were neither as amusing nor as easily solved as those television problems were. And somehow we never seemed to have the witty wisdom at our fingertips that those parents always had.

"When we became a blended family, Paul was fourteen, Jason was eleven, Sarah was ten, Nicholas was nine, Ashley was eight, and Christy was six. We worked hard at establishing a pattern of candor, cooperation, and communication among all eight of us. It was hard to keep from bursting into tears when someone glibly offered criticism in an especially sensitive area. So because Ed and I recognized the serious adjustments ahead for all of us, we tried to impress the kids with the need to temper their candor with love and consideration for one another's feelings. Together we worked out rules for the household and decided what discipline would be applied if those rules were broken."

"Paul, Jason, and Nicholas came to us with no idea of what to expect," Ed said. "They were confused and afraid, but they also had some pretty wild, unrealistic expectations. And they had memories—some pleasant, but many quite painful. Nicholas felt at home right away. He loved Donna and he loved me. Jason's adjustment was not quite so easy, but he did adjust. Paul, however, became obnoxious. He began testing us the day he arrived and never stopped. He made life especially miserable for Donna."

The pain showed on Donna's face as she said, "There was a time when I honestly believed that with enough love I could overcome any obstacle. I don't believe that anymore. If a child doesn't want to become a part of a family, no one can force him to do it. The child must adopt his parents every bit as much as his parents must adopt him."

"I'm certain that a lot of Paul's problems were caused by the conflicting loyalties he felt," Ed said thoughtfully. "I can understand that. He had lived with his mother for most of his life.

"Finally, in desperation Donna and I took Paul to a counselor. Unfortunately we didn't give much thought to the man we chose. He was a counselor whose main philosophy was that a person's primary concern should be his own happiness and comfort. He told Paul that he should have free run of the house without any restrictions from us. He even went so far as to scold Donna and me for undermining Paul's creative ambitions by disciplining him. Can you believe it? Of course we never went back to that counselor again. But the damage was already done. What little control I had over Paul was gone.

"When he was sixteen, Paul ran away and went back to live with his mother. She made the most of the situation. Paul quit school and found a full-time job. His mother took his paychecks to help pay off her stack of overdue bills. While his mother went out with her boyfriends, Paul served as a free baby-sitter for her three-year-old.

"It wasn't long before Paul got fed up with that arrangement. He was back in our home in two months. But his heart wasn't with us. Whenever anything happened that didn't suit him, he was off again. Finally I had to decide whether it was right to risk sacrificing my marriage and the emotional well-being of the other five children in a seemingly futile effort to help Paul. What could I do but commit him to the Lord and then let him go? Last year I had to make the most difficult decision of my life: I had my son put into a foster home."

"Wherever he goes and whatever he does," Donna said thoughtfully, "Paul is surrounded by our love and our prayers. I'm sure that in time he'll come around. When he does, we will be waiting for him with open arms."

After a pause Donna added, "When we talk to the kids about the importance of living for the Lord while they are young, they sometimes point to our own lives and say, 'When you were our age you did all the things you tell us not to do, but everything worked out all right for you, didn't it?' I truly believe that God allowed our heartbreaking situation with Paul so that the other children will see that Ed and I didn't get off scot-free. Where there is sin, its consequences are sure to follow."

"That's not to say that Paul had no choice in his actions," Ed quickly added. "Of course he did. But the fact remains that I wasn't there during his formative years. The Bible speaks of the sins of fathers being visited upon their children. This is hard for us to accept even though we see it again and again."

Long ago Cain asked the question, "Am I my brother's keeper?" For the Jacksons, the answer is yes. The Cruzes and the Wolffs agree. So do the Corneliuses and the Zimmermans. But taking in relatives and making them your own is not always an easy thing to do. It takes patience, determination, understanding love, and a great deal of dependence upon the Lord.

"All children need loving guidance," said Donna Jackson. "That's the whole idea of parenting: love, understanding, and honesty. If your family has these, it doesn't matter whether the child is yours, mine, or ours.

"Our family has a special verse that we claim as our own. It's Colossians 2:6: 'And now just as you trusted Christ to save you, trust him, too, for each day's problems.' What more can we ask?"

OPEN FORUM

Jack Kelley: Cheryl and I have both been married before, and we both brought children into our marriage. We have had some real heartrending experiences when our kids have come home from a visit with their other parents completely elated by the good time they had. But when it really comes down to it, they know that we're their parents. Their hearts are with us. Without realizing it, we have brought on much of our own pain. We've put ourselves through unnecessary anguish.

Dr. McDill: We all do that at times, don't we? But the very fact that your children came home and talked freely to you is a credit to your good parenting.

Jack Kelley: We encouraged them to talk and to share their experiences with us. We felt that the more open we were in allowing them to express themselves, the better it would be for all of us. The less we tried to influence their feelings, the better it worked out and the more honest they were with us.

Dr. McDill: How right you are! We all so badly need that openness.

Cheryl Kelley: Our oldest kids are sixteen and eighteen, and they know all about their father. He's not as bad as some, I suppose, but he is no trophy. We do not approve of his lifestyle, and when the boys were in their early teens we wouldn't let them see him at all. That really caused problems and rebellion. Since they resented our trying to tell them what their father was like, we decided they needed to see it for themselves. We called him and, through clenched teeth, told him we would like him to spend some time with his sons.

Dr. McDill: If you had it to do again, would you do anything differently?

Jack Kelley: I think we would allow the relationship with their father to develop more naturally. He wasn't really that interested in them anyway, so he wouldn't have taken the trouble to see them more than once or twice a year. Maybe then it wouldn't have become such an obsession with them.

Cheryl Kelley: Two years ago we had drug problems with one of the boys. But as soon as we let him get to know his father, the problems virtually disappeared.

Jack Kelley: Not knowing his father really bothered that boy. He used to say, "The man could die or lose a leg, and I wouldn't even know about it!"

Cheryl Kelley: The eighteen-year-old can go out with his father and have a nice time, but he can also see that in many ways he is actually more mature than his father is. Even the sixteen-year-old is beginning to see the reality. Lately he's been saying, "Don't worry, Mom. I don't want to be like him." We don't like the idea of this man influencing our boys, but we grit our teeth and pray that whatever limited influence he does have won't wipe out the years of influence we have had.

Jack Kelley: Kids actually are quite resilient and perceptive. We're teaching our children God's Word and his wisdom. Now we must trust God to bring them safely to adulthood.

QUESTIONS FOR DISCUSSION

1. What special problems does a family who adopts a relative have?
2. Do you think Ed and Donna Jackson could have done anything to help Paul adjust to their new blended family?
3. How could the Jacksons have gone about making a better choice in a counselor? (Also see chapter 12.)

10.   *A Parent Alone*

"I like children," said Jackie Schulman, a twenty-five-year-old, self-employed piano tuner. "I'm not married—maybe I never will be—but I think I'd make a super mother.

"In an evening music class I became acquainted with a single woman who adopted an eight-year-old orphan from Brazil. The two of them share a house with another single woman who also has an adopted child. Talking to this lady and seeing how well things have worked out for her has made me think seriously about adopting a little girl of my own.

"When I called the adoption agency to ask about the proper procedure for such an adoption, I could hardly get anyone to talk to me. I was quite bluntly informed that if I ever were to get approved—which was doubtful in itself—I would be placed at the bottom of their list of prospective parents because I'm single.

"I had it all worked out. My best friend and I share a rented house, and there is plenty of room for a child. Though I'm certainly not rich, my income would easily be enough to support myself and a little girl. My working hours are flexible and could be adjusted around the child's school hours. But no one seemed interested in hearing my qualifications. It was never said in so many words, but the answer that came across to me was 'Forget it. We aren't in the market for single parents.'"

A single person will undoubtedly have a more difficult time obtaining a child than a couple will. Most singles who want to adopt children are women. Agencies that place children with single people indicate that women outnumber men twenty-five to one as adoptive parents. Although historically most adoptions by single parents have been through agencies, independent adoption by single parents has become much more common recently.

Jackie Schulman had very little going for her as a potential adoptive parent. First, she was too young. Women in their late thirties and forties are preferred because it is felt that by then a person is more likely to be comfortable with his or her singleness and ready to settle down with a child to enjoy the daily routines of domestic life. Second, Jackie's financial base was not adequately stable. With almost no savings, her income depended entirely on her ability to find work consistently. Third, although she had thought about adjusting her hours to coincide with the child's time in school, she had not taken into consideration summer vacations, school holidays, and times when the child would need to stay home because of illness. Fourth, Jackie is a renter. Agencies definitely prefer and sometimes insist that their adoptive parents be homeowners. Fifth, because all of Jackie's close friends are unmarried women, she has no way of surrounding a child with good two-parent family models or with consistent male companionship. Even her own family has little to offer in this respect.

But even if Jackie were an older, financially secure homeowner who was surrounded by happy two-parent families, her struggle to have a child placed in her home would be far from easy. The goal of almost all adoption agencies is to place every child in a stable, two-parent home. They know that parenting a child alone is difficult. Nevertheless, the trend is toward more single-parent adoptions, at least with hard-to-place children or children from other countries.

Asked whether her agency accepted applications from single persons, a social worker in charge of placement said, "We certainly do. In fact we have some children available who we feel might more easily adjust to a single-parent home." Then she explained that despite the increase in single-parent adoptions in recent years, these placements are still relatively few in number.

Many criteria are important for single people who want to adopt. They must have experience with children and fully understand all that is involved in child care. They must realize that parenting is a twenty-four-hour-a-day, seven-day-a-week job. They must be healthy, both physically and emotionally. They must be realistic and mature. They must have financial security, for they will be their children's sole provider. They must be able to make adequate arrangements for day care while they are at work, especially for those times when their children are ill.

The first question adoptive parents must ask themselves is "What can I do for this child?" not "What can this child do for me?" Many times prospective single parents are trying to meet their own need for companionship. While this is an understandable need, it is not an adequate reason to seek to adopt. The only acceptable motivation is an earnest desire to love and care for a child.

DISCOURAGING CIRCUMSTANCES

Discouraged by her circumstances, Jackie Schulman abandoned the idea of adoption. Sheila Carswell, however, had good reason to persist. A thirty-seven-year-old elementary schoolteacher who was obviously comfortable in her role as a single adult, Sheila came much closer to fitting the picture of an ideal single parent.

"When I approached a private adoption agency about the possibility of adopting a child, I realized that such a placement would be neither quick nor easy," Sheila said. "But I was convinced that I would be a good mother, so I was determined to try. I appreciated the realistic honesty of the social worker with whom I spoke. She warned me at the outset that among adoption applicants, the prospective single parent is at the bottom of the heap. Agencies prefer good two-parent families.

"I didn't ask for an infant or a toddler because I know

that such children are easily placed with couples. And because I'm a schoolteacher, a school-aged child would fit more easily into my life. Not only our hours but also our vacations would be the same. If the child should have to miss school because of illness, my sick leave would allow me the time off to care for the child.

"The social worker who interviewed me asked questions about every imaginable area of my life. Some of the questions were really incredible! Why hadn't I ever married? Would I marry if someone were to ask me? How stable did I consider myself to be? What was my real reason for wanting a child? What needs could I meet in a child better than someone else could? How would I manage to raise a child by myself? What kind of a child would I accept? These are just a few of the dozens of questions that were fired at me.

"When the social worker finally told me that in her estimation I was well qualified and emotionally prepared to become a single parent, I heaved a sigh of relief. Then she told me about a couple of little girls who were available but because of their ages, nationalities, or physical problems would have little chance of ever being placed for adoption. 'It just may be,' she said, 'that one of those girls is the right one for you.'

"From the very beginning, my parents and two younger sisters were against my plans to adopt," Sheila explained. "They were afraid that everyone who met me and my child would automatically assume that I had been divorced or, even worse, that my child was illegitimate. Again and again they chided me for refusing to accept being a single, childless schoolteacher as my lot in life.

"The counselors at the agency felt that my family would have to play a major part in the life of any child I might adopt, so a social worker was sent to talk with my parents and my sisters and brothers-in-law. She sensed immediately the bitterness and hostility they felt.

"A few weeks later I was notified that my application for adoption had been turned down. According to the social worker, I had many excellent qualities and would probably have made a very good mother. My rejection, she said, was due entirely to the fact that my child and I would have received no emotional support from my family. In fact, in her opinion, they would actually have caused extra problems in an already difficult situation. I argued, I pleaded, and I explained, but the decision was final. There is little flexibility in regulations when it comes to single-parent adoptions!"

Independent, single-parent adoptions are not much easier. As in any independent adoption, the adoptive parent is selected by a birth parent, almost always the mother. In a large majority of cases, one of the primary motives of the birth mother to place her child for adoption is her desire for the child to have a two-parent home which the birth mother cannot provide. It is not uncommon for a birth mother to say "If I were willing to have my child raised by a single mother, I would raise him myself!"

However, independent adoptions by single adoptive parents do happen, and they are not as rare as they were just a few years ago. In selecting an adoptive home for a child, a birth mother typically is looking for many of the same attributes as is an agency.

DETERMINATION THAT PAID OFF

Most single men and women who consider adoption either become discouraged at the outset and never pursue it, as in Jackie Schulman's case, or else, like Sheila Carswell, they are turned down because they fail to meet the agency's strict criteria. Only a few single people make it to the point of having a child actually placed with them through an agency. When it does happen, it is a real testimony to the resilience and determination of the adoptive parent. Or, as Juanita Hart says, it is a real testimony to the providential hand of God.

"I have two adopted children," said Juanita, a reporter for a major metropolitan newspaper. "Robin, who was four when I got her, is now fourteen; Andy, adopted as an infant, is almost seven. God was preparing the way for me to get my children long before I had any thought of adopting or any way of doing so.

"After graduating from college, I left my North Dakota farm home and came to Los Angeles to seek my fortune in the big city. I started attending a small church where I was befriended by a widow named Betty Morgan. She was about my mother's age.

"My big plans and dreams were soon shattered when I found that I couldn't even get an interview, much less a job, with the local newspaper. Broke and discouraged, I was ready to forget my dreams, swallow my pride, and go back home—a failure at the age of twenty-three. But Betty wouldn't hear of it. She encouraged me, listened to me, sympathized with me, advised me, and plied me with free home-cooked meals.

"When I had been in Los Angeles less than a year, I contracted hepatitis. Since I was much too ill to care for myself, Betty took me in to live with her. By the time I was finally well again, I had no apartment, no job, and no money. So I stayed on with Betty.

"The next year, after I succeeded in landing a job as a rookie reporter, the rent on our apartment was raised so drastically that we could no longer afford to stay there. Betty had some money in the bank, and at her suggestion we used it as a down payment on a little house. Shortly afterward a friend of Betty's asked us to keep three thousand dollars of her money in our bank account. She wanted to protect the money from her alcoholic husband. The result was a padded account that made us look much wealthier than we were.

"By this time I was twenty-six years old and was doing well in my job at the newspaper. Betty, however, was bored with staying home alone all day. She was also feeling guilty about not being able to contribute to the house payments. So she suggested that we take in a foster child.

"It sounded like a great idea to me. I've always loved children. Our home was approved, and within two months four-year-old Robin was brought to us.

"Robin was a victim of child abuse. This was the fourth

time she had been removed from her mother. Each time previously Robin had been returned to her mother, but this time was the worst ever. The bruised and bleeding little girl had watched in terror as her mother was handcuffed and dragged, kicking and screaming, into a police car. Robin spent three hours being stitched up and bandaged in a hospital emergency room. She arrived at our house confused, frightened, and hurting. She cried all night.

"By morning Robin had settled down. She told me, 'The policeman said he would find me a really nice mommy. You must be her.' From then on I was 'Mommy' and Betty was 'Grandmommy.'

"Robin loved Betty and me, and we adored her," Juanita continued. "We took her everywhere we went even though she was never really comfortable outside the house. As soon as we came home, she would run inside and cry, 'Mommy, Mommy, lock the door!'

"Although all her family lived within twenty miles of our house, two whole months went by before any relative made an effort to contact Robin. They just didn't seem to be interested. When her mother and grandmother finally did come—unannounced—Robin would not go near them. She was terrified that they had come to take her away. They were granted visitation rights, but Robin steadfastly refused to see them. Even when I picked her up and carried her into the room where they were, she totally ignored them, acting as if they weren't there. She wouldn't even open the gifts they brought her. Naturally they wouldn't accept any responsibility for her feelings toward them. Instead they blamed me, claiming that I was deliberately turning her against them.

"Practically every day Robin would ask me, 'Do you promise you'll be my mommy forever?' I can't tell you how badly I wanted to make her that promise, but how could I? Even though both Betty and I wanted to adopt Robin, her mother wouldn't release her—especially not to me. Moreover, her mother called me one night in a drunken rage and screamed, 'You'd better never take my daughter away from me! If you do, I'll fix you for good!' I don't know where that woman is now—she had been in and out of prison—but I can tell you that we have really had to commit ourselves to the Lord's care and safekeeping.

"Our caseworker was well aware of my desire to adopt Robin," said Juanita. "She warned me that if I didn't fight hard for her, Robin was sure to be returned once again to her family. The caseworker helped me by accumulating evidence that Robin's family was unfit to raise her. It took several years, but finally, by court order, Robin was declared free for adoption.

"Now this is the exciting part! Listen to how the Lord's providential preparations all came together so that we could keep Robin. Because Betty was able to be home twenty-four hours a day, and because Betty and I had bought the house, and because I had a ready-made 'extended family' in my group of friends at church, and because we still had the other woman's money in our bank account, I was approved as an adoptive single parent. It took more than four years, but at the age of nine, Robin was legally declared my daughter.

"From the time Robin first arrived, everything in our house revolved around her," Juanita continued. "When she was seven years old, I began to feel that she would really benefit by having another child around. Our foster home was licensed for three children, so Betty and I decided to ask for another child. I didn't want anyone who would compete with Robin, however. She was still too fragile emotionally for that. Rather, I wanted someone she could love and help care for, someone who could teach her the joys of giving. So we decided to ask for a baby boy.

"When I told our social worker what we had in mind, she actually laughed out loud and said, 'You're crazy! The agency will never place a baby boy with you.' But the Lord had put it in my heart that this was what he had for us, so every morning and every evening Betty and Robin and I prayed together that God would give us our baby boy. We had to wait and pray for six months, but finally it happened. Our social worker called one morning and said, 'You win! Your baby boy is ready for you. Shall I bring him over?'

What a silly question! All three of us were waiting on the front porch when they arrived.

"But the baby who was placed in my arms was not the baby I had pictured for all those months. Four-week-old Malcolm Alfonse was not an attractive infant. His skinny little body was filthy and full of sores. His head was covered with an awful case of ringworm. When he arrived, he was crying at the top of his lungs, an activity he continued almost nonstop for two whole weeks. For a long time Robin stood and stared in silence at this pitiful little creature. After all our praying, I was certain she was terribly disappointed. Finally she spoke. 'Malcolm Alfonse?' she asked. 'He looks more like an Andy to me.' And from then on, he was Andy.

"It's hard to believe, but at the tender age of four weeks Andy was already a veteran of two foster homes and one adoptive home. In his short life he had been abused, neglected, and rejected. Finally because no one else seemed to want him, he was offered to us.

"But that little fellow was the best thing that ever happened to Robin. Perhaps because he had been so mistreated and unwanted, she could really identify with him. But they also looked alike. I'm a blue-eyed blond and Betty is very gray, but both Robin and Andy have raven-black hair and dark brown eyes. One night I tiptoed into Robin's room to kiss her goodnight. There she was with little Andy all snuggled in bed with her. Looking up at me, she said, 'Andy and I belong together, don't we, Mom?' We were just finding out what God had known all along.

"When Andy had been with us for a year, I told his caseworker that I would like to adopt him. She was irate. 'There is no way I would allow you to adopt that little boy,' she fumed. 'There isn't even a man in your house. What makes you think that you can take in foster children and then automatically adopt them? I'm going to remove him from your home immediately!'

"I was shocked by her reaction, and I was terrified that she might actually make good on her threat," Juanita continued. "But God had put Andy in our home, and no one could take him away without God's permission. Again Betty and Robin and I, along with our Christian friends, banded together in prayer. If God wanted Andy with us, he would have to intervene. If he didn't want us to keep Andy, he would have to give us the strength to accept his will and to give our baby up.

"Then, completely unsolicited, Robin's caseworker stepped in on our behalf. Praising Robin's extraordinary adjustment, she recommended that I be allowed to adopt Andy. The agency had already approved me as an adoptive parent for Robin, so what could they say? Andy joined our family. God had done it again!"

THE STRUGGLE GOES ON

In our society with its high number of divorces, millions of children are being raised in single-parent families. The children who are adopted by a single parent are sometimes more fortunate than those others, for they at least are spared the trauma of going through a divorce. Then too, their single parents have been hand-picked for their ability to cope with single parenthood.

But the fact remains that very few single people have the tenacity and the determination to fight for the right of adoptive parenthood. For a single person, the decision to adopt is complicated by the fact that the children who are placed in such homes are generally those who have little chance of being placed elsewhere. These children often have emotional scars that take a long, long time to heal. Isn't it ironic that single parents, who confront the difficult task of raising a child alone, are usually given the children who need the most help?

Today the major qualification for prospective adoptive parents, single or married, is that they have the potential for helping children to develop into sound, mature adults. The difference is that the single person is far less likely to get the chance to parent a child.

QUESTIONS FOR DISCUSSION

1. Under what circumstances might a single parent be the family of choice for an adopted child?
2. Do you think that Sheila Carswell should have continued her quest for a child through another agency or through an independent adoption? How might she have gone about it?

11.   *Growing Together*

Every family has its own story, unique and special. It has its own dreams and hopes, its own triumphs and shared joys. It also has problems, disappointments, and struggles. And every family changes. As each member grows and develops, so does the family as a whole. This is the way families are, and those that include adopted children are no different.

In this chapter we look at some of the issues that are sure to arise as your family lives and grows together. It is vital that the lines of communication between you and your child be kept open so that there can always be a means for honest, loving, tolerant sharing. Many problems generally associated with adoption can be avoided or minimized by sharing your feelings, by listening when your children want to talk, and by answering their questions as honestly as you can.

If you maintain an open family relationship, the time will come when your children will ask questions about adoption. Your approach to these questions should be no different than to their questions about human relationships, sex, faith, and other issues of growing and learning. Present the answers comfortably and truthfully. Don't worry about the actual words; they are not nearly so important as the feelings and attitudes you communicate. Even without eloquent explanations you can communicate your love to your children. You can let them know that they belong with you and that you are glad they do.

One of the first concerns many adoptive parents face is whether or not to tell their children that they are adopted. Today almost all adoption authorities agree the children should be told, and the earlier, the better. If you don't tell your children, sooner or later they will probably find out from someone else. Such a disclosure is tragic and unfair, and it could give your children the impression that you are ashamed of adoption and perhaps ashamed of them. It will also undermine your credibility. After all, if you weren't honest with your children about something as important as their adoption, how can they trust you to be honest about anything else?

The easiest and most successful way of handling the matter is to deal with it as an accepted fact of family life. It is important that your children be allowed to grow up with this knowledge. From the beginning their adoption should be an open, accepted, and understood fact. Talk about it from time to time in a casual, matter-of-fact way that is natural and comfortable for you.

You need not go into detail at first. Your children will not understand and will not be interested. It is enough for them to hear the word "adoption" and to associate it with warmth, comfort, security, and love. They will let you know when they are ready for more information by asking more questions. Follow their lead.

Be careful, however, not to carry your talk of adoption too far. Overemphasizing it can be just as bad as ignoring it. If you are always talking about your children's adoption, you will be emphasizing that they are different. This is certain to make them uncomfortable. The key is to strike a balance. Don't remind them too much, but mention it often enough to be sure that the idea is accepted and natural.

OPEN FORUM

Karen Alvarado: The older of our two adopted children is three. I feel that I probably should be telling her about her adoption, but I just don't know when or how to do it.

Terry Cohen: Don and I started using the word "adoption" when our daughter was just a baby. When we thought she was old enough to understand, we explained what adoption meant. I think she was about three years old at the time.

Don Cohen: If you wait too long, your child may hear it from someone else first.

Karen Alvarado: Sometimes I actually forget that she is adopted.

Ken Randle: It sounds to me as if you may be uncomfortable with the word "adoption." Our approach was to be free in our use of the word. We didn't go out of our way to use it constantly, but when it came up naturally, we didn't try to avoid it.

Karen Alvarado: How would my daughter know how I feel about adoption? She's only three.

Ken Randle: You would be amazed at how much little children can learn from what they overhear. They can sense your attitudes just by the way you say something or by the way you avoid saying it.

Katherine O'Neill: Our son enjoys explaining adoption to his little sister. He can remember going with us to get her. It was a happy time for him. He tells her, "Mommy and Daddy really wanted you. We all prayed about it, and God brought you into our family."

Steve Wilkinson: We recently had our first discussion with our two-and-one-half-year-old son, Jason, on this subject, and I was surprised at how easily and naturally it worked out. Our pastor, who is also an adoptive parent, had advised us to look for the first excuse to tell Jason. We were in the supermarket, and Jason was in the seat in the grocery cart. A pregnant woman walked by, and Jason told me he thought she was very fat. I explained to him that she wasn't fat. There was a baby in her tummy, and that is where babies come from, their mother's tummy. He asked me if he had come out of his mommy's tummy, and I told him "No, you did not come out of Mommy's tummy, because her tummy is broken. You were adopted." He just said "Oh," as if it were the most natural and understandable thing in the world. He hasn't asked any further questions, but when he does, we want to be ready to answer truthfully but positively.

Greg Swanson: We have some books on adoption around the house for the children to look at. Not only do they encourage questions, but they also tend to give adoption an air of acceptance.

Dr. McDill: I like the approach of waiting until the child asks questions. It's important to catch that moment of readiness. Otherwise you may be giving data that your child isn't ready to handle. It's better to wait for that moment of readiness than to be burdened with the dilemma of deciding when to tell, how to tell, and so forth. When the questions do come, keep the answers simple. Be prepared for that right moment with correct answers. Otherwise your child may draw a totally incorrect conclusion from your silence or hesitation.

THE NEED FOR UNCONDITIONAL LOVE

"I hate you! I don't like it here! I'm going to find my real mother and move in with her!"

If your adopted children have ever shouted things like this, you know how shocking, confusing, and painful such pronouncements can be. When this happens it is important to remember that it does not mean you have failed as a parent. It is easy to react to the words your children speak and to miss the real message. When your children accuse you of not loving them or say they don't love you, they are probably really asking, "Do you love me no matter what I do?" or "Are you really my parents?" or "Do you care enough to make me obey the rules?"

Adopted children, especially ones who have been unwanted in the past, have an enormous need to know they are loved unconditionally. If they don't have a backlog of experience that tells them they are valuable, they cannot take it for granted. They need to hear you tell them so again and again. You will be able to find many opportunities to say such things as "I love you," "You look so nice today," or "You did that job so well! Thank you for helping me."

But be careful that you don't say the words unless you really mean them. Strained or phony compliments will be recognized immediately for what they are, and they will do more harm than good. Your consistent warmth, security, and loving discipline guide your children to a secure sense of belonging and to feelings of self-worth. Day by day through your loving care you are giving your children the emotional strength and stability they need to face the realities that life will inevitably bring their way.

One of these realities is a possible contact with a birth mother or other relative. Many adoptive parents possess letters written by a child's biological parents at the time of birth, left with instructions that they be given to the child at a specific age. For many these letters are a real source of worry. Several of the parents with whom we spoke had questions about such letters.

OPEN FORUM

Katherine O'Neill: When we got our first child we were given a letter from his thirteen-year-old mother with instructions that it be given to him on his thirteenth birthday. She wrote that she loved his father very much but that they couldn't raise a child because they were just children themselves. She said her parents thought it would be best for her to finish school. She added that if he ever wanted to look her up, she would be happy for him to do so. Our son is now almost thirteen, and I don't really want to give the letter to him. How much do we owe the child who gave birth to our son? Must we follow her directions?

Roger Crawford: You have adopted the child, so he's your responsibility. You have to do what you think is best for him. You have no obligation to his birth mother.

Greg Swanson: We have two letters, one to us and one to our child. The one to our child came with express instructions that it be presented unopened to him on his sixteenth birthday. Since we have honored her request not to open the sealed envelope, we have no idea what is in the letter.

Rob Alvarado: That's a ticking time bomb!

Dr. McDill: I can see very little good coming from a letter like that.

Greg Swanson: We just wonder morally what we should do. The birth parents were married, and the letter she wrote to us was really neat. But the adoption agency did declare them unfit parents.

Victoria Meyers: Since your real obligation is to your child, not to his mother, I think that you should open the letter yourself and see what it says. Then you can decide whether you want to give it to him at all.

Dr. McDill: A confused, new mother—a little girl—wrote that letter. Whatever she put in it seemed appropriate at the time, but now she may feel very differently. There could be things in there that would cause great harm and damage.

Ken Randle: I couldn't justify the dishonesty of opening my child's letter. I would give it to him unopened.

Mr. Donnelly: I wonder if you would still feel that way if you had met with as many birth mothers as I have. They are often very confused and mixed-up. I would be concerned about what my child would find in such a letter. I agree with Victoria; I would open it and make a judgment based on its contents. But I wouldn't be hypocritical about it. I would tell my child that I disregarded the instructions because, loving him as I do, I wanted to be sure that I was doing the right thing for him.

Dr. McDill: In the end you must keep in mind that your responsibility lies with the child. You must decide what you feel would be the best for him, then do it without feeling guilty.

Mr. Donnelly: I would go one step further. You were selected to adopt your child because someone, either the birth mother or the agency social workers, felt that you had sound judgment and that you would exercise that judgment in the child's best interest. We should never apologize for using our best judgment for our children. You do have an obligation to the birth mother to comply with her reasonable requests to the extent that you can do so without compromising your responsibilities as a parent. However, if your parental responsibilities and the wishes of the birth mother come into conflict, your judgment as a parent must take priority.

WHEN TEASING HURTS

"Why are children so cruel?" asked one adoptive mother. "Why do they tease adopted children so unmercifully?"

Children can be terribly thoughtless and cruel in their treatment of other children. If the teasing draws a reaction from the child, the offenders can become downright vicious. Adopted children have no corner on getting teased, however. What they do have is a sensitive area of vulnerability. When this sensitive area is attacked, a child can be hurt deeply.

OPEN FORUM

Howard Vaughn: Both of our daughters have experienced a lot of painful teasing from other children at school and a lot of jeers on the playground. Once our older daughter was told, "No wonder your real mother gave you up. You were too ugly to keep!" My daughter is actually a very lovely girl, but that comment hurt her so badly that I'm not sure the wound will ever heal completely.

Katherine O'Neill: Once our daughter was called a derogatory variation of "illegitimate." Fortunately she talked to me about it. It so happens that she was an illegitimate child, so I took that opportunity to tell her the circumstances of her birth. But I also assured her that this had no bearing whatsoever on who she is or on her personal worth.

Dr. McDill: You did the right thing. I once had a patient who came to me for counseling because she had a terrible relationship with her mother. During treatment she angrily stated, "I hate my mother because I'm illegitimate!" I was certain she *wasn't* illegitimate, so I asked her where she had gotten such an idea. It seems that as a young child she had overheard some older children refer to a classmate as illegitimate, so she asked her mother if she was also. Her mother just said, "What a silly question!" Since her mother hadn't actually denied it, the girl assumed it was true. You can see the damage that can be caused by failing to fully answer and discuss a child's questions.

Ken Randle: I teach in a junior high school, and I can attest to the fact that many kids say anything that pops into their heads. They don't stop to think that their remark may hurt someone else. To them it's just a joke.

Dr. McDill: You cannot protect your children from hurtful comments. But you can arm them against their harmful effects by providing them with a healthy self-concept and a great reserve of love from which they can draw.

IN QUEST OF THE PAST

When your children begin to ask questions about their adoption, it may distress you to find that many of those questions concern their biological parents. You will undoubtedly be asked, "Why did they give me up?" In answering this question it is important that you emphasize the fact that your children's being "given up" was in no way their fault. Whatever they are or are not had no bearing on their birth parents' decision to allow their adoption. Though you may know very little—maybe nothing at all—about the birth parents and their problems, you can honestly say that there were many people who cared enough about your children to see that they were placed in a family that really loves and wants them. Your children are where they belong: safe and sound in your home. You can also say that for some reason beyond their control, the people to whom your children were born could not take care of them. You can fill in as many details as you know and feel that your children can handle at the moment.

No one sets out to be a bad parent. We all do the best we can to cope with the demands of life. But there are people who, no matter how they try, do not have the capacity to be good parents. Some realize their limitations and voluntarily relinquish the responsibility for their children. Others can only demonstrate their inability to parent, and in these cases the courts must step in and remove the child. The important thing is that it is because people cared about them that children are freed for adoption.

Virtually all adopted children want to know about their birth parents: what they looked like, how old they were, their interests and talents and abilities. Some adoptive parents have a more difficult time dealing with these questions than others do. There are some who absolutely refuse to discuss their children's past, even going so far as to deny that their children were adopted.

"My daughter doesn't ask questions about her birth parents," said one mother emphatically. "She just isn't interested. She knows she's our child and that's enough for her."

Just because your adopted children don't talk about their past does not mean they don't think about it. They do. And they need to have some explanation and answers. If you are comfortable in talking with your children about their past, they will also be comfortable. On the other hand, if they sense that raising certain questions threatens or embarrasses you, they may try to protect both you and themselves by avoiding those uncomfortable subjects. You may think that you are able to hide your feelings from your children. Be careful: Children understand a whole lot more than we think they do.

The ability of children to handle information about their background changes as they mature. By the time they reach adulthood, they should have all the information you have, even though their birth parents may have had some very serious problems and an unpleasant history.

Many adopted children were born to unmarried parents. If this is true of your children, you may worry about how you should describe their beginnings to them. If you simply say, "Your birth mother wasn't married," you will be giving a straightforward, honest answer, yet you will not be condemning the birth mother. If this answer is not complete enough, your children will ask you more questions.

When your children begin to express curiosity about their background and heritage, let them know that this is a natural desire. Reassure them that there is no reason for them to feel hesitant or ashamed. Some experts feel that if adopted children knew more about their biological parents, they would feel less need to search for them.

Perhaps it is fear that makes adoptive parents feel insecure and uncomfortable about dealing with their children's background—fear that their children will someday find their birth parents and like them better. An expression of interest by their children may be viewed by the adoptive parents as a sign of failure on their part or ingratitude on the part of their children.

In reality, the desire of many adopted teenagers and adults to learn about their heritage or to meet their birth parents usually arises out of a personal need, not out of failure on the part of the adoptive parents.

Adoptive parents usually want to know whether the adoption records can be legally opened. Most states have enacted laws to protect the confidentiality of everyone involved in an adoption. For all intents and purposes, adopted children are reborn into their adoptive families and have birth certificates to prove it. All traces of their beginnings are erased, leaving the children, the birth parents, and the adoptive parents free from ghosts out of the past. The best interest of the adoptee is the guiding principle for legal,

147

administrative, and legislative decisions concerning adoptions.

Currently, however, some groups are putting increasing pressure on legislatures to allow adult adoptees to have free access to their adoption records. Whether this would be a good or a bad thing has been hotly debated. On the one hand, it must be remembered that at the time of the adoption most birth parents and adoptive parents were promised confidentiality. It is also possible that what would be revealed in those records might be quite disappointing or even harmful to the adoptee, especially if it led to a meeting with the birth parents. On the other hand, many people feel strongly that adults are capable of calculating the risks and should be allowed to make their own choices.

In spite of the confidentiality of the birth records, many adoptees find a good deal of information about their backgrounds. Adoptees' best initial source of information is their adoptive parents. In recent years many organizations have been established that offer adolescents or adults practical assistance in searching for background information or for birth parents.

Is such information and the possibility of locating the birth parents good or bad? There is no pat answer to this question. Whatever your opinion, you will be able to find studies, statistics, articles, and books to support it.

Many adoptees express concern as to whether their birth parents would want to see them. (This is discussed at greater length in chapter 14.) One teenager asked, "Why would they want me now if they didn't want me then?"

"If I ever do meet them, they would probably tell me to get lost," said another.

"I'm not bothered by the fact that my child wants to search for her roots," one adoptive father said. "That's natural. But it seems to me that for the good of everyone involved, this is an impulsive curiosity that should be controlled. We all have impulses that we must learn not to give in to—like punching someone in the mouth or telling a person to lay off the dessert because he's already too fat. But isn't maturity learning to control these impulses?"

"What makes parents of adopted kids think that all their kids want to find their birth parents?" asked one sixteen-year-old boy. "My birth parents may be great people, but I don't want to meet them. I just want my real parents, the ones who raised me."

"There are some doors that should never be opened," said an adult adoptee, "because once they're opened, they're too difficult to shut. Sometimes they can never be closed again."

A social worker questioned, "Why are adoptive parents so afraid the biological parents are going to want their child back? That's less likely than being killed in an airplane crash. They have probably read too many romantic reports of ecstatic reunions. I'm sure they happen occasionally, but not nearly so often as we are led to believe. It's unrealistic to think that all those years can just be wiped out."

Nevertheless, there are instances when very disturbed, rebellious teenagers and young adults meet their birth mothers and immediately settle down to a normal life. Some adoptees, it seems, are unable to come to terms with who they are until they have had that contact with their beginnings. But this isn't always the case. It is important to distinguish between a real need to know and a form of quasi-searching in which adolescents go through a period of threatening their families with the idea of searching for their birth parents. This is very much like other teenagers who threaten to run away from home. Adoptive parents, however, seem particularly vulnerable to such threats; when they overreact, it appears to have the effect of reinforcing the power of the teenagers' threatenings.

"If I ever did meet my birth parents, it wouldn't change the way I feel," one teenager said. "My parents are my parents, and I'd never consider leaving them. They raised me and I love them."

There are a few adoptive parents who encourage and personally become involved in their children's search. One mother initiated it. At the beginning her son was mildly involved, but after several months he told her that he really wasn't interested. His mother continued the search alone. "The time will come when he will want to know," she said, "and when he does, I will have something to tell him."

As part of her search this mother attends the meetings of a local adoptees search organization. "I think all adoptive parents should become acquainted with one of these," she said. "They would get a completely different perspective of the adoptee's search."

"My daughter has lived with me for fourteen years," said another mother. "Her relationships with other people don't affect her relationship with me. That's already well established. Eventually she is going to have to live her own life. She has another set of parents and that concerns her. Because of this, I want her to find out as much as she can about it, and I will help her."

What is the answer? Most adoptive parents find that they have mixed feelings when they discover their children's interest in searching for their birth parents. Initially they may be hurt and angry. Usually, however, the relationship between the adoptive parents and their children is strong enough to withstand the strain of a search. The adoptive parents can provide vital emotional support at this time when one of their children's greatest fears is that they will hurt the parents they love.

Most adoptees do not get very far in their search, and even fewer ever make contact with their birth parents. In most cases a search proves disappointing. You and your children should be prepared for this. They will need your empathy and support in the face of disappointment.

OPEN FORUM

Rachel Nichols: Our two children are very different. The younger one is full of questions, but the older one says little. She just doesn't seem to be interested. I guess it's a difference in their personalities.

Cheryl Kelley: One of our children shows no interest at all in her birth mother or in any of the family records we have. But when she gets angry at her brothers and sister, she will say, "You're not really my family!" She obviously thinks more about it than she feels like sharing.

Marian Crawford: Our older son is adopted, and the younger one was born to us. I worried all through my pregnancy that I would love my birth child more than my adopted one. Not long ago the older boy asked, "Mom, do you love me as much as my brother?" I could honestly and happily say, "Yes, I do." I'm telling the truth when I say that I feel no difference.

Lorraine Swanson: Our son's first question was, "Did I come from your tummy?" I said, "No, you came from someone else's tummy, but God made you just for us."

Patrick O'Neill: Our son said, "My birth mother must have really hated me. Why else would she have given me up?" What would be the best response to a question like that?

Rachel Nichols: We encountered that same situation. It was hard for me to say, but I answered, "I don't know her reason for giving you up, but I know she must have loved you. It took love to allow you to be adopted into a home where you would be well cared for." I felt like adding, "But I'm a much better mother." Fortunately I resisted the temptation.

Don Cohen: We told our child that her birth mother surely loved her and that she would have kept her if she could have done so. It seems important to avoid running down the biological mother. Kids need to feel that they were born of essentially good and loving people and that they were not rejected because of who they are.

Rachel Nichols: We got our girls when they were tiny babies. Their birth mothers could not have known them long enough to like or dislike them.

Mr. Donnelly: That's a good point. Particularly a few years ago before open adoption achieved its current prominence, in many cases a birth mother who indicated that she planned to put her child up for adoption never even saw the baby.

Lorraine Swanson: Our child really was given up because he wasn't wanted. He had a birth defect that his parents just couldn't handle.

Ken Randle: You still could tell him that he was given up because his parents weren't able to care for him. Whether the reason was physical or emotional or whatever, the birth parents were unable to care for their child in most cases.

Judy Randle: A psychologist we consulted warned us about some things not to say. "Your mother was too ill to care for you" may cause a child to worry whenever his adoptive parents get sick because he may fear that they won't be able to care for him either. "Your mother died" can cause the same kind of worry—that these parents will also die and leave him alone. He may even think that he caused his mother's death. If you say, "She was too poor to take care of you," he may get scared everytime he hears you complain about the high price of food. Or he may feel the need to search for his birth mother to take care of her.

Patrick O'Neill: Then what should we say?

Judy Randle: The psychologist suggested that if we don't know the answer, we should merely say, "I don't know the reason, but it must have been a good one." In our case that's the whole truth. We really don't know.

Roger Crawford: Our son's parents were married, but they divorced when he was three, and his mother decided to give him up. They have since remarried and had two more children. The whole thing is a very bad situation involving drugs and crime. Without going into the details, we just told our son that they couldn't care for him.

Dr. McDill: When children say such things as "My mother must have hated me," they may be voicing some specific feelings rather than inquiring about their birth mother's reasons for allowing them to be adopted. I think I would approach the situation from the idea of what the child is feeling about himself. Is he unhappy about something? Is he feeling unworthy? What specific feelings brought this up? This may be more helpful than giving a cut-and-dried factual answer.

Katherine O'Neill: I wish we hadn't been given so much information about our children's backgrounds. I can't see how it will ever do any good, and it really makes me feel uncomfortable having to wade through some direct questions when I would much rather be able to say truthfully, "I don't know."

Ken Randle: The older the children get, the more they want you to paint in the background of the birth mother. Sooner or later you're going to have to describe someone to fill in that shadow.

Judy Randle: As our children got older and began to ask questions, we regretted the casual way we had dismissed and forgotten the information we were given at the time of the adoptions.

Ben Meyers: Our social worker volunteered very little. We had to dig and pressure her for everything we got. But we figured if we don't need it, fine; if we do, we'll have it.

Dr. McDill: I agree. It's important to find out as much as possible about the ancestry and heredity of a child at the time of adoption rather than to say it doesn't matter and regret it later.

Betsy Vaughn: Our attorney wrote comprehensive letters for both of our girls telling everything that was known about their backgrounds. When they began studying genealogy in school and were supposed to make out a family tree, it was really nice to have that letter.

Rob Alvarado: One of our girls comes from an unbelievably sordid background involving drugs, crime, and prison. I'm afraid that such knowledge would be catastrophic to her self-image.

Dr. McDill: You can only answer as honestly as you can, perhaps choosing to leave out the worst details.

Rob Alvarado: I would have to lie in order to say anything good!

Jack Kelley: Do you really think honesty would be so harmful?

Rob Alvarado: Yes, I really do. And in time she'll surely ask. I guess I'll just have to make up something. A lie would be better than the truth.

Everyone: No! Don't lie!

Ken Randle: You're looking at this from a three-year-old's point of view. It will be a number of years before you actually have to deal with this problem. When your daughter is older, both you and she will be better able to handle it.

Roger Crawford: I'm in favor of giving a little bit of information over a long period of time, not piling it all on in one shocking session. Answer the little questions first. Then add more as she asks and you feel that she's able to handle it.

Ken Randle: Sometimes we overreact and answer more than the child is asking.

Jack Kelley: When she does ask, if you feel your daughter is still too young, you could just say, "I don't think you're old enough to handle the answer right now. Ask me again next year, and if I feel you're old enough, I'll tell you about it." An older child who really feels good about himself and has a secure family background can handle anything.

Rob Alvarado: I don't know. . . .

Jack Kelley: Is there anything about your family background that, if you were told today, you couldn't handle?

154

Rob Alvarado: No, I think I could handle anything. But I'm thirty-four years old. My daughter won't wait until she's my age to ask.

Jack Kelley: By the time she's seventeen or eighteen with the background you're giving her, she'll do fine. I'm speaking from experience. Our oldest two are that age. They have been told the sordid details of their backgrounds and they have managed quite well.

Dr. McDill: I want to stress again that moment of readiness. Don't try to explain what the child is not ready to hear. And, please, *don't* be dishonest! If the child later finds out that you lied to him, it will be far worse than whatever sordid details you may have avoided disclosing.

Jack Kelley: What is it in the psychological makeup of adoptees that makes them so intent on finding those other parents?

Dr. McDill: From a biblical standpoint, a separation accompanied by a very real sense of loss occurred at the time of the Fall. This inherent lostness, this forsakenness, is certainly part of it. During adolescence children begin to move away from identifying with their family and move toward peer identification. They begin searching for an independent identity. For adopted children, however, this search includes another set of parents. You mustn't feel threatened by this. It's completely normal. Your response should be, "I'm glad to see you are growing up and getting your own ideas about things. I'm happy about that. Tell me about your feelings."

Greg Swanson: This makes me awfully uncomfortable. How would the rest of you feel about your children undertaking a serious search for their birth parents?

Karen Alvarado: For the daughter who comes from such a terrible background I would be strongly against it. For the other one I would be more neutral.

Betsy Vaughn: I'm dreading it for both our children. Neither one would be welcomed by her birth mother.

Mr. Donnelly: Children have a romanticized vision of what their birth parents ought to be like. In most cases, were they to see the reality, many would be extremely disappointed if not downright shocked. This is not to say that many reunions with birth parents are not happy, because many of them are very joyous events, and I have spoken to many adoptees and birth parents who have very positive feelings about the reunion. But there are also reunions which are devastating experiences for all concerned, so the greatest of care must be exercised.

Katherine O'Neill: The family of our daughter's birth mother knows nothing about the child. If she should someday locate that mother and appear at her door, it would be a disaster. How can a birth mother ever make a new life for herself if she has to worry about that stranger stepping back into her life and breaking her heart?

Victoria Meyers: I remember seeing in Ann Landers's column a letter that was written by a woman who had given up her child. She said that if her birth child ever reappeared, it would probably break up her marriage. If that happened, she said, she would sue everyone involved.

Betsy Vaughn: The child must realize that the decision to adopt was made with everyone's best interests in mind. For fifteen or twenty years parent and child have gone their separate ways. That other person has a right to her new life.

Howard Vaughn: Once that contact is made, no matter how it turns out, it can never be undone.

Dr. McDill: I would recommend that any contact certainly be put off until adulthood. Dealing as an adult to an adult would be much better than dealing as a child to an adult.

Mr. Donnelly: Even the most radical groups pushing for the availability of birth records are opposed to making them available to anyone under eighteen.

Patrick O'Neill: An adult may well be satisfied simply to see the birth parents and not to push for actual contact. Someone less mature might be more likely to take it too far and cause real problems.

Don Cohen: Many people seem to be more interested in learning about their identities than they are in finding a new set of parents.

Judy Randle: When our daughter was in college, she called our lawyer and asked him to find out all he could about her birth parents. He got some information together, but before he gave it to her he asked, "If we go through with this, if you ever meet your birth mother, what do you think it will prove? Will you be happier? Will she?" After thinking it over, she told him that she had decided to forget the whole thing.

Jack Kelley: Our children have a drastically different lifestyle than their other parents. They have very little in common.

Terry Cohen: Our daughter has talked about wanting to meet her brother some day. She also says she wants to see what her mother looks like. She has this wild plan to find out where the woman lives and, posing as an encyclopedia saleswoman, to go knock on her door. I asked her what she thinks would happen if the woman were to open her door and see a carbon copy of herself standing there. She didn't give me an answer, but she must have thought about it, because she hasn't mentioned it again.

Cheryl Kelley: Is it possible that the less the mystery surrounding those other people, the less the curiosity?

Dr. McDill: I definitely think so. Mystery builds obsession. I would downplay the mystery in every way possible. Instead, the parents must encourage the building of a strong relationship between the child and our heavenly Father. This is the best life structure possible, and it will aid in the best possible development.

157

Allen Nichols: If we had thought there was any chance of the adoption records' being opened, we would never have adopted in the first place. We were guaranteed total anonymity, and we feel that promise must be honored.

Howard Vaughn: What is the law? Can an adoptee get access to those birth records?

Mr. Donnelly: This varies from state to state. In Hawaii, for example, the records are accessible under most circumstances, even if the parties were guaranteed anonymity at the time of the adoption. That is the exception, however. In most states, the records cannot be opened except in the case of a dire need such as a medical condition. In a few states the laws are different in the case of independent adoptions. But these laws are currently under attack by many adoption-rights and right-to-know groups that are lobbying very intensely for new legislation. If laws on this do get passed, their constitutionality will be challenged. The right to privacy is a recognized constitutional right. The right of adoptees to know their birth parents is not. Some states have tried to compromise on this issue, with varying degrees of success. In California, for instance, one of the relinquishment forms signed by every birth mother in every adoption since 1984 has asked her whether she wishes to authorize the state to reveal her name, last known address, and telephone number to her child should the child request this information after reaching the age of twenty-one. If there is a mutual desire for a reunion, the state will provide the information. But if the desire is not mutual, the state will not release the information. I think this is a wise approach—it maintains the right to privacy but allows the child and the birth mother to waive that right if they wish. By the age of twenty-one, the adoptee should be able to make the decision, and I feel that the adoptive parents should be out of the decision-making loop.

Ben Meyers: If an attorney still knows the whereabouts of the birth mother, could an older adoptee ask the lawyer to communicate with the mother and discover if she would be interested in meeting?

Mr. Donnelly: Yes, I have done that. A letter would be sent stating: "The other parties to the adoption would like to make contact. If you are interested, let me know. If I don't hear from you, I will assume you want to remain anonymous." That is clearly the way to proceed. No one has the right to infringe upon the privacy of another.

QUESTIONS FOR DISCUSSION

1. Do you think it's wise for parents to initiate a search for their children's birth parents? Why or why not?
2. If your adopted children asked no questions about their background, what would you do?
3. Which situation discussed in this chapter would be the most difficult for you to handle? Why?

12.   *Help!*

All parents worry about how their children will turn out, and that includes adoptive families. Because they love their children, parents want them to be happy. They also want to be able to look at them and feel a sense of satisfaction and pride.

As your children grow, you are bound to face problems with them. All parents do. Most will be the normal, everyday problems of rearing children. But as an adoptive family you should be prepared to encounter more questions and more insecurity than others. Don't let this discourage you. Many authorities are quick to point out that there is a very high success rate among adoptive families who are willing to openly share their love, satisfaction, and pleasure as well as their frustrations, disappointments, and pain.

In some families disappointment, unhappiness, and frustration seem to be the predominant emotions. What are the problems that weigh them down? What can they do to help themselves? When they are no longer able to help themselves, to whom should they turn? In this chapter we seek answers to these difficult, sometimes painful questions.

THE INFLUENCE OF HEREDITY

"Our experience with adoption has been a painful disappointment," said a fifty-two-year-old woman. "If we had it to do again, we wouldn't adopt. It's too risky. A child inherits his behavior from his birth parents and there is nothing anyone can do about it."

160

No one will dispute the fact that an adopted child inherits a great deal biologically. Both adoptive parents may be short and heavy with dark brown hair. But if the child was born into a family of tall, thin, red-haired people, it will not take a genetics expert to tell us whom he will look like. An outgoing, athletic family may adopt a son who develops into a quiet, introspective poet. Your influence and encouragement will have a strong effect, but it won't make a football star of a person who has neither the talent nor the interest to play the game. Of course, such differences often occur in biological families as well.

All parents need flexibility and a willingness to accept their children's individuality, but adoptive parents especially so. It is unfortunate when people go into adoption with preconceived ideas of what their children will be like. Children have a way of surprising us. They seldom seem to turn out the way we picture them.

Adoptive parents must accept the fact that they will have limited knowledge of their children's heredity. This truth complicates their desire to understand and encourage their children's natural inclinations, to be aware of possible hereditary personality problems, and to be forewarned about inherited medical problems, including allergies, mental problems, diseases, and physical disorders.

"Most adoptive parents have higher-than-average intelligence," stated an adoptive father who is involved in counseling other adoptive parents. "But some adopted kids come from just the opposite background. The environment in which they are raised will influence their development, but their inherited limitations will still be there. To be realistic, adoptive parents must recognize this."

Learning is a complex undertaking. Factors besides inborn intellect are physical and emotional well-being, the amount of support and encouragement received, and the child's temperament and attention span. Studies indicate that when children born to mentally inferior mothers were placed in their adoptive homes before the age of two, they reached educational, social, and occupational levels very much like their adoptive parents. While a child's innate ability sets an upper limit to what can be achieved, it is not the sole deciding factor.

Even so, there seems to be a disproportionately high percentage of learning problems among adoptees. Some claim that this is also true of behavior problems. Some adopted children fit into the categories that cause children to be labeled "high risk" for learning and behavior problems without their adoptive parents even being aware of it. Children are considered high risk if—

- Their mothers had virus infections (such as measles) during the first three months of pregnancy.
- Their mothers had difficult and prolonged labor during birth.
- They were deprived of oxygen during birth.
- They are hyperactive.
- They were born to mothers who smoked and drank alcohol excessively during pregnancy.
- They were born to habitual drug users.
- They were born to mothers who had poor prenatal care.
- They were premature or post-term babies.
- They have severe allergies.

Just because children display one or more of these conditions does not mean they will have learning or behavior problems. But if children fall into the high-risk category, their parents should be aware of the possibility. If any problems do show up, early identification and treatment make a successful outcome much more likely.

Learning disabilities are the least recognized of all handicaps. A major, federally funded research project found that 16 percent of all schoolchildren have some sort of learning disability. Although such children usually have an average or above-average intellect, they are unable to process what they see. This shows up as an inability to pay attention, to concentrate, to understand, to remember, or to properly control their activity. Children with such problems usually have trouble with reading, writing, or math. Because of their low tolerance for frustration and their inappropriate behavior, they are often considered simply "disciplinary problems." Frequently they are shunned and ridiculed by their peers.

Unless they receive professional help, these children seldom learn to live and work, to love and play as other children do. As they grow older, the inability of many of them to think logically compounds their problems. Typically, children with learning and behavior disabilities may drift in and out of contact with a variety of teachers, social workers, and school psychologists who are often unable to give them the help they need so badly. Some of the children grow up to lead fairly normal lives, but many others barely manage to scrape by. It is particularly sad that so many are never able to develop their natural talents and abilities.

So what can adoptive parents do? They can become informed. They can keep in close touch with their children's progress in school. If they have reason to suspect a problem, they should have it checked out by the school psychologist or some other qualified professional. Accurate diagnosis and professional treatment are the most important remedies.

FACTORS OTHER THAN HEREDITY

What about traits and tendencies that are not commonly regarded as strictly biological? Can a child be genetically predisposed to alcoholism? To criminal behavior? To mental illness? There are no clear answers. Studies have been done but they present conflicting and inconclusive results. Even those professionals whose expertise is in this area are unable to agree on the relationship between heredity and other factors. To the extent that a consensus exists, it is that there may be a genetic predisposition to certain kinds of behaviors, such as antisocial, criminal, or compulsive behavior, but that these predispositions can either be overcome or encouraged by the environment.

You can do nothing about your children's heredity, but you can do much to provide them with a positive, nurturing

Christian environment. Concentrate on what you can do and trust God for the rest.

Perhaps the greatest challenge of parenthood is to help children to develop their unique potential and use it in the best ways possible. The temperament with which your children were born can be either a liability or an asset, depending on how it is developed and used. The strongest, most promising trait is the flipside of the weakest. The restless child has the same characteristic as the adult who, with boundless energy, keeps the Sunday school program running smoothly. The shy, introverted child can become that rarest of persons, the good listener. The frustratingly strong-willed child whose stubbornness drives you to distraction has the same temperament as the person you praise for having the strength of character and concentrated drive to accomplish great things. What is most crucial is not a person's inborn temperament so much as the way in which that temperament is channeled.

There is a real danger in attributing your adopted children's problems to their biological past and refusing to explore other possible causes. The specific genes that carry the master plan for any person can come from any combination of a host of distant, unknown, long-dead ancestors. There is no reason to assume that children will be like their parents. We are all aware of cases where one child in a family of several stands out as strikingly different in appearance, temperament, or abilities.

By contrast, in many adoptive families there are remarkable instances of family likeness. People who live together tend to adopt one another's mannerisms and habits. To a certain extent, because of shared ideas and attitudes, people even grow to think and act alike.

So while heredity is certainly important, it is the opinion of many professionals that the most significant influence on children's futures is the environment in which they are raised. The aims, examples, and daily training their parents give them will go a long way toward shaping children into the people they will be as adults. The best potential in the world will lead to nothing if it is not encouraged and developed.

Some of you will vigorously disagree on this issue. "We gave our adopted son every advantage," one father told me. "We were the very best parents we knew how to be. But that boy has been in trouble since he was thirteen. He is now twenty-two, and I see no sign of a change in him. Either he was genetically programmed for antisocial behavior, or my wife and I are terrible failures as parents."

Many families share this man's heartache, adoptive or not, Christian or not.

Why is it that in a family of three children—sharing the same genetic background, home environment, and family expectations—there may be two loving kids and one who is an endless source of problems and hurt? Why is one child cooperative and conforming while a sibling is obstinate and rebellious? The fact is that God has made each of us responsible for what we do with life. Some people have great obstacles to overcome while others have seemingly endless advantages, but in the end we each bear the responsibility to decide what we will do with our lives. Parents can train and pray and influence and teach, but children themselves do the choosing.

THE ROLE OF THE FATHER

One other issue is relevant to the problems relating to heredity and environment in the lives of adoptive children. That is the role of the father.

When a father is actively involved in his child's early life, both dad and child benefit greatly. Researchers at Boston Children's Hospital Medical Center indicate that even very young babies behave differently with their fathers than they do with their mothers. They play gentle, cooing games with their mothers, but with their fathers they perk up and get ready for louder, more playful action. Michael Yogman, a pediatrician at the medical center, stated, "Fathers have a unique role to play in their babies' lives—one that complements the mother's role." This holds true long past infancy.

Taking the responsibility of fathering seriously may mean that your priorities will need some rearranging. You may have to retrain yourself in the area of emotional responses. Many men feel awkward and uncomfortable about showing love and affection to their children, especially their sons.

"I guess we men have never been taught to express our emotions as women have," said one father. "It's too bad. I think we've been cheated out of an awful lot!"

Most adoptive fathers take their role of fathering very seriously. Maybe the reason is that they want and prepare for fatherhood during the adoption process in ways that biological fathers might not. They have had to endure disappointment and waiting. They have been carefully screened to ensure that they are well suited and qualified. One adoptive father said, "Most any man can be a father, but it takes a really special one to be a daddy."

As a father, are you loving, affectionate, responsive, involved, available, and approachable? Or distant, aloof, and always busy? Do you consider parenting to be primarily a mother's task? If your view of fathering is limited to a game of baseball with the children on Saturday and taking the family on a two-week vacation in the summer, you are missing out on a great deal. So are your children.

Some psychologists maintain that there is a correlation between a person's view of God and that person's relationship with his or her father. The modeling done by a father can influence his children in basic spiritual concepts and in their attitude toward faith. This modeling involves largely implicit, not explicit instruction; it is powerful, for good or for ill. Fathering is serious business with eternal implications.

DRUG USE BY BIRTH PARENTS

Perhaps the most frightening issue in adoption today is the prevalence of drug use by the birth parents, especially the birth mother. We are only now beginning to understand some of the implications of drug use during pregnancy.

Studies, released almost daily, are painting an increasingly ominous portrait of the prospects for children born to drug abusers: They tend to be smaller than other newborns and are at much higher risk for premature delivery. They tend to have arrested development of their neurological systems, which can cause many problems including a heightened risk for sudden infant death syndrome, also known as "crib death." They are at greater risk for mental retardation.

The most common symptom suffered by the children of drug abusers is a marked tendency toward juvenile neurological problems such as hyperactivity, attention deficit disorder, dyslexia and other learning difficulties, and multiple sclerosis.

Drug-abusing birth mothers aren't the only concern, either. A recently released study found a link between drug use by the father and many of these same symptoms in their children. Certainly a complete drug history of the birth mother is extremely important and should be obtained if it's at all possible. If a drug use history of the birth father is available, all the better.

Some drugs seem to be worse for unborn babies than others. The worst of all seem to be cocaine and LSD. Yet it does not necessarily follow that the "harder" the drug, the worse it is for the baby. Perhaps the most addictive and harmful drug known is heroin, yet many doctors feel that heroin is not nearly as harmful to unborn babies as cocaine.

So far we know of no agency or independent adoption organization which routinely tests birth mothers for drugs. Most conscientious adoption agencies and adoption lawyers, however, will have a birth mother tested if there is reason to suspect she may have been using drugs during the pregnancy.

In a relatively new drug test, a few strands of the birth mother's hair are clipped and sent to a lab which tests for the presence of drug traces. The major advantage of this test is that it can screen for drugs taken months before. Because hair grows about one-half inch per month, if the birth mother's hair is at least five inches long, the test can detect whether she used drugs within the past ten months, the entire length of her pregnancy. While this test is expensive, many adoptive families feel that the peace of mind it gives them is well worth the cost.

Birth mothers who voluntarily choose to place their expected children for adoption are usually women of conscience, not the kind of people who are likely to abuse drugs. Mothers whose children have been taken away because of neglect or abuse (and who are likely to be unavailable for drug tests) pose a much greater risk to their children. How ironic that where a drug test is needed most, it is usually unavailable.

ADOLESCENCE

The greatest challenges in parenthood come during your children's adolescence. In our complex world, adolescence is a time of turmoil and confusion in the struggle for a personal identity. Adolescents have a need to gain their independence. Because it is important that they establish themselves as individuals separate from their families, it is almost inevitable that problems will arise during this transition from childhood to adulthood.

Birth children may be at a loss to explain their parents' "unfair behavior." Adopted children think they have an explanation: They reason that they are living with strangers. What a perfect excuse for explaining every problem.

"My mother won't let me do anything!" a fifteen-year-old girl complained. "She doesn't trust me at all. She doesn't even try to understand me. I think it would be different if she were my real mother—if I had been born to her."

That reasoning doesn't account for the fact that non-adopted friends are experiencing the exact same trials. Teenagers' minds, however, are not always open to logic or to facts, especially if the facts don't agree with their feelings.

The greatest quest of the teenage years seems to be the search to "find oneself." This desire often becomes intertwined with normal rebelliousness and a desire for independence. Questions from your teenagers about their background are inevitable. For adopted teenagers, some of these questions can be nearly impossible to answer. Very likely only limited information will be available about their birth family, and that may just serve to make them more curious than ever. An unknown factor about the past cannot easily be incorporated into a sense of self, so many adopted teenagers feel a need to search for their biological parents. Adolescence, however, is no time to begin such a search. But because teenagers need reassurances of their own worth, it *is* a good time to reassure your children that it was not through any fault of theirs that they were released for adoption.

SELF-ESTEEM

Low self-esteem is a big problem for many people. We are so precious and worthwhile to God that he was willing to sacrifice his own Son to redeem us. Yet we persist in thinking of ourselves as inferior, never quite measuring up to everyone else. Children have this problem, too, and adolescents most of all. Since they have to deal with the perception that they may have once been rejected, it is not surprising that adoptees seem to be especially vulnerable to feelings of self-doubt.

The problem of low self-esteem is due in part to the society in which we live. For us a person's worth is measured against idealistic standards of physical attractiveness, athletic prowess, high intelligence, and social acceptability. These standards are artificial and foolish. We all know that. But if we are honest we have to admit that to some extent all of us are affected by them.

What can you do to help your adopted children develop a healthy self-concept? This is a complex problem, but the following five points may prove helpful:

- Examine the values you are fostering in your home. Whether we like it or not, we are all products of our society. We want beautiful, smart, popular kids just as much as the next person. But you must be completely accepting of your children even if they are somewhat less than perfect.

- Treat your children wisely. They deserve your unconditional love. Their positive points should be reinforced with sincere, spontaneous praise. And be especially careful about what kind of joking and teasing goes on in your home. Never poke fun at anyone's weak spots. If anything intended as play is disturbing to a child, end it at once.

- Help your children to compensate for their weaknesses. It is not possible to remove all your children's obstacles or to shield them from every hurt. It is foolish even to try. But you can help them discover and take advantage of their strengths while deemphasizing their weaknesses.

- Encourage your children to assume responsibility and independence. This will naturally be progressive. As your children mature and prove their dependability, they should be rewarded with increased responsibility and independence.

- Discipline wisely. Overpermissiveness can create feelings of insecurity. If you never discipline your children, it will increase their feelings of not belonging and of not really being loved. By contrast, inconsistent or cruel punishment can permanently damage their self-image. Just what are the elements of wise discipline? First, establish the rules in advance. Second, be consistent; a broken rule should *always* mean punishment. Third, your children should not be punished for mistakes or accidents. Fourth, after punishment has been meted out, reassure your children that you still love them just as much as ever. Fifth, be sure the punishment fits both the infraction and the child's age.

If you are successful in developing healthy self-concepts in your children, you will have given them a priceless treasure. You will have given them the armor to protect themselves from the bumps and bruises of life.

MENTAL ILLNESS

Several decades ago, a mental health researcher made the startling discovery that one-fourth of all the patients in mental hospitals were adoptees, although adoptees account for far less than one-fourth of the population. That researcher and many since have concluded that adopted children are uniquely at risk for debilitating mental disorders; however, this research was badly flawed from the start. Perhaps the greatest flaw was that the researcher made no effort to distinguish between adoptees who were adopted at birth and those who were adopted later in life. If children who were abused, molested, or neglected early in life; placed in foster care; shuffled from one foster home to another; and then adopted wind up in a mental hospital, what placed the children in that institution: the adoption, or what preceded the adoption?

More recent studies have focused upon this inherent flaw and have made some interesting discoveries. In a 1987 study, college-age adoptees were compared with their classmates from similar socioeconomic backgrounds. On the whole, the adoptees were happier, better adjusted, and felt more in control of their lives than did their non-adopted classmates. How did the researchers account for this startling discovery? Their hypothesis is that adopted kids are better adjusted because they have received superior parenting. Adoptive parents tend to be older and presumably more prepared for parenthood. After all, adoptive parents are parents by choice, not by biological accident.

That stated, every adoptive parent needs to be aware that many mental disorders, such as schizophrenia, can be hereditary. It is terribly important that the fullest possible health history of both birth parents be obtained at the time of the adoption. A complete health history of the birth father is not available in most cases. Often the health information on the birth father is provided by the birth mother and consists of, "Well, he looked healthy to me."

As a consequence, every person considering adoption should be aware that it is not only possible but likely that there will be gaps in the health information which may be available. This is a risk which any responsible adoption professional will try to minimize by obtaining as much information as is available.

OPEN FORUM

Rob Alvarado: I blame TV programs and movies for a lot of the misconceptions concerning adoption. I really resent the way they misrepresent adopted families, birth parents, and their problems.

Cheryl Kelley: So do I! The TV show I dislike the most is *The Brady Bunch.* At the height of its popularity people would tell us how much our family was like the Brady family. What a laugh! Anyone who has ever spent an hour in our home knows that the only possible similarity is that we're both blended families with a houseful of kids.

Mr. Donnelly: More offensive than that is the picture of birth mothers portrayed by the media. Whenever I see a birth mother portrayed on television, she is always shown as a teenager, unstylish, poorly groomed, not very bright, promiscuous, poorly educated, and easily taken advantage of. The reality is quite different. The typical birth mother I see in my office is twenty-three years old, a high school graduate, of above average intellect, and a very nice person. What must it do to the child's self-image to see the media's terribly misleading and derogatory image of a birth mother and think that his birth mother may be a loser like the one portrayed on the screen?

Betsy Vaughn: To me, the most disturbing stories are the ones that describe sentimental accounts of adult adoptees who are reunited with their birth parents. You see such stories on television, in the newspapers, and in magazines. They are presented in a sensational manner and are misleading. Kids get the idea that every woman who ever gave up her baby for adoption is anxiously awaiting his reappearance.

Jack Kelley: Even when children are raised in a happy, secure home and are well-adjusted, there seems to come a time when they need to know about their biological parents. At least that is how it has happened in our family.

Don Cohen: When our daughter was first adopted, I wrote out a letter telling her what it meant to us to have her come into our family. I told her how strongly we felt that God had sent her to us and how we had all planned and prepared for her arrival. I included everything I knew about her parents, her background, the details of the common-law marriage of her parents, and even about her father's desertion of the family. I also told her about her only biological sibling, a brother three years older than she. I emphasized that giving her up had been a hard but loving decision on her mother's part. We put the letter away with instructions that in the event of our deaths it was to be given to her. Otherwise we would give it to her when we felt that she needed to know that information.

Terry Cohen: It hurts to admit it, but Don and I have been disappointed in our adopted daughter. It is possible that we have been guilty of setting unrealistically high expectations for her, but I just wonder if some of her behavior problems are due to poor heredity. There are more and more people today who feel that all of us are more a product of our heredity than of our environment. As adoptive parents we must at least consider this possibility.

Jack Kelley: I can't accept that. We have seen fantastic personality and attitude changes in our children even though some of them were older when we all came together. We attribute the changes to the working of the Lord in their lives.

173

Howard Vaughn: Our girls don't look different from the other children, but both of them have problems with self-esteem. I think it's because their school classmates make demeaning remarks to them and let them know they are considered second-class because they're adopted. I'm afraid they are in for a pretty rough life if we can't do something about their low self-esteem.

Betsy Vaughn: They tend to be controlled by what their friends think. But we can't always choose their friends for them, especially now that they are getting older.

Dr. McDill: I deal a lot with problems of self-esteem. It's really quite a complex problem. You cannot merely bolster your children up with compliments. What you say will not agree with their feelings, and it is their feelings that they will believe. Instead, you need to let them know you have confidence in their ability to think and to reason out the facts. By asking, "What do you think about this?" or "What would you do in a case like that?" you will be demonstrating your confidence in their judgment. They will begin to think, "Hey, they really do want my opinion!" When they know you have confidence in them, they will begin to have confidence in themselves.

Howard Vaughn: That's good. We have been trying to pump them up with compliments, but it hasn't worked.

Dr. McDill: No, because their self-esteem has nothing to do with your opinion of them; it is what they think of themselves. There are many other factors involved, of course, but this is basic.

Greg Swanson: Does the whole "roots" thing have anything to do with a person's self-concept?

Dr. McDill: Yes, it does. We all have innate feelings of wanting to belong. We all try to find a historic root with which we can identify. I think this is at the bottom of the typical teenage quest to "find oneself."

Terry Cohen: Our daughter, the youngest of our three children and the only one who is adopted, was a real joy to us until she reached adolescence. Suddenly she was a different person: angry, resentful, and rebellious. Her greatest desire seemed to be to hurt and embarrass us. She has purposely sought out friends we were sure to disapprove of.

Don Cohen: She has been more hurtful to her mother than to me. The girl will hardly speak to Terry or allow her to touch her.

Terry Cohen: Two years ago, when she was eighteen, our daughter began to pressure us about finding her birth parents. We felt it was time to give her the letter Don had written when we first got her because it contained all the information we had. When she read it, it really seemed to help. I'm sure it was the Lord's timing.

Judy Randle: Do you blame adoption for your daughter's problems?

Terry Cohen: Yes, I do.

Judy Randle: That's interesting, because Ken and I have a strikingly similar situation in our family, but with a slightly different twist. We also have three children: two adopted and the middle one born to us. It is our child by birth who has been our big problem. At nineteen she shows no sign of changing her attitude.

Don Cohen: I guess in the end we parents can only give our children over to the Lord's keeping and prayerfully wait for a change in their behavior.

SEEKING OUTSIDE HELP

There are times when problems arise that are too big for parents to handle. In a time of crisis, what can they do? Where should they turn?

"Often I was at my wit's end with Tad," said the mother of a boy adopted at the age of ten. "One morning I was ready to turn him over to the welfare department or to anyone else

175

daring enough to take him. I cried and I prayed and I cried some more. Believe me, it's terrible to feel like a total failure as a parent! In desperation I called an acquaintance who had gone through problems with her own adopted son. She told me about a support group that had helped her. My husband and I started attending, and it made all the difference in the world."

"We had problems, real problems," one father said. "What we did was to find another Christian family who were going through the same things we were. Sharing with them was an enormous help to us. By talking and praying together we both became stronger. We really needed to know that there was someone who truly understood our pain. It's important for Christian parents to unite so that they can support and encourage each other when these problems erupt."

Self-help groups prove to be lifesavers for many parents, including adoptive parents. They can share tips and experiences and receive front-line help from people who have been there. Sometimes just knowing you are not alone, that your problems are not unique, is enough to enable you to cope with the situation you are facing.

How do you go about finding a support group? Your local adoption agency is probably your best contact; they will often be able to refer you to a group. Your minister might be able to put you in touch with people who are in a similar situation.

If you have reason to believe that the problems your child is experiencing are too serious to be handled by such a group, it is time to find an experienced counselor. It is possible that the professional will only need to assure you that your child's behavior is indeed normal and that you have no reason to worry. Nevertheless, if there really is a problem, a trained, experienced professional is the one who should help.

How do we find the right professional? Again, your local adoption agency is a good source of advice. Most agencies will offer counseling to families who need it even if the child was not adopted through them. Another possibility is to get referrals from several people who have had dealings with psychologists, psychiatrists, or family counselors and have been pleased with them. Ministers may be able to recommend professional counselors also.

IS IT IMPORTANT TO INSIST ON A CHRISTIAN COUNSELOR?

Without a doubt a trained, competent, experienced Christian should be the counselor of choice. You would both be building on the same foundation. You would be able to base your quest for an answer on sound, biblical principles. Christian counselors have resources that non-Christians know nothing about. They can draw on the guidance of the Holy Spirit and share the unconditional, unending love of God. You will be able to pray and talk together in a way that would not be possible with someone who does not share your relationship with Christ.

This is the ideal. But it is not always possible to find a trained, competent, Christian counselor. In such a case it is better to work with a non-Christian who knows what he or she is doing than to work with a Christian who has no training or experience. Whether or not a counselor is a Christian, it is vitally important that you hold the same basic values.

In the end you must accept your children for who they are. Let them know that there is nothing they can do that will make you stop loving them. God is loving and forgiving, and he has unlimited patience. You must try to demonstrate the same qualities. With God's help you can.

For reasons we cannot understand, God sometimes chooses to allow Christian parents to suffer through the actions of their children. When we see nothing but our hopeless problems, when we groan under the weight of our pain, it is reassuring to know that God has the answers. He knows the reasons. When we are forced to acknowledge our helplessness, we must lovingly let our children go and trust them to the safekeeping of God. We can only pray that they

177

will be brought to the point where they themselves will make the decision to come to him.

OPEN FORUM

Ken Randle: I am sure there never was a parent who wasn't periodically faced with problems. Children can't get their growing done without going through stages, and some of those stages can be very irritating and upsetting. Parents should learn all they can about child development so they will be better prepared to understand and to accept the different kinds of behavior they see in their children.

Roger Crawford: Every parent, by birth or by adoption, runs the risk of having a rebellious or difficult child.

Dr. McDill: In my opinion, it's a mistake to regard adoption itself as a source of probable difficulty. That's not to say, however, that adopted children don't have certain areas of increased vulnerability.

Cheryl Kelley: I think it's harder to raise an adopted child than a biological one. The rewards are just as great, but the periods of failure seem to hit a lot harder.

Lorraine Swanson: The most painful adoption-related problem for us is the negative attitudes of our relatives. It isn't only what they say; often it's what they leave unsaid or what they say by their actions. We were aware of their feelings from the beginning, but we were afraid that if we put any pressure on them, they might completely break off their relationship with us. We decided we could deal with their attitude more easily than we could deal with a brick wall between us.

Greg Swanson: As they got to know our son, their negative attitude softened a little. But it didn't disappear. We have learned to accept it and to live with it.

Dr. McDill: How does your son react?

Lorraine Swanson: He's only six. He doesn't seem to notice.

Rachel Nichols: How do you react when your child comes home from school and out of the blue says, "You're not my real mother!"

Marian Crawford: He was probably just needling you. That's happened to me. Once when I gave my son canned spaghetti for lunch he announced, "I don't like spaghetti, and I won't eat it, and you can't make me because you're not my mother!" I said, "Well, since I'm not your mother I guess I don't need to fix you anything else." When he got really hungry he came back and sheepishly said, "Uh, Mommy . . ."

Rob Alvarado: It's not unusual for a child, biological or adopted, to say, "I hate you!" If you let a comment like that get to you, the child will use it again and again. He is just looking for a button to push.

Roger Crawford: Another possibility is that he is asking, "How can you be my mother if I wasn't born to you?"

Katherine O'Neill: When our daughter said, "You aren't my real mother," I acknowledged the fact that I had not given birth to her. But I added that I was the one who did the loving and the caring, the one who was raising her. So I agreed in part, but I pointed out the difference.

Marian Crawford: We are our children's real parents in every sense except the biological one, and that's what we want them to understand.

Allen Nichols: Before we can convince *them*, we must first convince ourselves.

Mr. Donnelly: People often come to me and say, "When you talk to the real mother . . . ," and I say, "Wait a minute! Nine months does not a real mother make."

Terry Cohen: Real parents are the people who care for a child, comfort him and soothe him, feed him and play with him, take him to school, and sit up all night with him when he's sick. Biological or adoptive, all parents have to grow to be real parents through their daily loving care of the child.

Don Cohen: It is being loved and cared for that makes a family. The experiences shared day by day bind them together and help the child to understand what it is to be part of a family.

Allen Nichols: Whether you are born into a family or adopted into it, once you are there you are a real part of that family. I feel that I have a greater understanding and appreciation of God's love for me because of the love I feel for my children.

Don Cohen: We consider our adopted daughter to be a chosen child, but not chosen by us. God chose us to be her parents. We didn't have a choice in our natural children, and we didn't have a choice in her either.

Terry Cohen: We explained our daughter's place in the family to her by telling her, "Mommy and Daddy came by marrying each other, the other children came by birth, and you came by adoption. How we came into the family isn't important. What is important is that we are all together just as God planned it."

Rob Alvarado: I dislike the term "real mother."

Cheryl Kelley: When our children were younger, the littlest one said something about her "real" mother. The oldest boy turned to me and said, "What are you, Mom? Our plastic mother?"

Rachel Nichols: What would be a better designation than "real" mother?

Terry Cohen: The current term of choice seems to be "biological" mother.

Greg Swanson: That's O.K. for us, but a little child couldn't say that.

Betsy Vaughn: I don't like "natural" mother because that makes me feel like an unnatural mother.

Allen Nichols: Not necessarily. Maybe you're a supernatural mother.

Katherine O'Neill: I have heard "your other mother" used, but I don't like that because it seems to indicate that the first parents are still available somewhere. It makes them seem as real and as vital to our children as Patrick and I are.

Rob Alvarado: I like "birth mother." It's easy to say, and it gets the true picture across.

Marian Crawford: Several times my son has said things like "My *real* mother would understand." That can be upsetting when I hear it too often or at the wrong times.

Judy Randle: Once I overheard my daughter and her friend talking in the next room. The friend said, "She's not your real mother. You're adopted." I loved my daughter's answer. She said, "So what if I'm adopted? She is still my real mother."

QUESTIONS FOR DISCUSSION

1. Under what circumstances should you seek out a professional counselor?
2. Can you think of other ways to locate a good counselor in your area?
3. Which problem in this chapter would be the most difficult for you to handle? Do you have any other suggestions toward a solution for that problem?

13.

No Longer My Child

"It has been more than thirty years," Claudia Greenley, a tiny gray-haired grandmother, said quietly. "Why is it that I still can't talk about David without tears? It was such a terribly painful experience that even after all this time the hurting still hasn't stopped. I don't suppose it ever will."

People love to tell success stories of their experiences with adoption and of the great joy their children have brought into their lives. Many inspiring books have been written about families who have adopted several little ones, sometimes with great physical or mental handicaps. Overcoming great odds, these people have been able to weld the children together into a happy, healthy, loving family. The message seems to be "With enough faith and enough love, you too can overcome any problems." But there are families whose adoption experiences have ended with dashed dreams and broken hearts. Their stories are seldom told.

Fortunately the percentage of unsuccessful adoptions is quite small. When failures do occur, they are generally confined to cases involving handicapped or older children— the ones who are most likely to bring deep-rooted problems into their new homes.

"Both my daughter, Elizabeth, and I were lucky to have survived her long and difficult birth," Claudia Greenley said. "The doctor told me that I must never risk another pregnancy. I was more than disappointed—I was absolutely devastated! Henry and I had always planned on having five or six stairstep children, and I just couldn't adjust my thinking to raising our little girl alone.

"When Elizabeth was two years old, Henry and I decided that we could still have our big family. We would adopt. In those days there were many babies available. But Henry was in the army, and we were moved around so often that we were never able to meet the agencies' residency requirements.

"Finally, after four years of frustration, I went to an adoption agency in the area to which we had just moved and literally begged them to give me a child. I was told that if we would be willing to take an older child, one could be placed with us immediately. I went home and talked it over with Henry. Since Elizabeth was by then six years old, we figured that an older child would fit in just fine. I knew how much Henry would enjoy a son—he loves camping and fishing and all kinds of sports—so at my suggestion we requested an older boy.

"David arrived the very next week. He descended upon our quiet, well-ordered home with all the grace of a hurricane. He was ten years old and small for his age, but awfully strong. He was endlessly energetic and unbelievably loud. We all stared in wonder at this strange boy who roared in and took over our home."

"In his own eyes," Henry Greenley interjected, "David was the greatest. He thought he deserved the best of everything. When we went out to dinner, which we enjoyed doing often, he always ordered the most expensive meal on the menu. When other boys came to play, the whole neighborhood could hear David bossing them around. And school was a problem from the very beginning. David was a terrible bully, always getting into fights. He did very little schoolwork. I knew I had to discipline him, but whenever I did, he would scream and swear at me, then stomp off to his room to pout. David surely didn't fit my idea of what a son should be."

"But he was good to Elizabeth," Claudia added quickly. "She loved him dearly and followed him everywhere, just like a puppy. And David was always gentle with her. He really did love his little sister."

"If he truly cared about Elizabeth," Henry said, "she was the only one who ever got through to him. To everyone else he was nothing but trouble."

"I tried so hard to love him," Claudia said, "but he really made it hard. Whenever he didn't get his way he would yell, 'You don't love me! I'm going to run away!' That scared me so much that I did everything I could to meet his demands. In an effort to prove our love we bought David all the expensive toys that were so important to him, even though it was a real financial hardship for us. But then he shocked us by systematically destroying every single toy! One time he traded an expensive electric train for a baseball mitt and a pocketknife. Then he used the knife to slash the mitt to pieces. He really scared me when he did things like that.

"The stress David put on our family started to cause problems between Henry and me. We could see that our family was in trouble, but we didn't know where to turn for help. We weren't Christians at the time and didn't attend church, so we had no minister to counsel with us. We called David's caseworker at the adoption agency, but she just shrugged off our problems and told us to be patient and to give David more time and more love."

"That was a laugh!" Henry said bitterly. "By that time any love I ever felt for David was long gone."

"The breaking point came when Henry told me that unless David was gone by the end of the week, he would take Elizabeth and move out," Claudia said. "I felt terrible about returning David to the agency, but what could I do? I admit, however, that once I was forced to make the decision, I felt better than I had since the day David arrived. It was as if the weight of the world had suddenly been lifted from my shoulders.

"Still, you cannot imagine the guilt I've carried all these years. I'm certain that David was never adopted again. I just can't help but think that we might have been able to work things out if only we had been given some help." She paused. "But maybe I'm wrong. Maybe nothing could have helped us."

COMPETENT COUNSELING

The Greenleys' story points up the absolute necessity of competent, sympathetic counselors who are readily available when problems first become evident. Today most adoption agencies are willing and able to provide this assistance, and most adoption attorneys are quick to refer clients to reputable and experienced counselors. Other sources of help include ministers, physicians, school personnel, and the local department of mental health. While a Christian counselor may be preferable, God can also work through a non-Christian. In either case it is essential that the person be a competent, qualified professional who shares your philosophy of life. Had the Greenleys had access to such a person, perhaps they could have come to understand the causes of David's actions. Perhaps they could have learned to help him to trust and to love. Perhaps, despite all the problems, they could have found a permanent place for him in their family.

"When we adopted David," said Claudia Greenley, "we had no concept of God's guidance in such a personal matter, so the idea of asking him for help never occurred to us. We had been unfortunate enough to have gotten a very troubled child. It was embarrassing and frustrating to be unable to handle David, and we were ashamed to have failed so miserably. Had we been Christians, had we entered into the adoption with prayer and with some sense of divine guidance, maybe then things would have turned out differently."

Maybe, but not necessarily. From the very beginning the adoption of twelve-year-old Patty by Peter and Carol Ann Messina was surrounded by prayer.

"From the time I first saw Patty," Carol Ann said, "I realized that she was a fascinatingly complex person. She's a beautiful girl with a sweet nature. She is also loud and boisterous and at times can be most annoying. She moved into a foster home in our neighborhood and was immediately befriended by our two daughters, who were ten and fourteen at the time.

"Patty had spent most of her life in foster homes—she

couldn't even remember how many. One day when she was swimming in our backyard pool, I overheard her talking to my younger daughter. 'You sure are lucky to have a real home,' she said. 'I get moved around so much I don't even unpack my clothes anymore.' My heart went out to that poor girl. Can you imagine a child growing up homeless and unwanted?

"When summer came, Patty was over constantly. She really was a dear, but she also had some irritating habits. I didn't realize how often I was making such remarks as, 'If Patty were *my* child, I would . . . ,' until my younger daughter finally retorted, 'If you think you could help Patty so much, why don't we just adopt her? She's at our house all the time anyway, and no one else wants her.'

"My daughter's comment and my mothering instinct set us all to thinking. Perhaps God had brought Patty into our lives because he wanted her to be a permanent part of our family. We had all been praying for Patty for quite a while, but now our prayers changed. We started asking God for clear, definite direction. If he wanted Patty to join our family, and if he would be in the union, we asked that he open a way for us to adopt her. We also asked that he give us a sign to assure us that we were doing the right thing. If the adoption was not his will, we prayed that the doors would be unmistakably closed.

"With the opening of school that fall, Patty was around less frequently. Still she came over almost every evening to have our girls help her with her homework. She had always been a poor student in school, Patty told us. It was obvious that her personal study skills were nonexistent. But we were quite impressed at the effort she seemed to be making.

"Then one morning during the week before Thanksgiving, Patty burst into our house at seven-thirty. Though it was almost impossible to understand her through her sobs, we were finally able to gather that her foster father had taken a job in another city and the family would soon be moving away. Patty was to be moved to still another foster home. Sinking into a kitchen chair, she buried her face in her hands and wept. 'You're my best friends in the whole world,' she cried. 'Now I won't ever see you again!'

"How my heart ached for that little girl! She looked so small and helpless and vulnerable. Without taking the time to think it through, I blurted, 'Maybe you could stay here with us.' Patty stared at me in disbelief. So did everyone else. Surely this was our sign from the Lord. He was assuring us that he did want Patty to be with us. That very week the arrangements were made."

"When Patty came into our family she had never been exposed to spiritual things," said Peter Messina. "She had no spiritual awareness at all and very little interest. But once she began attending church with us and got to know the other kids in Sunday school and the youth group, she seemed to enjoy it and to fit right in. It was hard for her to sit through the church service, but then I guess that's understandable. Though she never actually protested, she fidgeted and wiggled and checked my watch a lot. Even so, she apparently heard and understood a lot more than we realized. She was never one to share her thoughts with us, but she would occasionally ask me questions like, 'Does God love me too?' and 'How do you know God is real?' and 'Can anyone who wants to, be God's child?'

"I answered her questions as honestly as I could, trying to encourage her without being pushy. Our daughters were a great help. Their faith is sincere and matter-of-fact, and Patty was open to anything that came from them."

"Patty was always rather cold and distant to me," Carol said. "She rejected every effort I made to hug or kiss her. I was sure that with enough motherly love I could win her over, but the more affectionate I was to her, the more difficult the situation became. Before long Patty became openly rude and disrespectful to me. That was especially hard for me to handle because she was so open and loving to Peter and the girls. What was I doing wrong? I tried everything I could think of to improve our relationship, but nothing helped. It was the most frustrating, most exasperating experience of my life.

"When the friction continued to increase, Peter took Patty to see a psychiatrist suggested by her school counselor. After a few sessions he assured Peter that physically Patty was a healthy, alert, intelligent girl. But he also said that she was deeply troubled. Having been cruelly and painfully abused and rejected by her birth mother, Patty was placed in a foster home. There she was further abused by her foster mother. Because of these painful experiences, Patty had developed a deep distrust—almost a hatred—for women. Though she badly needed love and security, she had long ago learned not to expect much from an adult, especially one who calls herself 'mother.' For me ever to establish any kind of a positive relationship with Patty, I would need an endless supply of patience and a boundless reserve of love. Even then, any hope of a real mother-daughter love developing between us was probably unrealistic.

"I can't tell you my dismay at hearing the psychiatrist's report. My mind was flooded with questions. Could I possibly raise a child under such circumstances? Could I give Patty all the patience and love she needed? Were we making a mistake by adopting a child with such problems? I had no answers, so I took the situation directly to the Lord. First I reminded God that neither Peter nor I had ever searched out a child to adopt; it was he who had brought Patty to us. Then I reminded him that from the very beginning our whole family had sincerely prayed for his will and his guidance in this matter. I reminded him, too, that to the best of our ability Peter and I were following his leading. So why, I demanded, was everything turning out bad?

"Soon difficulties began to arise between our girls and Patty. Although she was twelve years old, Patty was so irresponsible and unpredictable that we dared not leave her without adult supervision even for a short time. That meant that either we had to restrict our own daughters' privileges to match the limited ones we were able to give Patty, or else we had to listen to Patty's accusations that we were showing partiality to our own girls. We finally settled on an uneasy compromise: Sometimes we restricted the other girls' freedom, and at other times we maintained a different set of rules for them than for Patty. The results were terrible. Our girls resented Patty, and Patty resented them.

"Academics also became a problem. Our girls have always been excellent, motivated students. Patty was just the opposite. We tried hard to avoid comparisons, but Patty felt hopelessly outclassed by her straight-A sisters."

"Soon after Patty moved in with us," said Peter, "I was awarded a contract on which I had been working for almost a year. The only problem was that I would have to be out of the state for the next few months. This couldn't have come at a worse time. Carol Ann was having real problems with Patty, and the girls were complaining about her more every day. It seemed that I was the only one to whom Patty could relate. I almost decided to turn down the contract, but then I reasoned that with my being absent from the situation at home, perhaps Patty would be drawn closer to Carol Ann. It didn't work out that way."

"Those four months were the most miserable time of my entire life!" exclaimed Carol Ann. "I had absolutely no control over Patty; she just ran wild. I scolded and I punished. I even tried the positive approach. Cookie baking is a favorite activity at our house, so I would tell Patty, 'If you do your jobs quickly, you can help me make cookies.' That child would respond by walking slowly to her room, sitting down on the bed, and refusing to do a single thing. I'm sure it was that she just didn't want to be involved in any activity that included me. That really hurt. It also angered and frustrated me. No matter how hard I tried, I could not win that girl over.

"More and more I resented the time and attention I was wasting on Patty. She took so much out of me that I was unjustly sharp and impatient with the other girls. It just wasn't fair to them or to me. Every morning I would wake up promising myself that I wouldn't allow anything to upset me that day. Whatever was done, whatever was said, I would take it all in stride. But before the girls were even off to school, I would be angry and someone would end up in tears."

"When I returned home after my four-month absence, I couldn't believe the situation I found awaiting me," Peter said. "I could hardly recognize my formerly happy, loving, cheerful family. Now everyone was moody and touchy. One night after Carol Ann and I had gone to bed, our two daughters tiptoed into our bedroom and locked the door behind them. Lying down on our bed, they burst into tears. We hugged them close and soon we were crying too. The older girl sobbed, 'Remember how happy our family used to be? Please, please, can't we be like that again?'

"We remembered the events that had brought us to the adoption. We recalled all the prayers and good intentions that had gone into it. Then Carol Ann suggested that we pray about it. And we did pray, the four of us together, long into the night. The more we prayed, the more certain we became that for the good of our family, Patty would have to go.

"I called the agency the next morning while the girls were at school," Carol Ann said. "That evening we all gathered by the fireplace in the living room and we told Patty of our decision. Peter explained that we just couldn't be the family she needed. Patty asked if we liked her; we said we did. She asked where she would go next; we said we didn't know, but wherever it was, our prayers would go with her. Then she started to cry, and none of us could think of anything to say. It was Patty who finally broke the silence, but all she said was, 'I'm going to miss my friends.' Peter took her back to the agency the next day, and we haven't seen her since.

"I'm embarrassed to admit it, but I felt a wonderful sense of exhilaration when Patty was finally gone. Still, it's amazing how often she comes to my mind. And whenever I think of her I stop what I'm doing and say a prayer for her. Even though she's no longer with us, in a strange way she remains a part of our family. I guess she always will. We did all we could do for her. It's just that the time came when we had no choice but to hand her over to the Lord. Her future is in his hands."

Perhaps because we were raised on fairy tales, we want every story to have a happy-ever-after ending, especially where children are concerned. Unfortunately, in real life things don't always happen that way. They didn't for Henry and Claudia Greenley, and they didn't for Peter and Carol Ann Messina. They didn't for David, and they didn't for Patty.

MAKING A FINAL COMMITMENT

When you adopt children, you make a commitment to do your very best to become parents to them from the first moment they move into your home. You are not legally bound by this commitment, however, until the adoptions become final. Once they are final, it's as if those children had been born to you. You are responsible for them in good times and in bad, in joy and in sorrow, in sickness and in health, until they are grown. There is, with rare exception, no turning back.

Actually, there are only two exceptions to the permanence of a finalized adoption. First, there have been several cases in which an agency failed to disclose a child's known psychiatric problems to a prospective adoptive family. Several of these families have sued the agency to rescind the adoption, using a theory lawyers call "wrongful adoption," which is a form of fraud. Not only have these adoptions been rescinded, but the adoptive parents have been awarded money damages for the wrongful conduct by the agency.

The other exception is a very difficult one to cope with emotionally. In a few states by law or by court precedent an adoption can be rescinded by the adoptive parents through court action if the child suffers from a "mental illness" which was undiagnosed at the time of the adoption and which is so severe that had it been known at the time of the adoption the child would have been considered "unadoptable." The adoptive parents must file a court action to rescind the adoption within five years after the adoption is made final.

To "unadopt" a child is one of the most heartbreaking

experiences imaginable, both for the child and for the adoptive parents, and all parties must come to terms with an enormous amount of guilt and an overwhelming sense of failure. Fortunately, these cases are quite rare.

If you have any doubts about being able to make a permanent life with a specific child, voice your concerns at once. Don't put it off until the adoption becomes final. In many cases you can delay the finalization until you are sure.

Meanwhile, get help immediately. Most adoption agencies have backup resources that can offer counseling, advice, and other types of assistance that they hope will help you work out a solution. Even if your child was not adopted from a local agency, a local agency will do its best to help. Everyone there wants the adoption to work.

Failed adoptions are unfortunate and sad for everyone involved. But sometimes a placement just doesn't work out. When this happens it's best to face the situation honestly. By continuing in an impossible relationship, you are creating a no-win situation. Remember that an adoption that was begun surrounded by prayer should end the same way.

If you are faced with the agonizing realities of a failed adoption, please understand that there is such a thing as "successful failure." What appears to be a dismal failure when viewed through our eyes may actually be success when seen from God's point of view.

"I recently got a phone call from a friend of mine who is a schoolteacher in a nearby town," Carol Ann Messina reported. "Patty is in her eighth-grade class this year. She is also in her Sunday school class. Patty is now in another foster home and seems to be doing very well. Her foster parents are an older couple who treat her like a daughter. She is the only child in their home. That sounds like a perfect situation for Patty.

"My friend also told me that Patty talked to her about her faith in Jesus. Patty says she accepted him as her Savior while she was living with us. Her new foster parents aren't Christians, but Patty goes to church every Sunday. Once she told my friend, 'God is helping me to work out all my problems.'"

"We know without a doubt that God put Patty in our home," Peter added. "He put her here even though he knew from the beginning that she wouldn't be able to stay with us. Many, many times we have asked, 'Why did God set us up for such a failure?' I think I'm finally beginning to understand. This was God's way of bringing Patty to himself. It really is true: God never, ever makes mistakes."

QUESTIONS FOR DISCUSSION

1. In your opinion, would David Greenley's adoption have worked out differently had Claudia and Henry handled it better? What could they have done?
2. When Carol Ann Messina learned that there was little hope of her ever being able to establish a loving mother-daughter relationship with Patty, how might she have made the best of the situation?
3. In determining their daughters' degree of freedom, the Messinas compromised by sometimes overly restricting the responsible girls and at other times maintaining different sets of rules for the girls. What might have been a more successful approach to Patty's lack of responsibility?
4. What would you do in a situation like the Greenleys'? How about the Messinas'?

14.   *The Children Speak*

Despite the many things that make them different and unique, there remains one constant principle in all adoptive families: The most important person in any adoption is the adopted child. That child's feelings, concerns, and well-being must be the primary consideration of everyone involved. But because adults tend to limit their view of adoption to their own perspective, the questions and concerns of the children often go unanswered, their gentle wisdom and touching insights passing unnoticed. We do well to pause and listen as the children speak.

In this chapter you will read the thoughts and ideas about adoption from more than fifty children between the ages of seven and fifteen. A few adults who grew up in adoptive homes were also included in these discussions, as were some nonadoptive children who had particular thoughts on the subject based on their observations of classmates, friends, and relatives. With few exceptions, the children who participated in these discussions had been adopted in traditional, closed adoptions, and as a result had little or no information about their birth parents. The children of open adoptions tend to deal with many of the same issues, but most experts feel there is a difference in the degree and magnitude of these concerns. Children of open adoptions possess at least some information concerning the birth parents so curiosity and fantasy play a smaller role in their perceptions of being adopted.

The positive feelings and attitudes toward adoption expressed by the majority of the children were impressive.

194

One nine-year-old boy expressed it this way: "If people can't have a baby, then they should adopt one like my mom and dad did. There are lots of people who can't raise their own babies because it's too hard a job for them. I'm sure glad my parents wanted to adopt me. If no one wanted to, how could I ever have been in a family?"

"So what if I'm adopted?" asked a twelve-year-old girl. "My parents raised me and that's all I really care about. They love me and are very kind to me. They are my only real parents."

The idea of being special or chosen was a common theme, especially among the preadolescent children, perhaps because this is how their adoption was explained to them.

"I feel special to be adopted," said a seven-year-old girl. "Adopted isn't something everyone is."

"Adopted kids are chosen," stated a ten-year-old. "They are picked out because they are special."

Another ten-year-old said, "My parents aren't like most people who get their kids whether they want them or not. They wouldn't have gotten me if they didn't really want me."

"I'm not adopted," explained a boy in junior high school, "but I'm an only child because my mom can't have any more children. I've always wanted my parents to adopt another child so that I wouldn't be the only one. Lately they have been talking a lot about adopting a boy around seven or eight years old." Then he added, "I think more people should adopt older children. Babies aren't the only ones who need homes."

"My stepdad is trying to adopt me," reported a twelve-year-old boy. "I sure hope it goes through, because he's already like a real dad to me. My other dad is trying to stop the adoption, but I don't know why. He never sees me or calls me on the phone or anything. I think he's just trying to punish me because I still love my mother and he doesn't."

Several adolescent children shared the view of a fourteen-year-old girl who said, "I wish I knew my birth parents. But if I did know them, it wouldn't change the way I feel about my adopted parents. I'll always love them most of all

195

because they really wanted me and they took me when I needed a family."

"I think about my first mother a lot," a thirteen-year-old said thoughtfully. "I wish I had a picture of her. If I just knew what she looked like I'd be satisfied."

"I don't care about those other parents so much," said a fifteen-year-old boy, "but I wish I knew if I had any brothers or sisters. If I do, I would like to meet them. We might end up being really good friends."

Some responses, however, were not so positive. Interestingly, most of the negative comments came from adolescents. "I'm afraid my friends won't like me if they know I'm adopted," a twelve-year-old explained. "Like one time my best friend said, 'I sure would hate to be adopted, because then I wouldn't have any real parents.' I didn't say anything, because I didn't want her to find out I was adopted. I don't want anyone to know."

"I feel really mad at my real parents," declared a fourteen-year-old boy. "They cheated me out of the chance to be a normal kid who lives in a normal family. I don't want to be 'special' as everyone is always saying I am!"

An even stronger opinion was voiced by a thirteen-year-old girl. "I hate being adopted, and I think most other adopted kids do too," she said. "Sometimes I am kind of mean to my parents. I say bad things about them because I'm angry about being adopted. I have a brother and a sister who were born into our family and I feel like I'm different from them."

"Sometimes I feel I'm not wanted," said a fifteen-year-old boy. "I just don't feel that I really belong. My brothers are adopted, too, but they seem to fit in better than I do. Sometimes I feel like I'm living with a bunch of strangers."

A surprising number of birth children either wish they were or believe that they are adopted. Some of them can be very hard to convince otherwise. This comment by an eleven-year-old girl was not uncommon: "My mother says that I'm not adopted, but I think I am. In lots of ways I seem like an adopted kid, and that's just how my parents treat me."

IMPRESSIONS AND FANTASIES

What exactly is an adopted child like? Not surprisingly, children's ideas are generally determined by the personalities of the adopted children they know. Here are some of the comments nonadoptive kids used to describe their adoptive counterparts:

"Adoptive kids are usually competitive."

"They're always loud."

"They're too quiet."

"Adopted kids act wild."

"Adopted kids hit or kick or bite when they get mad."

"They are poor students."

"They work hard."

"They never work."

"They're mean like Teresa who is adopted."

"They're nice and gentle."

It sounds as if the variations found among adopted kids are exactly the same as those found in any other group of children. "My real parents might be nicer to me than my adopted parents are," suggested an eight-year-old boy. "They would probably get me more toys and stuff that I want."

But a fifteen-year-old girl observed, "I used to think that my birth parents would love me more than my adopted parents do. I guess all adopted kids think that. But now I know better. My birth parents probably wouldn't be nearly as nice to me because they wouldn't want me as much."

"I think my first parents are probably movie stars," ventured an eight-year-old girl.

"Maybe my first father played football for the Dallas Cowboys," said a nine-year-old boy. "That's what I want to do."

"I used to dream that my birth parents were something special—famous or rich or important—but I grew out of that," recalled a fourteen-year-old boy. "Actually they probably weren't as good as my own parents are. They sure didn't love me as much."

197

Fantasizing about birth parents is common among adopted children, and it is very frustrating to many adoptive parents. How can any human being ever hope to compete with the rich, handsome, famous, perfect parents of a child's imagination? It seems that the best thing parents can do to help their children move from a world of fantasy to reality is to share with them the truth about their biological pasts. Informed children are far less prone to fantasize than those who are kept in the dark.

"I was an unwanted baby born to a fifteen-year-old girl," related a thirty-four-year-old mother of two. "Fortunately for me, it wasn't so easy to get abortions in those days or I probably wouldn't be alive today. By means of adoption I became part of a wonderful Christian family that was overjoyed to get me. It was God himself who arranged for us to be together. The family in which I was raised was, is, and always will be my real family."

TO KNOW THE TRUTH

Today, almost without exception, professionals stress the importance of being honest with children about adoption. The kids agree. Without exception they said they want to be told the truth, and they want to know it from the beginning.

"My parents told me about my adoption when I was still really little," a ten-year-old girl said. "I'm glad they did. Can you believe that some parents don't even tell their children?"

"I got mad when I was told," said an eight-year-old boy, "because I was already in the first grade. My parents should have told me before that. I should have known when I was a baby."

Many share the opinion of a fifteen-year-old who said, "Parents should never, ever lie to their child about being adopted. If they would lie about something like that, how could their child ever believe anything else they say? Kids don't like parents who lie to them."

"Nobody had to tell me I was adopted," a thirteen-year-old girl stated. "I can remember it. I was so glad to get a family who wanted to keep me forever. It's really hard for me to say 'I love you' to my parents, but I think they know how I feel." She paused. "At least I hope they do."

In an effort to anticipate and diminish some of these issues, there has been a marked trend in recent years toward open adoptions that are marked by a relationship between the adoptive parents and the birth parents. Many of the most conscientious adoption professionals have been requesting that each birth mother write a letter to her child telling why she placed the child for adoption. These letters are usually written to the comprehension level of a five-year-old child, since it is typically at that age that a child begins asking questions about the birth parents and is capable of understanding the answers. These letters do not need to be elaborate. In fact, it is better to keep them as simple as possible. A fairly typical letter of this kind follows:

Dear Carolyn,

This is a very difficult letter for me to write. As I write this, you are just a tiny baby with a sweet smile and a full head of dark hair. Placing you for adoption is the hardest thing I have ever done, or probably ever will do. I know you will not be a tiny baby very long, and that you will have many questions about your adoption. I am writing this letter so that you will know that, above all else, I love you dearly. I am placing you for adoption, not because I don't love you, but because I love you so much that I want you to have more of a life than I can offer you right now. I have spent many hours in tears making this decision, but this is what I have to do because it is best for you.

My name is Donna and I'm nineteen years old. I am five feet four inches tall, and have light brown hair and blue eyes. I am enclosing a picture of myself and your father. The reason I decided to place you for adoption is that I wanted you to have a two-parent home, enough money to support you well and a chance to get a good education. I couldn't provide you with those things. Also, I know I'm not where I should be spiritually. I'm just not ready to be a mother.

Your father and I aren't married. His name is Jim and he is twenty-three. He has brown hair and brown eyes, and he's about six feet tall.

Please, please never think I didn't love you very much. My love for you was the main reason I've decided to let you be adopted. I chose Roger and Cheri to be your parents because they are good people who I think will be wonderful parents. They will provide you with the good home you deserve but I can't give you. So don't be sad. Have a wonderful life and be sure to listen to your parents because they love you very much, too, and I am sure they will be very wise and good parents. When you grow up and are twenty-one years old, if you would like to meet me, I would be honored to get to know you and see what a fine person you have turned out to be. I have already talked this over with your parents, and it is okay with them. If you would rather not meet me, that's okay too. You will not be seeing me for at least twenty-one years, but you will always be in my heart and in my prayers.

> With much love,
> Your birth mother, Donna

WANTING TO KNOW WHY

One of the most common concerns shared by adopted children is their struggle to find a satisfactory answer to the question, "Why was I given up by my birth parents?" The happiest children seem to be those who have come to terms with the explanation they were given by their adoptive parents. Many others, left to figure it out for themselves, assume they were rejected because of some failure on their part. It is concern over this issue which has caused many adoption experts to recommend that each birth mother write a letter to the child.

"Obviously someone didn't want me," declared an eleven-year-old boy. "It makes me mad that that woman just dumped me without even telling anyone why."

"I always wondered why my birth mother gave me up,"

a fourteen-year-old pondered. "Was I ugly or no good or what?"

"I told my friends that I thought I was given up because I was ugly," related a thirteen-year-old girl, "and one of them said, 'Maybe so, but you are what you are.' That made me really feel bad. Another friend said, 'It's not what you look like that matters; it's what you are.' But my best friend, Kristin, told me, 'That couldn't be the reason. Mothers who give up their babies for adoption don't even see them first.' I hope Kristin is right."

Most children who do not know the facts attempt to guess their birth mother's reason for not keeping them. A large percentage of the children interviewed, especially the younger ones, agreed with the nine-year-old who reasoned, "Those first parents are probably dead. Adopted kids must be orphans." Many others shared this view of a thirteen-year-old girl: "My mother was probably too young and just couldn't handle a baby."

Where motive is concerned, most of the children were willing to give the biological mother the benefit of the doubt. They generally agreed that it had probably been very hard for her to give up her baby.

"She was probably too poor to keep me," a seven-year-old boy suggested. "She probably wanted me to be in a family that could afford to give me a nice home and warm clothes and good food and nice toys."

"My first mother probably wanted me to have a better home than she could give me," reasoned an eleven-year-old girl.

A twelve-year-old said, "My parents told me that my birth mother must have loved me very much because she let me be adopted into a family that could give me a better life than she could."

"My mom told me that my birth mother agreed with her and my dad that children should grow up in families with two parents who really care for them and can give them a good home," said a fourteen-year-old girl. "They say that she couldn't give me that, so she arranged for me to be adopted by a family who could."

One twelve-year-old had a different idea. "I don't even try to guess why my first mother gave me up. I'm going to wait until I get older. Then I will just find her and ask her."

REGARD FOR BIRTH MOTHERS

The kindness and sensitivity with which most children seem to regard their birth mothers is a credit to the gentle handling of a delicate situation by the adoptive parents.

"I'm sure my first mother didn't want to give me up," an eleven-year-old boy reflected. "It was probably a very hard thing for her to do. She did it for my own good, so that I could be raised in a family with parents who could take good care of me."

"She must have felt awful," observed a seven-year-old. "She must have cried and cried. I feel sorry for her."

A fifteen-year-old said, "She must have been terribly confused. I'm sure she was sad and hurt. And frightened too. She must have been scared to death. That decision was probably very hard for her to make. You know, she was exactly the same age as I am right now. I can't imagine having to make a decision like that."

"I think she felt pressured to give me up," declared a twelve-year-old girl. "Then she probably felt guilty because she had done it."

A number of children commented on the feelings of guilt that they attribute to their biological mothers. A fourteen-year-old said, "That must have been the hardest decision she ever had to make. She must have felt like she was torn into two pieces. She probably felt awfully guilty because she didn't know if she was doing the right thing or not. I never want to have to make a decision like that."

"I think adopted children should be grateful to the people who let them be adopted," said one ten-year-old. "Some mothers probably couldn't make the decision to give their babies up, so their kids had to grow up in a bad home."

"I really wish I knew if my mother had to give me up or if she just wanted to," said a twelve-year-old girl. "If she wanted to, I would be mad at her; but if she had to do it, I would feel sorry for her."

GROWING UP ADOPTED

Many adoptive parents feel that their adopted children have a harder time growing up, suffer more problems, and have more troublesome self-doubts than nonadoptive children. The opinions of adopted children are divided. One twelve-year-old said, "Adopted kids just have the same problems as everyone else," but another one declared, "All my problems are because I'm adopted." A thirteen-year-old boy said, "The thing is, adopted kids just have one more thing to think about."

"My parents talk too much about my being adopted," commented an eight-year-old girl.

"My mother always says that I have more problems than other kids," stated a fifteen-year-old boy, "but in my opinion she's the one who causes the problems. She protects me too much. She wants to control my whole life. Why does she have to worry all the time? What's wrong with me that she can't just leave me alone?"

Evidently parents are not the only offenders. A nine-year-old boy told about his fourth-grade schoolteacher who, on the first day of school, had all the adopted children in the class stand up. There were three of them. "He told us that he had been adopted, too, so he could really understand us and our problems. The teacher said we would all be special friends that year. It was embarrassing."

A thirteen-year-old who was not an adopted child observed, "I think that some adopted kids make their own problems. They are always talking about their adoption. They keep on bragging about it like it's a great big deal or something."

Most of the adopted children agree. "I'm not ashamed of

being adopted, but why talk about it all the time?" a twelve-year-old boy asked.

"My parents don't talk to other people about adopting my sister and me," said a nine-year-old. "If we want to tell people, we can, but they leave it up to us. We don't talk about it very much, but sometimes we do."

"I think about being adopted," said an eleven-year-old, "but I don't talk about it much because I think it bothers my parents. Sometimes I'd really like to talk to them about my adoption. I'd like to ask them some questions. But I don't, because I don't want to make them feel bad."

"Do you want to hear something funny?" laughed a ten-year-old girl. "Sometimes people who don't know that I'm adopted say I look just like my mother and sister. I don't tell them that I wasn't even born in the same family. I wonder what they would say if I did?"

TO TEASE OR NOT TO TEASE

Many parents express concern about the teasing their adopted children have to endure. Others, however, say that they are unaware of a problem. As for the adopted children themselves, only a few spoke of being teased by friends or schoolmates.

"The kids who get teased are the ones who are always talking about being adopted," observed an eleven-year-old girl.

"Everybody gets teased about something," a thirteen-year-old boy said. "If it's not about being adopted, then it's about having big ears or being dumb in math or something else."

"I've never heard anyone tease my adopted brother or my adopted friend, and I'm really glad," said a ten-year-old boy. "I'd get mad if anyone did."

But there were those who have encountered teasing, and they related some painful experiences. "I have a black friend who was adopted by a white family," said a fifteen-year-old boy. "People tease him by saying, 'Salt and pepper don't mix.' It's embarrassing to him."

"Sometimes people tease me by saying that I had to be adopted because I wasn't good enough for my real parents," said a nine-year-old.

A seven-year-old said, "One time my best friend got mad at me and said I was fat and stupid and adopted. So I got mad back and said she was ugly and dumb."

"Some boys in my class at school used to say that the reason I had to be adopted was because I was so ugly that when I was born my mother took one look at me and died of fright," said a twelve-year-old girl.

"My brother is the one who teases me," an eight-year-old girl commented. "When he gets mad he calls me a stupid adopted little kid. He's just as adopted as I am, but he never says anything about that!"

VULNERABLE BY ADOPTION

Yet according to the kids, there are some areas in which adopted children seem to be especially vulnerable. "I think adopted kids suffer more psychologically, like feeling guilty and inferior and helpless," suggested a fifteen year-old-girl.

"Adopted kids can feel as if they aren't loved as much as other kids," said a nine-year-old.

A fourteen-year-old boy said, "Sometimes adopted kids don't get along too well with their parents." He paused, then added, "Of course, my brother has the same problem and he's not adopted."

"I think adopted kids sometimes stop obeying their parents because they feel that the adopted parents aren't their real parents and they wonder why they should have to obey them," said a thirteen-year-old.

Several children talked about having inner conflicts and questions, but many said they did not discuss their concerns with anyone for fear of hurting their adoptive parents' feelings.

"I can't help worrying about why I wasn't wanted," said

a nine-year-old girl. "Once I said something about it to my mom, but she said I shouldn't have such silly thoughts. Then she changed the subject. I still worry about it, but now I don't tell my mom."

"My sister isn't adopted like me," observed an eight-year-old boy. "I always wonder which one of us my parents love the most."

"I just wish I could know for positive sure that my parents love me and accept me just as much as they would if I had been born to them," explained a young teenager. "I really wish I knew, but how could I ever ask my parents something like that?"

A fourteen-year-old girl said, "Lots of times I wonder how my first mother looked and what she was like. But I'm afraid it would hurt my parents if I asked them, and I love them too much to do that."

"Sometimes at night I get to thinking about my natural parents, wondering who they are and why they gave me up, and I just can't get to sleep," commented a twelve-year-old girl. "I guess I would have to say that my biggest problem is insomnia."

An eleven-year-old girl mused, "I wonder what my natural parents look like. I wonder if they're nice. Most of all I wonder if they ever think about me and wonder what I'm like."

WONDERING . . . SEARCHING

Wondering about birth parents seems to be the greatest single common denominator among adopted children. Unfortunately, the subject can be threatening to many adoptive parents.

"I just wish I knew what my birth mother looks like," said an eleven-year-old girl. "I wonder if she's good at drawing and bad in spelling like me. I wish I could see her and find out for myself."

A few children seem to be totally disinterested in their biological parents. "I never asked questions," said a twenty-five-year-old woman, "because there was nothing to ask. My mom and dad and sister are my family. What else do I need to know? I never had any desire to find my birth parents. I still don't."

"Everyone thinks I should try to find my birth mother," said a fifteen-year-old girl, "but I don't want to. My parents have been very good to me, and I'm happy with things just the way they are. I don't want to change anything."

A fourteen-year-old reasoned, "If I ever did see my birth mother, what in the world would I say to her?"

When contemplating an actual search, many young people wisely consider the birth parents' viewpoint. Most feel that the birth parents would not be anxious to see their children again.

"I was adopted by parents who wanted me," explained a fifteen-year-old. "Why should I bother my birth parents? They didn't want me in the first place, and I'm sure that they wouldn't want to see me now."

"I think my birth mother would be horrified if I suddenly came to see her," declared a fifteen-year-old. "She probably has a new family by now. How could she explain me to them?"

"I think my first mother would be mad at me for coming to see her," said a ten-year-old girl. "She would probably tell me to get away from her house and stay away."

"If I came to see her," suggested a thirteen-year-old, "it could ruin her whole life. It wouldn't be fair for me to do it."

"When she gave me up," observed a twelve-year-old boy, "she gave up for good. It wouldn't be fair for me to show up and make her explain me to her husband and kids."

"That woman has a constitutional right to her privacy," declared a twenty-nine-year-old adoptee.

"I would be afraid to just knock on my birth mother's door," said a thirteen-year-old girl. "She probably wouldn't even let me in. Why should she? I'm a complete stranger."

"My mom told me that my biological mother is very intelligent," said a fifteen-year-old girl. "She gave me up so that she could finish school. I'd like to know what she did with her life, what kind of job she's in. But she probably wouldn't want to see me." She added, "I'm curious, but I'm not looking for a new mother. I like my present one just fine."

"I'm afraid that if I searched for my birth parents I would only end up hurting my adoptive parents," said a twelve-year-old. "And I wouldn't hurt them for anything in the world!"

This concern was echoed by many adoptive children who feared that their real parents—the ones who had adopted and raised them—would feel hurt, unloved, dissatisfied, jealous, unwanted, left-out, or afraid of the competition. A few thought such a search would be discouraged by their adoptive parents because of concerns that the children could be hurt if they discovered something bad about their birth parents. Some thought that their adoptive parents might not mind such a search, and a few felt that their parents might encourage and help them.

"I knew that my mother was dead and my father gave me up for adoption because he couldn't take care of me all alone," stated a fourteen-year-old girl. "I was really depressed and I used to cry a lot. My adoptive parents thought it would be good for me to meet my father, so they helped me find him. I was scared when I found out where my real dad lived. But when I called him, he was glad to talk to me. I met him, and we hugged and kissed. He said he would call me and he did. Now I visit him on a regular basis. I'm really glad I know him."

Whatever the reaction of the adoptive parents, for many children the desire to know persists. As one fifteen-year-old boy said, "All I want is to *see* my birth mother. I don't want to move in with her!"

"I've seen TV programs and I've read articles about kids who have searched out their birth parents," said a fourteen-year-old girl. "Those stories always seemed to have happy-ever-after endings. But I really don't think it happens that way very often."

It doesn't. Few experiences end happily. Most ultimately fall somewhere between disappointing and disastrous.

"I asked my parents' lawyer about finding my birth parents, and he said it was very hard because of the sealed records," said a fifteen-year-old. "He said most searches are unsuccessful."

"Most searchers probably just get tired and give up," suggested a fourteen-year-old. "Maybe they really don't want to find their birth parents as much as they think they do."

"If I ever found my other parents," said a twelve-year-old, "I would probably end up getting the door slammed in my face. I'm sure there would be a sad ending for me."

"Most adopted kids would probably be very disappointed if they did find their birth parents," observed a thirteen-year-old boy. "The parents probably wouldn't be at all what the kid thought they would be."

"My mom showed me an article she read about a man who searched out his birth mother," stated a thirteen-year-old. "The whole thing turned out badly for everyone. In the end he said he wished he had never started his search. I never will."

"I have the very best kind of parents right now," explained a fourteen-year-old boy. "They listen to me when I want to talk, they answer me when I ask them questions, and they leave me alone when I want to be left alone. They love me just as I am because I'm their son. Why would I ever want to look for any other parents?"

QUESTIONS FOR DISCUSSION

1. From what the children expressed, do you think it is important for adoptees to be given all the information available on their background? In what ways can that information help them? In what ways may it be of harm?
2. Is it possible for adoptive parents to create a situation free and open enough to allow their children to be able to express these thoughts to their parents? If not, why not? If so, how might this be accomplished?

15.   *Conclusion*

Now you have today's adoption story. You have heard
the good news and the bad news. There have been words of
encouragement and words of discouragement. It is important
to see both sides. To accept the positive and refuse to see the
negative is unrealistic and can only lead to disappointment.

If this were a movie, you could take your adopted
children into your arms and as a family happily fade into the
sunset. But real life is not like that. Your family experiences
will sometimes be pleasant, at other times unpleasant. Your
family will go through these experiences, good or bad,
together. Sometimes you and your children will enjoy each
other. At other times you will grow impatient. It is the
experiences you share day by day—the smiles, the laughter,
the sighs, and the tears—that bind you together into a real
family.

What, then, are the most important things to remember
about the current adoption scene? They can be summed up in
eight points.

1. In adoption the welfare of the children must be the
first and foremost consideration of everyone involved. It may
well be that receiving your children, holding them in your
arms, and sharing the joy of their entry into your family are
the happiest moments of your life. We hope that is so.
Nevertheless, an adoption is no longer considered to be
merely a means of finding a baby for a specific family. It is
finding the right home for a specific child. Understanding this
will help you to be more patient with the questions, the

screening, the home study, and the waiting you may be asked to endure.

2. There definitely are children available. It may not be the two-day-old girl with blond curls who you had pictured in your dreams, but there are plenty of children. Give some consideration to the minority children, those with handicaps, and the older children who are available and waiting for homes. You may discover that one of these children is just perfect for you. It has happened that way in many families.

3. Not everyone should adopt. It is vitally important to examine your motives honestly and determine why you want to adopt. Be sure your reasons are valid ones. Then take a long, realistic look at your present family situation. Be sure that a child would fit in and be a welcome part of your family. Remember that when the newness wears off, the child will still be there and will still be yours.

4. Maintain a family where love, openness, honesty, and a strong faith in God are a natural way of life. Many of the problems that exist between adoptive parents and their children, just as in nonadoptive families, can be traced to an absence of communication, lack of open sharing, and misunderstandings.

5. Anticipate problems. It is not being overly pessimistic to expect that problems will occur. Happy-ever-after endings belong in fairy tales, not in real life. If you anticipate problems, you will be better equipped to handle them when they hit. And you will be less likely to react in word or action in ways that you will regret later. If the problems never materialize, so much the better.

6. There are no guarantees. Like biological children, your adopted children may or may not turn out the way you want them to. Parenthood holds no guarantees. Nor does life. Love means accepting others for who and what they are and not demanding that they change to fit into all your dreams and expectations. We have an awesome responsibility to "train up a child in the way he should go." But once we have trained our children, we must be willing and prepared to let them go to make their own decisions and lead their own lives.

We cannot and should not accept responsibility for the lives they choose to build for themselves.

7. God has the answers. When problems come that seem too painful to bear, and when your questions seem unanswerable, you must trust God to work it all out. That is more easily said than done. But easy or hard, it is the truth. To deny it is to deny either God's total love for you or his sovereign power over your life. God is not bound by the limits of understanding and short-sightedness as we are. He sees the finished picture, and he promised that it will be beautiful. Trust him to be true to his promises. Let him prove his faithfulness.

8. A grafted family tree can be every bit as strong, beautiful, and fruitful as any other family tree. Don't let anyone tell you otherwise. You will hear good adoption stories and bad ones. You will hear happy accounts that will warm your very soul, and you will hear sad ones that will wrench your heart. Listen to them all, but do not lose your perspective. Determine that your family's story will be one of the good ones.

The fact that your adopted children were not born to you should not make the least bit of difference in your day-to-day living. You will care for them, teach them, encourage them, love them, and discipline them exactly as you would if they were yours by birth. If you allow the fact that your children are adopted to color your daily dealings with them, you will be putting an unnecessary strain on your relationship.

Do your best for your children. Help them to develop what they have within so that they will be able to cope with their future. No parent can do more.

We have looked at some of the special needs and problems your adopted children may have. Some are related to their adoption, but most are not. That they are adopted is a fact of your children's existence. They and you must learn to accept this fact. You cannot change it, and you shouldn't try. But neither should you exaggerate the importance of this fact. There is nothing to be gained by overemphasizing your children's adoption and making them feel different.

Whatever your adoption experience, it is unique. That's because you are unique, and so are your children. You will not feel exactly the same as any other adoptive parent, nor will you act exactly the same. But there are some things that you will have in common. All adoptive parents want to raise their children to become responsible, contributing members of society. They all want to share a happy family life with them.

Children are a gift from God. They are also our greatest and most precious natural resource. Through adoption children become cherished members of your family. And they will surely make your life richer and fuller as well.

OPEN FORUM

Karen Alvarado: Our little girl had her third birthday last week. We had a big day—a party with her little friends in the afternoon and then a big family dinner in the evening. She fell asleep on my lap. As I tucked her into bed I prayed, "Bless the girl who gave birth to Jodie. Please let her know that this little girl is safe, happy, and very dearly loved. Give that girl happiness, too, and somehow bring her to yourself."

Judy Randle: When you see them so peaceful and happy, it's easy to forget the hard times and the frustrations and struggles, isn't it? All you can think of is how deeply and richly God has blessed your family.

Roger Crawford: Whether we give birth to our children or adopt them, we don't own them. They're only on loan to us from the Lord God. It's our job to raise them, to teach them and love them wisely, to parent them the very best we know how, and to root and ground them in the Lord. If we do these things, we will have accomplished the job that he has called us to do. Then we must be willing to commit them to God for safekeeping. Our children will be better people because of us, and our lives will be better and more complete because of them.

APPENDIX A

State Policies on Adoptions

State policies on independent adoption are complex and constantly changing. Perhaps the best summary available on these policies is contained in the following charts and notes published in 1987 by the American Public Welfare Association (APWA), a highly regarded organization headquartered in Washington, D.C.

This information is intended only as a general guide. Laws and policies regarding adoption can be changed in any state at any time. You should refer specific questions to a licensed adoption agency in your area or to an attorney who is familiar with your state's current adoption laws and policies.

ABBREVIATION GUIDE TO CHARTS

A series of codes and abbreviations are used in the charts. Their definitions appear below:

Code/ Abbreviation	Definition
°	For further information contact the Interstate Compact on the Placement of Children (ICPC) office in your state.
X°	Consult notes on your state at the back of the charts.
	Blank spaces in a given category indicate that the state provided no response to this part of the question.

Code/Abbreviation	Definition
100A	Form ICPC-100A
C.P.	Child-Placing Agency
D	Day
H	Hour
M	Month
NA	Not Available
P.A.	Public Social Service Agency (State and/or Local)
S.W.	Social Worker
W	Weeks
Y	Year

I. LAWS   A. Independent Adoption Laws

State	1. Independent adoption is legal within state YES	NO	OTHER	2. Independent adoption is legal *into* state YES	NO	OTHER	3. Independent adoption is legal *out from* state YES	NO	OTHER	4. Independent adoptions may lawfully be made by: i. Mother YES	NO	OTHER	ii. Lawfully made by father YES	NO	OTHER	iii. Lawfully made by other relative YES	NO	OTHER
ALABAMA	X			X			X			X			X				X	
ALASKA	X			X			X			X°			X			X		
ARIZONA	X			X			X			X			X				X	
ARKANSAS	X					X			X	X			X				X	
CALIFORNIA	X			X			X			X			X				X	
COLORADO			X°			X°			X°	X			X					
CONNECTICUT		X° illegal							°									
DELAWARE		X				X	X											
DIST. OF COLUMBIA																		
FLORIDA	X			X				X				X		X			X	
GEORGIA	X			X			X						X				X	
GUAM																		
HAWAII	X			X			X		°	X			X					
IDAHO	X			X			X			X			X			X		
ILLINOIS	X			X			X											
INDIANA			X°	X			X			X°			X°			X°		
IOWA	X			X			X			X			X			X		
KANSAS	X			X			X			X			X				X°	
KENTUCKY	X°			X°			X			X			X				X	
LOUISIANA	X			X			X			X			X			X		
MAINE	X					X°	X		°	X			X				X	
MARYLAND	X			X			X			X			X			X°		
MASSACHUSETTS		X°			X			X										
MICHIGAN		X°																
MINNESOTA		X°				X°			X°		X			X			X	
MISSISSIPPI	X			X			X			X			X			X		
MISSOURI	X			X			X											
MONTANA			X			X			X	X			X				X	
NEBRASKA		X°		X			X			X			X					
NEVADA	X°			X°			X°			X			X			X°		
NEW HAMPSHIRE	X°			X			X			X			X				X	
NEW JERSEY																		
NEW MEXICO	X			X			X			X			X			X°		
NEW YORK	X			X			X											
NORTH CAROLINA	X			X			X			X			X				X	
NORTH DAKOTA		X			X		X											
OHIO	X			X			X			X			X					
OKLAHOMA	X			X			X			X			X			X		
OREGON	X			X			X											
PENNSYLVANIA	X			X			X			X			X			X		
PUERTO RICO																		
RHODE ISLAND	X			X			X											
SOUTH CAROLINA	X			X			X											
SOUTH DAKOTA	X			X			X			X			X			X		
TENNESSEE	X			X			X			X			X					
TEXAS	X			X			X			X			X				X°	
UTAH	X			X			X			X			X					
VERMONT	X			X			X			X			X			X		
VIRGIN ISLANDS																		
VIRGINIA	X			X			X			X			X					
WASHINGTON	X			X			X											
WEST VIRGINIA	X					°			°	X			X			X		
WISCONSIN	X			X			X			X		X		X			X	
WYOMING	X			X			X		°	X			X				X	

State	iv. Lawfully made by unlicensed person YES	NO	OTHER	v. Lawfully made by doctor YES	NO	OTHER	vi. Lawfully made by lawyer YES	NO	OTHER	vii. Lawfully made by clergy YES	NO	OTHER	viii. Lawfully made by court YES	NO	OTHER	5. In indep. adoption non-licensed intermediary may arrange placement YES	NO	OTHER
ALABAMA		X			X			X									X	
ALASKA	X			X			X									X		
ARIZONA		X			X		X				X		X				X	
ARKANSAS		X		X			X			X°			X°				X	
CALIFORNIA		X			X			X			X			X			X	
COLORADO													X°				X	
CONNECTICUT																		
DELAWARE																	X	
DIST. OF COLUMBIA																		
FLORIDA		X		X			X										X	
GEORGIA		X			X		X				X		X				X	
GUAM																		
HAWAII				X			X			X								X°
IDAHO	X			X			X			X			X			X		
ILLINOIS																		
INDIANA	X°			X°			X°			X°			X°			X		
IOWA	X			X			X											X°
KANSAS		X°			X°			X°			X°			X°				
KENTUCKY			X°			X°		X°				X°		X		X°		
LOUISIANA	X			X			X			X			X			X		
MAINE		X		X			X			X			X					
MARYLAND		X		X			X									X		
MASSACHUSETTS																	X	
MICHIGAN																		
MINNESOTA		X		X			X										X	
MISSISSIPPI	X			X			X									X		
MISSOURI																		°
MONTANA		X		X			X			X							X	
NEBRASKA																	X	
NEVADA		X		X			X			X							X	
NEW HAMPSHIRE	X°			X			X			X			X				X	
NEW JERSEY																		
NEW MEXICO		X		X			X									X		
NEW YORK																	X	
NORTH CAROLINA		X		X			X			X			X			X		
NORTH DAKOTA																	X	
OHIO																	X	
OKLAHOMA	X			X			X			X			X			X		
OREGON																	X	X°
PENNSYLVANIA	X			X			X									X		
PUERTO RICO																		
RHODE ISLAND																X		
SOUTH CAROLINA										X				X		X		
SOUTH DAKOTA	X			X			X									X		
TENNESSEE																X		
TEXAS		X°		X°			X°									X		
UTAH													X			X		
VERMONT	X			X			X			X			X			X		
VIRGIN ISLANDS																		
VIRGINIA																	X	
WASHINGTON																		X°
WEST VIRGINIA	X			X			X			X			X				X	
WISCONSIN		X			X			X			X		X					X°
WYOMING	X°			X°			X°									X		

I. LAWS   A. Independent Adoption Laws (cont.)

State	6. In indep. adoption non-licensed intermediary may physically arrange placement			7. Compensation is allowed to *birth mother*			7a. Compensation to birth mother is allowed by *direct* payment			7a. Maximum amount of compensation allowed			7b. Compensation to birth mother is allowed by *indirect* payment		
	YES	NO	OTHER	YES	NO	OTHER	YES	NO	OTHER	YES	NO	OTHER	YES	NO	OTHER
ALABAMA		X		X											
ALASKA	X			X											
ARIZONA		X				X°	X						X		
ARKANSAS		X			X				X				X		
CALIFORNIA		X				X°			X°			X°	X		
COLORADO		X						X							
CONNECTICUT															
DELAWARE		X		Private = Illegal											X
DIST. OF COLUMBIA															
FLORIDA		X						X			X		X°		
GEORGIA	X				X			X						X	
GUAM															
HAWAII			X°			X°									
IDAHO	X				X			X						X	
ILLINOIS								X							
INDIANA	X			X					X°						
IOWA			X°	X				X					X		
KANSAS				X			X						X		
KENTUCKY	X					X°		X				X	X		
LOUISIANA	X				X			X					X		
MAINE															
MARYLAND		X						X							
MASSACHUSETTS		X			X			X					X		
MICHIGAN															
MINNESOTA		X			X			X			X			X	
MISSISSIPPI	X							X					X		
MISSOURI			°					X					X		
MONTANA		X				X		X							X
NEBRASKA		X		X					X°						
NEVADA		X		X			X						X		
NEW HAMPSHIRE		X		X				X					X		
NEW JERSEY															
NEW MEXICO	X			X			X			X			X		
NEW YORK		X						X					X		
NORTH CAROLINA		X			X			X			X			X	
NORTH DAKOTA		X			X			X			X			X	
OHIO		X				X°			X°			X°			X°
OKLAHOMA	X			X			X			X			X		
OREGON		X										X°			X°
PENNSYLVANIA	X			X										X°	
PUERTO RICO															
RHODE ISLAND	X			X				X					X		
SOUTH CAROLINA	X				X			X			X			X	
SOUTH DAKOTA	X				X			X					X		
TENNESSEE		X							X				X		
TEXAS		X			X				X°					X°	
UTAH	X				X			X					X		
VERMONT	X			X			X			X			X		
VIRGIN ISLANDS															
VIRGINIA						X°		X			X				
WASHINGTON			X°	X°											
WEST VIRGINIA		X		X				X					X		
WISCONSIN			X°	X°											
WYOMING	X			X			X					X	X		

I. LAWS   A. Independent Adoption Laws (cont.)

State	i. Indirect payment: prenatal medical expenses			ii. Indirect payment: housing/food			iii. Indirect payment: clothing			iv. Indirect payment: travel			v. Indirect payment: hospital/delivery fees			vi. Indirect payment: legal fees		
	YES	NO	OTHER	YES	NO	OTHER	YES	NO	OTHER	YES	NO	OTHER	YES	NO	OTHER	YES	NO	OTHER
ALABAMA	X			X			X			X			X			X		
ALASKA	X			X			X			X			X			X		
ARIZONA	X			X			X			X			X			X		
ARKANSAS																		
CALIFORNIA	X			X			X			X			X			X		
COLORADO	X					X		X				X	X			X		
CONNECTICUT																		
DELAWARE			X								X				X			X
DIST. OF COLUMBIA																		
FLORIDA	X			X			X			X			X			X		
GEORGIA	X				X			X			X		X				X	
GUAM																		
HAWAII																		
IDAHO	X				X			X			X		X				X	
ILLINOIS	X			X					°			°	X			X		
INDIANA	X							X°								X		
IOWA	X				X			X			X		X			X		
KANSAS													X			X		
KENTUCKY	X			X			X			X			X			X		
LOUISIANA	X			X			X			X			X			X		
MAINE																		
MARYLAND	X				X		X				X		X					
MASSACHUSETTS	X																	
MICHIGAN																		
MINNESOTA		X		X			X				X				X		X	
MISSISSIPPI	X			X			X			X			X			X		
MISSOURI	X			X			X				X		X			X		
MONTANA																		
NEBRASKA																		
NEVADA	X			X			X			X			X			X		
NEW HAMPSHIRE	X			X			X			X			X			X		
NEW JERSEY																		
NEW MEXICO	X			X			X			X			X			X		
NEW YORK	X				X			X				X	X			X		
NORTH CAROLINA		X			X			X				X		X			X	
NORTH DAKOTA		X			X			X		X				X			X	
OHIO			X°			X°			X°			X°			X°			X°
OKLAHOMA	X			X			X			X			X			X		
OREGON																		
PENNSYLVANIA	X			X			X			X			X			X		
PUERTO RICO																		
RHODE ISLAND	X			X			X			X			X			X		
SOUTH CAROLINA	X				X			X			X		X			X		
SOUTH DAKOTA		X		X				X		X			X				X	
TENNESSEE	X					X°			X°			X°	X			X		
TEXAS	X					X		X				X	X			X		
UTAH	X			X			X			X			X			X		
VERMONT	X			X			X			X			X			X		
VIRGIN ISLANDS																		
VIRGINIA																		
WASHINGTON																		
WEST VIRGINIA	X			X						X						X		
WISCONSIN																		
WYOMING	X			X			X			X			X			X		

State	vii. Indirect payment to attorney for making/arranging placement			viii. Indirect payment to attorney for preparing/filing legal proceeding			8. Our state law provides for fixing responsibility for custody or meeting child's needs			9. Voluntary adoption consents are acceptable/valid			9a. Voluntary consents can be given prior to child's birth		
	YES	NO	OTHER	YES	NO	OTHER	YES	NO	OTHER	YES	NO	OTHER	YES	NO	OTHER
ALABAMA	X			X			X			X			X		
ALASKA	X			X			X						X		
ARIZONA	X			X				X		X				X	
ARKANSAS															
CALIFORNIA		X		X				X		X				X	
COLORADO		X		X				X				X		X	
CONNECTICUT	–														
DELAWARE			X			X						X			X
DIST. OF COLUMBIA															
FLORIDA	X			X			X			X				X	
GEORGIA		X				X				X				X	
GUAM															
HAWAII							X			X					X
IDAHO		X					X			X				X	
ILLINOIS	X			X									X°		
INDIANA	X°			X°				X		X				X	
IOWA		X			X		X					X		X	
KANSAS				X				X		X				X	
KENTUCKY		X°		X						X		X		X	
LOUISIANA		X		X				X		X				X	
MAINE								X°		X				X	
MARYLAND		X		X			X							X	
MASSACHUSETTS										X				X	
MICHIGAN												X°		X	
MINNESOTA		X				X				X				X	
MISSISSIPPI	X			X			X							X	
MISSOURI	X			X										X	
MONTANA								X				X			
NEBRASKA								X		X				X	
NEVADA		X		X				X		X				X	
NEW HAMPSHIRE	X			X				X		X				X	
NEW JERSEY															
NEW MEXICO	X			X			X			X				X	
NEW YORK		X		X						X				X	
NORTH CAROLINA		X				X		X		X				X	
NORTH DAKOTA		X				X									X°
OHIO			X°			X°	X			X				X	
OKLAHOMA	X			X				X		X				X	
OREGON														X	
PENNSYLVANIA	X			X				X		X				X	
PUERTO RICO															
RHODE ISLAND	X			X								X	X°		
SOUTH CAROLINA		X		X				X		X				X	
SOUTH DAKOTA		X		X				X				X°		X	
TENNESSEE	X			X				X		X				X	
TEXAS		X		X						X			X°		
UTAH	X			X				X		X				X	
VERMONT	X			X				X		X				X	
VIRGIN ISLANDS															
VIRGINIA								X		X				X	
WASHINGTON										X				X	
WEST VIRGINIA								X		X				X	
WISCONSIN								X				X°		X	
WYOMING	X			X				X		X				X	

I. LAWS   A. Independent Adoption Laws (cont.)

State	9b. Voluntary consents can be given at any time after child's birth			9c. Consent can be given no sooner than X hr./day after birth			10. Both parents must be parties to adoption and give consent or court action to rule out need			11. Child must give consent if over X years.			12a. Consent cannot be revoked after signing		
	YES	NO	OTHER	YES	NO	OTHER	YES	NO	OTHER	YES	NO	OTHER	YES	NO	OTHER
ALABAMA	X						X			X 14Y					X
ALASKA							X				X			X	
ARIZONA		X		X 72 H			X			X 12 Y			X		
ARKANSAS			X	X 12 H					X	X 10 Y					
CALIFORNIA			X°			X°	X			X 12 Y					X°
COLORADO		X			X		X			X12 Y					X°
CONNECTICUT															
DELAWARE				X		X			X			X			X
DIST. OF COLUMBIA															
FLORIDA	X					NA			X°	X 12 Y					X°
GEORGIA	X						X			X 14 Y			X		
GUAM															
HAWAII			X	X 3 D			X			X 10 Y				X	
IDAHO	X°						X			X 12 Y					
ILLINOIS		X		X 72 H			X			X 14 Y			X°		
INDIANA	X					X			X°	X				X	
IOWA		X			X		X				X				
KANSAS	X						X			X 14 Y			X°		
KENTUCKY		X		X 5 D		X°	X		X	X 12 Y					X
LOUISIANA		X		X 5 D					X	X 13 Y				X	
MAINE	X						X			X 14 Y					
MARYLAND	X						X			X 10 Y					
MASSACHUSETTS				X 4 D			X			X 12 Y			X		
MICHIGAN	X						X			X 14 Y					
MINNESOTA	X							X		X 14 Y					
MISSISSIPPI		X		X 3 D			X			X 14 Y			X		
MISSOURI		X		X 2 D			X			X 14 Y					X°
MONTANA							X			X 14 Y					X
NEBRASKA	X								X	X 14 Y			X		
NEVADA		X		X 72 H			X			X 13 Y			X		
NEW HAMPSHIRE		X		X 72 H			X			X 11 Y					X
NEW JERSEY															
NEW MEXICO		X		X 72 H			X			X 10 Y			X°		
NEW YORK	X					X	X			X 14 Y				X	
NORTH CAROLINA	X					NA	X			X 12 Y				X	
NORTH DAKOTA															
OHIO		X		X 72 H			X			X 12 Y					X
OKLAHOMA	X			X 10 D			X							X	
OREGON	X					X°	X			X 14 Y					X°
PENNSYLVANIA		X		X 72 H			X		X°	X 12 Y					X°
PUERTO RICO															
RHODE ISLAND	X			X 15 D			X°			X 14 Y					NA
SOUTH CAROLINA	X							X°		X 14 Y			X°		
SOUTH DAKOTA	X			X 15 D			X°			X 12 Y					X°
TENNESSEE	X									X 14 Y					
TEXAS	X°-			X°			X			X 12 Y			X°		
UTAH	X						X°			X 14 Y			X		
VERMONT	X						X			X 14 Y					
VIRGIN ISLANDS															
VIRGINIA		X		X 10 D			X			X 14 Y					X°
WASHINGTON	X			X 48 H			X			X 14 Y			X		
WEST VIRGINIA		X		X 72 H			X			X 14 Y			X		
WISCONSIN		X			X		X					X°			X°
WYOMING	X			NA	X		X			X 14 Y					X

Item columns:
- **12b.** Consent cannot be revoked after X days
- **12c.** Consent cannot be revoked after X months
- **12d.** Consent cannot be revoked after adoption petition is filed
- **12e.** Consent cannot be revoked after interlocutory decree is issued
- **13.** Consent cannot be revoked at any time prior to finalization

State	12b YES	12b NO	12b OTHER	12c YES	12c NO	12c OTHER	12d YES	12d NO	12d OTHER	12e YES	12e NO	12e OTHER	13 YES	13 NO	13 OTHER
ALABAMA							X			X			X		
ALASKA	X 10 D				X		X					X		X	
ARIZONA									NA			NA			NA
ARKANSAS	X 10 D													X	
CALIFORNIA			X°						X°			X°			X°
COLORADO			X°						X°			X°	X		
CONNECTICUT															
DELAWARE		X					X			X					X
DIST. OF COLUMBIA															
FLORIDA			X°						NA			NA			NA
GEORGIA	X 10 D													X	
GUAM															
HAWAII			X°						X°	X		X°			X°
IDAHO	X 30 D							X				X	X		
ILLINOIS														X	
INDIANA		X			X			X				X°			X°
IOWA	X°													X	
KANSAS			X°					X						X	
KENTUCKY		X					X				X				X
LOUISIANA	X 30 D				X			X		X				X	
MAINE															
MARYLAND	X 90 D													X	
MASSACHUSETTS		NA												X	
MICHIGAN	X°										X			X	
MINNESOTA	X 10 D													X	
MISSISSIPPI		X						X			X			X	
MISSOURI			X°						X°	X°		X°			
MONTANA														X	
NEBRASKA														X	
NEVADA														X	
NEW HAMPSHIRE												X	X		
NEW JERSEY															
NEW MEXICO			X°										X		
NEW YORK	X 45 D				X		X				X			X	
NORTH CAROLINA	X° 30 D			X°			X			X				X	
NORTH DAKOTA															
OHIO		X					X			X	X				X°
OKLAHOMA	X 30 D			X			X				X			X	
OREGON							X							X	
PENNSYLVANIA															X°
PUERTO RICO															
RHODE ISLAND		NA					NA			NA		NA			X
SOUTH CAROLINA							X°				X				X°
SOUTH DAKOTA		X					X			X		X	X		
TENNESSEE	X 15 D								NA			NA	X		
TEXAS	X°					X°	X°					X°			X°
UTAH														X	
VERMONT	X° 50 D								NA	X		NA		X	
VIRGIN ISLANDS															
VIRGINIA			X°						X°			X°			X
WASHINGTON	X 2 D			X 12 M			X				X				X°
WEST VIRGINIA														X	
WISCONSIN			X°						X°			X°			X
WYOMING									X			X			X

I. LAWS   A. Independent Adoption Laws (cont.)

Item / State	14. Must be "informed consent" name of adoptive parents on document at time signed by birth parent			15. Consents to be issued before court			15a. Consent to be executed before court; birth mother must appear at hearing			15b. Consent to be executed before court; both birth parents must appear at hearing		
	YES	NO	OTHER	YES	NO	OTHER	YES	NO	OTHER	YES	NO	OTHER
ALABAMA		X						X			X	
ALASKA		X						X			X	
ARIZONA		X			X				NA			NA
ARKANSAS		X			X							
CALIFORNIA	X					X°			X°			X°
COLORADO		X				X°		X		X°		
CONNECTICUT												
DELAWARE			X				X			X		X
DIST. OF COLUMBIA												
FLORIDA		X		X								
GEORGIA		X			X			X			X	
GUAM												
HAWAII		X		X					X°			X°
IDAHO		X				X°	X			X		
ILLINOIS		X		X								
INDIANA		X		X				X			X	
IOWA		X		X				X			X	
KANSAS		X		X				X			X	
KENTUCKY		X				X			X			X
LOUISIANA		X		X				X			X	
MAINE				X								
MARYLAND		X		X				X			X	
MASSACHUSETTS		X		X					NA			NA
MICHIGAN		X		X								
MINNESOTA	X			X				X			X	
MISSISSIPPI		X		X				X			X	
MISSOURI		X		X			X				X	
MONTANA	X					X						
NEBRASKA	X			X								
NEVADA	X			X								
NEW HAMPSHIRE		X		X						X		
NEW JERSEY												
NEW MEXICO	X			X								
NEW YORK		X		X				X			X	
NORTH CAROLINA	X°			X				X			X	
NORTH DAKOTA						NA						
OHIO		X				X°			X°			X°
OKLAHOMA	X			X			X°			X°		
OREGON		X		X				X			X	
PENNSYLVANIA		X		X					NA			NA
PUERTO RICO												
RHODE ISLAND		X		X								
SOUTH CAROLINA		X		X								
SOUTH DAKOTA		X		X			X				X	
TENNESSEE			X°	X								
TEXAS		X		X				X			X	
UTAH		X					X°			X		
VERMONT		X		X				X		X		
VIRGIN ISLANDS												
VIRGINIA	X			X								
WASHINGTON								X		X		
WEST VIRGINIA		X		X								
WISCONSIN			X			X°			X			X
WYOMING			X	X					NA			NA

I. LAWS   A. Independent Adoption Laws (cont.)

State	15c. Consent to be executed before court; birth and adopt. parents must appear at hearing			16. Agency investigation needed *prior to* placing in independent adoption		
	YES	NO	OTHER	YES	NO	OTHER
ALABAMA		X			X	
ALASKA		X			X	
ARIZONA			NA			X°
ARKANSAS					X	
CALIFORNIA			X°			X°
COLORADO		X				X°
CONNECTICUT						
DELAWARE			X			X
DIST. OF COLUMBIA						
FLORIDA				X		
GEORGIA		X			X	
GUAM						
HAWAII			X°		X	
IDAHO		X			X	
ILLINOIS				X		
INDIANA		X				X
IOWA		X		X		
KANSAS		X			X	
KENTUCKY			X	X		
LOUISIANA		X		X		
MAINE					X	
MARYLAND		X		X		
MASSACHUSETTS			NA	X°		
MICHIGAN						X
MINNESOTA		X			X	
MISSISSIPPI		X			X	
MISSOURI		X		X		
MONTANA				X		
NEBRASKA					X	
NEVADA				X		
NEW HAMPSHIRE				X		
NEW JERSEY						
NEW MEXICO				X		
NEW YORK		X		X		
NORTH CAROLINA		X			X	
NORTH DAKOTA						
OHIO			X°	X		
OKLAHOMA		X		X°		
OREGON		X			X	
PENNSYLVANIA			NA	X		
PUERTO RICO						
RHODE ISLAND						X
SOUTH CAROLINA			X	X		
SOUTH DAKOTA		X		X		
TENNESSEE						
TEXAS		X			X	
UTAH		X			X	
VERMONT		X			X	
VIRGIN ISLANDS						
VIRGINIA	X				X	
WASHINGTON		X		X		
WEST VIRGINIA					X	
WISCONSIN			X	X		
WYOMING			NA		X°	

I. LAWS   B. Child-Placing Agencies Licensed in Your State That Allow:

State	1. Out-of-state licensed C.P. agency to conduct adoptive studies			2. Out-of-state licensed C.P. agency to accept relinquishments/receive child for placement			3. Out-of-state licensed C.P. agency to make adoptive placement			4. Out-of-state licensed C.P. agency to provide post placement supv.			5. Out-of-state licensed C.P. agency to: OTHER		
	YES	NO	OTHER	YES	NO	OTHER	YES	NO	OTHER	YES	NO	OTHER	YES	NO	OTHER
ALABAMA	X			X			X			X					X
ALASKA	X				X			X			X				
ARIZONA		X			X				X°		X				
ARKANSAS	X			X			X			X					
CALIFORNIA		X			X			X			X			X	
COLORADO		X			X			X			X				
CONNECTICUT	X°			X			X			X					
DELAWARE			°	X			X					°			
DIST. OF COLUMBIA															
FLORIDA		X		X				X			X				
GEORGIA		X		X				X			X				
GUAM															
HAWAII		X		X				X			X				
IDAHO		X		X			X				X				°
ILLINOIS		X		X				X°			X				
INDIANA		X		X				X°			X				
IOWA		X		X			X				X				
KANSAS		°		X			X				X			X	
KENTUCKY		X				X°	X				X				X°
LOUISIANA		X		X			X				X				
MAINE		X		X			X				X				
MARYLAND	X			X			X			X					
MASSACHUSETTS		X		X				X			X				
MICHIGAN		X		X				X			X				
MINNESOTA		X		X				X		X					
MISSISSIPPI	X			X			X			X					
MISSOURI		X		X				X		X					
MONTANA															
NEBRASKA	X			X					°	X					
NEVADA		X		X			X				X				
NEW HAMPSHIRE		X		X				X		X					°
NEW JERSEY															
NEW MEXICO		X		X			X			X					
NEW YORK		X°			X°			X°			X°			X	
NORTH CAROLINA		X		X				X			X				
NORTH DAKOTA															
OHIO		X		X				X			X				
OKLAHOMA		X		X				X			X			X	
OREGON		X		X				X			X				
PENNSYLVANIA	X			X			X					X°			
PUERTO RICO															
RHODE ISLAND		X		X			X				X				
SOUTH CAROLINA		X		X			X				X				
SOUTH DAKOTA			X°			X°		X°				X°			
TENNESSEE		X°				X°		X°				X°			X°
TEXAS		X°				X°		X°				X°			
UTAH		X		X			X				X				
VERMONT		X		X			X			X					
VIRGIN ISLANDS															
VIRGINIA		X		X			X				X				
WASHINGTON		X		X			X				X				
WEST VIRGINIA		X		X				X			X				
WISCONSIN		X°		X			X				X°				X
WYOMING			NA			NA			NA			NA			NA

I. LAWS   C. Adoption Proceedings

State	1. Non-residents may file adoption petition in state			2a. Adoption petitioners must personally appear at court at petition filing			2b. Adoption petitioners must personally appear at court in finalization			3a. Agency investigation/ report to court required in all adoption; or			3b. Agency investigation/ report to court required in independent adoptions		
	YES	NO	OTHER	YES	NO	OTHER	YES	NO	OTHER	YES	NO	OTHER	YES	NO	OTHER
ALABAMA	X			X					X				X		
ALASKA		X		X			X				X			X	
ARIZONA		X				X	X			X			X		
ARKANSAS	X												X		
CALIFORNIA		X		X			X			X					
COLORADO		X		X					X°	X°	X	X°			X°
CONNECTICUT		X					X°			X					X°
DELAWARE		X		X				X		X					NA
DIST. OF COLUMBIA															
FLORIDA	X					X°				X°	X		X		
GEORGIA		X		X			X				X		X		
GUAM															
HAWAII	X			X			X		X°	X		X°			°
IDAHO		X		X			X				X		X		
ILLINOIS		X		X			X		X°				X		
INDIANA	X°					X°			X°	X			X		
IOWA	X			X			X				X		X		
KANSAS	X			Judge's Discretion						X			X°		
KENTUCKY		X		X			X			X			X		
LOUISIANA	X°			X			X			X			X		
MAINE	X					X		X		X			X		
MARYLAND		X°				X		X			X		X		
MASSACHUSETTS	X			X			X			X			X		
MICHIGAN	X			X				X		X					NA
MINNESOTA		X		X			X			X°			X°		
MISSISSIPPI		X					X					X°			°
MISSOURI	X			X			X			X			X		
MONTANA		X						X					X		
NEBRASKA		X		X			X			X			X		
NEVADA		X				X	X			X					
NEW HAMPSHIRE	X			X					X°		X		X		
NEW JERSEY															
NEW MEXICO		X		X						X			X		
NEW YORK	X			X			X			X					
NORTH CAROLINA		X		X				X		X			X		
NORTH DAKOTA															
OHIO	X								X°	X°			X		
OKLAHOMA		X		X			X			X			X		
OREGON			X°	X					X°	X		X°	X		
PENNSYLVANIA	X			X			X			X			X		
PUERTO RICO															
RHODE ISLAND	X			X			X			X			X		
SOUTH CAROLINA	X			X			X			X			X		
SOUTH DAKOTA		X		X			X				X		X		
TENNESSEE		X		X				X				X°	X		
TEXAS	X			X					X°	X			X		
UTAH		X		X			X				X			X	
VERMONT	X			X			X				X			X	
VIRGIN ISLANDS															
VIRGINIA			X°	X				X			X		X		
WASHINGTON		X		X			X						X		
WEST VIRGINIA		X		X			X			X			X		
WISCONSIN		X		X			X			X			X		
WYOMING		X		X			X								

I. LAWS   C. Adoption Proceedings (cont.)

Column groups:
- **3c.** Agency investigation/report to court required in *relative adoptions (including stepparents)*
- **3d.** Agency investigation report to court required in *agency adoptions*
- **4a.** Interlocutory decree required *all adoptions; or*
- **4b.** Interlocutory decree required *independent adoptions*
- **4c.** Interlocutory decree required *relative adoptions (including stepparents)*

State	3c YES	3c NO	3c OTHER	3d YES	3d NO	3d OTHER	4a YES	4a NO	4a OTHER	4b YES	4b NO	4b OTHER	4c YES	4c NO	4c OTHER
ALABAMA		X		X				X		X				X	
ALASKA		X		X				X			X			X	
ARIZONA	X			X				X		X				X	
ARKANSAS		X		X											
CALIFORNIA								X		X			X		
COLORADO			X°	X			X°			X°			X°		
CONNECTICUT	X°			X											
DELAWARE	X			X				X		X				X	
DIST. OF COLUMBIA															
FLORIDA		X		X				X		X				X	
GEORGIA		X		X				X		X				X	
GUAM															
HAWAII			°	X				X		X				X	
IDAHO		X		X				X		X				X	
ILLINOIS				X				X		X				X	
INDIANA	X			X					X	X				X	
IOWA		X		X				X		X				X	
KANSAS		X°		X				X		X				X	
KENTUCKY	X			X				X		X				X	
LOUISIANA	X			X				X		X			X		
MAINE		X		X											
MARYLAND	X			X				X		X				X	
MASSACHUSETTS	X			X				X	NA			NA			NA
MICHIGAN	X			X			X								
MINNESOTA	X°			X°					NA			NA			NA
MISSISSIPPI		X°				X°		X			X				X
MISSOURI	X			X			X			X			X		
MONTANA															
NEBRASKA	X			X											
NEVADA								X		X				X	
NEW HAMPSHIRE		X		X				X		X				X	
NEW JERSEY															
NEW MEXICO	X°			X			X			X			X		
NEW YORK															
NORTH CAROLINA	X			X				X		X				X	
NORTH DAKOTA															
OHIO		X°		X				X		X				X	
OKLAHOMA	X°			X			X°			X			X		
OREGON	X		X°	X		X°	X			X				X	
PENNSYLVANIA		X		X					NA			NA			NA
PUERTO RICO															
RHODE ISLAND	X			X			X			X			X		
SOUTH CAROLINA	X			X				X		X				X	
SOUTH DAKOTA			X	X				X		X				X	
TENNESSEE				X				X		X					
TEXAS	X			X				X		X				X	
UTAH		X			X			X		X				X	
VERMONT		X		X				X		X				X	
VIRGIN ISLANDS															
VIRGINIA			X°	X				X		X					X°
WASHINGTON			X°	X			X			X			X		
WEST VIRGINIA	X							X		X				X	
WISCONSIN	X			X							X				X
WYOMING				X			X								

State	4d. Interlocutory decree required in agency adoptions — YES	NO	OTHER	5a (1). Final order in independent adoption can be entered: there is min. time requirement — YES	NO	OTHER	5a (2). Final order in independent adoption is *no less than:*	5b (1). Final order in relative adoption can be entered: there is minimum time requirement — YES	NO	OTHER	5b (2). Final order in Relative adoption in *no less than:*
ALABAMA	X			X			6 M	X			6 M
ALASKA		X		X				X			
ARIZONA			X	X			6 M	X			6 M
ARKANSAS				X			6 M				
CALIFORNIA			X°			X°				X°	
COLORADO	X°			X			6 M	X			6 M
CONNECTICUT								X			90 D
DELAWARE		X				NA		X°			
DIST. OF COLUMBIA											
FLORIDA		X					90 D	X			90 D
GEORGIA		X					60 D	X			60 D
GUAM											
HAWAII		X				X°				X°	
IDAHO		X		X	X		30 D	X			30 D
ILLINOIS		X		X			6 M				
INDIANA		X				X°				X°	
IOWA		X		X			180 D	X			
KANSAS		X		X			30 D	X			30 D
KENTUCKY		X				X				X	
LOUISIANA			X	X			6 M	X			6 M
MAINE											
MARYLAND		X		X°			15 D	X°			15 D
MASSACHUSETTS			NA	X°			6 M				
MICHIGAN						NA		X			
MINNESOTA			NA	X			3 M	X			3 M
MISSISSIPPI		X			X				X		
MISSOURI	X			X			9 M	X			9 M
MONTANA				X				X			
NEBRASKA				X			6 M	X			6 M
NEVADA		X		X			6 M	X			6 M
NEW HAMPSHIRE	X			X			6 M		X		
NEW JERSEY											
NEW MEXICO	X			X°			90/120 D	X°			90/120 D
NEW YORK					X		6 W	X			6 W
NORTH CAROLINA	X			X			12 M°		X		
NORTH DAKOTA											
OHIO		X				X°	6 M			X°	6 M
OKLAHOMA	X			X			NA	X			NA
OREGON		X									
PENNSYLVANIA			NA	X			40 D	X			40 D
PUERTO RICO											
RHODE ISLAND	X			X			6 M	X			6 M
SOUTH CAROLINA		X		X			6 M			X	
SOUTH DAKOTA		X		X			6 M	X			6 M
TENNESSEE		X		X			12 M	X			6 M
TEXAS		X		X°				X			
UTAH		X		X			6 M	X			12 M
VERMONT		X		X			6 M	X			6 M
VIRGIN ISLANDS											
VIRGINIA		X		X			9 M				
WASHINGTON	X				X				X		
WEST VIRGINIA		X		X			6 M	X			6 M
WISCONSIN			X	X			6 M	X			6 M
WYOMING				X			6 M	X			6 M

State	5c (1). Final order in agency adoption can be entered: there is minimum time requirement. YES	NO	OTHER	5c (2). Final order in agency adoption in no less than:	6. Specific number of supervisory visits are required prior to finalization YES	NO	OTHER	6a. If yes, give number of visits.
ALABAMA	X			6 M	X			2
ALASKA	X				X			2
ARIZONA	X			6 M	X			once a month
ARKANSAS					X			
CALIFORNIA	X°				X			4ag; 2bp; 2pt
COLORADO	X				X°			1
CONNECTICUT	X			90 D		X		
DELAWARE	X°			6 M to 1 Y	X			3
DIST. OF COLUMBIA								
FLORIDA	X			90 D	X			2
GEORGIA	X			60 D	X			
GUAM								
HAWAII			X°			X		
IDAHO	X			w/6 M sup.	X			6
ILLINOIS	X			6 M			X	1/M, after 3 M: quarterly
INDIANA			X°			X		
IOWA	X			180 D			X	No but IDHS policy = 3
KANSAS	X			30 D		X		
KENTUCKY			X			X	X	3 usually made
LOUISIANA	X			6 M	X			2
MAINE			X		X			varies
MARYLAND	X°			15 D		X		
MASSACHUSETTS					X			
MICHIGAN	X				X			
MINNESOTA	X			3 M		X		
MISSISSIPPI		X				X		3 in 6 M or 4 in 12 M
MISSOURI	X			9 M	X			12
MONTANA	X					X		
NEBRASKA	X			6 M				
NEVADA	X			6 M	X			3
NEW HAMPSHIRE	X			6 M	X			3
NEW JERSEY								
NEW MEXICO	X°			90/120 D	X			over 1 Y = 10; under 2 Y = 3
NEW YORK	X			6 W		X		
NORTH CAROLINA	X			12 M°				not req.; 4 usually made
NORTH DAKOTA								
OHIO			X°	6 M	X			4 Y
OKLAHOMA		X		NA			X	
OREGON								
PENNSYLVANIA	X			40 D			NA	
PUERTO RICO								
RHODE ISLAND	X			6 M	X			
SOUTH CAROLINA		X				X		
SOUTH DAKOTA	X			6 M	X			2
TENNESSEE	X			6 M			X	
TEXAS	X					X		
UTAH	X			6 M	X			3
VERMONT	X			6 M	X			3
VIRGIN ISLANDS								
VIRGINIA	X			6-1/2 M	X			3
WASHINGTON		X			X			1
WEST VIRGINIA	X			6 M	X			4
WISCONSIN	X			6 M	X			
WYOMING	X			6 M	X			

Placements That Must be Made Through The ICPC

State	1. Our state fixes responsibility for cost of planning responsibilities for placement			2. Local P.A. will provide birth parent counseling			3. Local P.A. will provide and assist birth parent complete ICPC-100A			4. Local P.A. will package complete materials on child, parent, and other relatives			5. Local P.A. will conduct prospective adoptive parent assessment		
	YES	NO	OTHER	YES	NO	OTHER	YES	NO	OTHER	YES	NO	OTHER	YES	NO	OTHER
ALABAMA	X			X			X			X			X		
ALASKA		X		X			X			X				X	
ARIZONA		X		X				X			X		X		
ARKANSAS	X			X				X		X					X
CALIFORNIA	X					X°			X°			X°	X		
COLORADO		X		X			X					X°			X°
CONNECTICUT			X°	illegal					X°			X°			X°
DELAWARE		X				°			°			°			X°
DIST. OF COLUMBIA															
FLORIDA	X			X			X			X			X		
GEORGIA			X°				X°			X			X		
GUAM															
HAWAII		X				°				X°		X°			X°
IDAHO		X				°	X			X			X		
ILLINOIS				X°			X°			X°			X°		
INDIANA		X				X°			X°			X°			X°
IOWA				X					X°		X			X	
KANSAS		X		X			X					°			X
KENTUCKY		X		X			X			X			X		
LOUISIANA		X		X				X		X					X°
MAINE	X°			X			X			X			X		
MARYLAND		X				X°			X°		X				X°
MASSACHUSETTS				X			X			X			X		
MICHIGAN				X			X					X°			X°
MINNESOTA		X				°	X		°	X			X		
MISSISSIPPI		X					X°			X°					X°
MISSOURI				X			X					X		X	
MONTANA		X		X			X					X		X	
NEBRASKA				X				X				X		X	
NEVADA		X		X			X			X			X		
NEW HAMPSHIRE		X		X			X			X					X°
NEW JERSEY															
NEW MEXICO	X			X			X			X				X	
NEW YORK				X			X			X			X		
NORTH CAROLINA		X		X			X			X			X		
NORTH DAKOTA				X			X			X			X		
OHIO	X			X			X			X			X		
OKLAHOMA		X		X			X			X			X		
OREGON						X°	X°			X°					X°
PENNSYLVANIA		X				X°			X°						X°
PUERTO RICO															
RHODE ISLAND				X			X			X			X		
SOUTH CAROLINA				X				X		X			X		
SOUTH DAKOTA	X			X			X					X		X	
TENNESSEE		X				X°	X°			X°			X		
TEXAS				X					X°	X				X	
UTAH		X		X				X		X			X		
VERMONT		X		X			X			X				X	
VIRGIN ISLANDS															
VIRGINIA							X°			X°					X°
WASHINGTON				X				X				X		X	
WEST VIRGINIA		X		X			X					X	X		
WISCONSIN		X		X								X°			X°
WYOMING		X		X			X			X			X		

II. POLICIES/REGULATIONS   A. Independent/Relative Placements That Must be Made Through The ICPC (cont.)

State	6. Independent licensed S.W. allowed to provide services: #2 through #5 on previous page			7. Licensed private C.P. agencies can/will provide services: #2 through #5 on previous page			8. Local P.A. charge service fees for #2 through #5 on previous page			8b. Amount of fees
	YES	NO	OTHER	YES	NO	OTHER	YES	NO	OTHER	
ALABAMA		X		X				X		
ALASKA	X			X				X		
ARIZONA			X	X			X			$150
ARKANSAS	X			X				X		
CALIFORNIA		X			X			X		
COLORADO		X				X°	X			$35/hr. – max. $500
CONNECTICUT		X				X°			X°	varies
DELAWARE		X		X				X		
DIST. OF COLUMBIA										
FLORIDA		X		X				X		
GEORGIA		X		X				X		
GUAM										
HAWAII		X		X				X		
IDAHO	X			X			X			
ILLINOIS		X		X				X		
INDIANA		X		X			X			varies
IOWA	X				X		X			
KANSAS	X			X					X	$55/hr.
KENTUCKY		X			X	X	X			
LOUISIANA		X		X				X		
MAINE		X		X°			X°			
MARYLAND		X		X				X		
MASSACHUSETTS			°			°		X		
MICHIGAN		X				X°		X		
MINNESOTA		X		X			X			varies
MISSISSIPPI			X°	X					X	depends on income
MISSOURI		X		X			X			
MONTANA		X		X				X		
NEBRASKA	X				X					
NEVADA		X			X		X			
NEW HAMPSHIRE		X		X				NA		
NEW JERSEY										
NEW MEXICO	X			X				°		
NEW YORK	X			X			X			
NORTH CAROLINA		X		X				X		
NORTH DAKOTA		X		X			X			
OHIO		X		X				X		
OKLAHOMA	X			X			X			$250
OREGON		X		X°						$670
PENNSYLVANIA		X		X					X°	varies
PUERTO RICO										
RHODE ISLAND		X		X				X		
SOUTH CAROLINA	X			X					°	
SOUTH DAKOTA	X			X			X			
TENNESSEE		X		X				X		
TEXAS	X°			X				X		
UTAH		X		X						
VERMONT		X		X				X		
VIRGIN ISLANDS										
VIRGINIA		X		X				X°		
WASHINGTON	X°			X				X		
WEST VIRGINIA	X			X				X		
WISCONSIN		X		X				X		
WYOMING			NA	X				X		

II. POLICIES/REGULATIONS   B. Independent/Relative Placements—Sending State Compact Administrators

State	1. Will process and forward 100A and other materials prior to child's birth			2. Will request local P.A. involvement and services of IIA. #1–#4 prior to birth			3. Our state law provides for fixing the responsibility for cost of returning child to sending agency		
	YES	NO	OTHER	YES	NO	OTHER	YES	NO	OTHER
ALABAMA	X			X				X	
ALASKA	X			X				X	
ARIZONA	X				X			X	
ARKANSAS	X			X				X	
CALIFORNIA	X					X°		X	
COLORADO	X					X°		X	
CONNECTICUT									
DELAWARE									
DIST. OF COLUMBIA									
FLORIDA	X			X				X	
GEORGIA	X			X					
GUAM									
HAWAII	X			X				X	
IDAHO	X			X				X	
ILLINOIS		X		X°					
INDIANA			X		X			X	
IOWA	X					X°		X	
KANSAS	X				X			X	
KENTUCKY	X		X	X				X	
LOUISIANA	X			X				X	
MAINE	X			X				X°	
MARYLAND	X					X°		X	
MASSACHUSETTS		X		X					
MICHIGAN			X			X°			
MINNESOTA	X			X					
MISSISSIPPI	X					X		X	
MISSOURI	X				X				
MONTANA	X			X			X		
NEBRASKA	X				X				
NEVADA	X			X			X		
NEW HAMPSHIRE	X				X			X	
NEW JERSEY									
NEW MEXICO		X			X		X		
NEW YORK	X			X					
NORTH CAROLINA	X			X				X	
NORTH DAKOTA	X			X					
OHIO			X°	X			X		
OKLAHOMA									
OREGON	X				X				
PENNSYLVANIA	X				X			X	
PUERTO RICO									
RHODE ISLAND	X			X					
SOUTH CAROLINA	X			X				X	
SOUTH DAKOTA	X				X			X	
TENNESSEE	X			X				X	
TEXAS			X°		X				
UTAH	X			X				X	
VERMONT	X				X			X	
VIRGIN ISLANDS									
VIRGINIA		X				X°			
WASHINGTON	X				X				
WEST VIRGINIA	X			X				X	
WISCONSIN			X°			X°		X	
WYOMING	X			X				X	

NOTES ON STATE CHARTS

This section presents additional explanations of the responses in the charts. The explanations were provided by individual states. They are identified by chart question number and have not been abridged or edited.

Also included is a state code citation for each state's corresponding adoption statute. This information will direct laypeople to the legal material they seek. For the most current information *always* check the annual supplement provided with each statute code.

Alabama

I.(A)(10)(a)   Sometimes

Adoption Laws: go to: Vol. 15, pg. 818. The pertinent material is in Chapter 10, Section 26, Section 1-10.

Alaska

II.(A)(7)   State is planning to implement fees in the future.

Vol. 5, Title 25, Chapter 23, Sections 10-240, pg. 27.

Arizona

I.A.6   Compensation is allowed to the birth mother for "... reasonable and necessary expenses ..." The statute does not prohibit the compensation being paid directly to her, assuming "compensation" includes within its meaning, reimbursement for expenses.

I.(A)(14)   Adoptive home must be certified by the court.

I.(B)(3)   Through ICPC, placement may occur, but supervision is by Arizona agency.

I.(C)(2)(a)   No one need *appear* at petition filing. The lawyer may mail it to the court if he or she so chooses.

I.(C)(2)(b)	Statutes require petitioner and child to appear ". . . unless the court orders otherwise."
II.(A)(7)	$150 charged by Juvenile Court in Phoenix.

Vol. 2, Title 8, Chapter 1, Section 101-128, pg. 965.

Arkansas

Vol. 5A, Title 56, Chapter 2, pg. 35 (of 1985 supplement).

California

I.(A)(6)	Limited to maternity connected medical or hospital and necessary living expenses of mother preceding and during confinement as an act of charity. Itemized report to court.
I.(A)(6)(a)	No maximum; must be reasonable.
I.(A)(7)(b) & (c)	Consents may be taken only after child is born, the mother has been medically discharged from the hospital, the petition has been filed and the petitioners and child have been seen and interviewed if the adoption is to take place in California. If adoption is to take place in another state, that state's laws and regulations will be followed except that consent will not be taken before birth or before mother is medically discharged from the hospital.
I.(A)(10) & (11)	Consent cannot be revoked after signing without court approval up until the granting of the adoption which is usually not less than 180 days from the filing of the petition but is usually longer. There are no interlocutory decrees in independent adoptions.
I.(A)(13)	Consents are taken before a judge only if the Indian Child Welfare Act applies in

	which case both birth parents must appear but not the adopting parents.
I.(A)(6)	Only to meet ICPC requirements. No preplacement evaluation required for independent adoptions when all parties reside in California.
I.(C)(4)(d)	Only when child is eligible for Adoption Assistance Program.
I.(C)(5)(a)-(c)	In independent and relative adoptions (excluding stepparent) there is technically no time limit except that the state department or one of the eight delegated licensed county agencies is given 180 days to make its report to the court on its investigation with its recommendation.
	In stepparent adoptions there is *no* time limit on how long the probation or welfare department has to make its investigation but the adoption cannot be granted until the report is filed.
	In agency adoptions, the petition is not filed until the agency is ready to consent to the adoption and it may be calendared any time after filing.
II.(A)(1),(2),(3)	On request of birth parent or receiving state.
II.(B)(2)	If requested by receiving state.

Civil Code Part 3, Vol. 6, Title 2, Chapter 2, pg. 459.

Colorado

I.(A)(1)-(3)	Parent placement only.
I.(A)(10)(a)-(e)	All Colorado relinquishments are court hearings. There is a ten-day appeal period after the hearing which must be on basis of improper procedures and not just a change of mind.
I.(A)(13)	Although Colorado courts may honor consents from other states, where it is

	legal for a child to be made available for adoption by consent, most judges will honor other states' laws but there have been problems over them accepting the process of terminating the father's rights in other states. The judge may ask for interim action.
I.(A)(13)(b)	Some courts permit father to sign a waiver. If only birth mother is present, usually father's rights are terminated through the Uniform Parental Act or Dependency Neglect filing.
I.(A)(14)	No adoptive investigation. If child is coming into the state, the family must obtain a family care home license prior to placement. This is not required if placement is intrastate.
I.(C)(2)	Two hearings required. Courts vary on requiring presence of adoptive petitioners at both hearings.
I.(C)(3)	Required by statute only for agency adoptions. Most courts require it for all other adoptions *except* stepparent—which are excluded from requiring a report.
I.(C)(4)	*Not* an interlocutory decree. A court order is issued at first hearing which is a certificate of approval of placement.
I.(C)(6)	For older children in public agency: Once weekly during first two months of placement; monthly until finalization afterwards. Rule is a state department one and not statutory.
II.(A)(3)	Forms given to parent to complete.
II.(A)(4)	Only with an order of the court of jurisdiction ordering the agency to do so.
II.(A)(6)	Will if there is an order of the court of jurisdiction.

| II.(B)(2) | If child is leaving state, will request local county to counsel parent(s) but not enforceable. If the child is coming into the state, no adoptive assessment unless there is a court order. A family home license is required for Colorado families. |

Vol. 8B, Article 4, Title 19, pg. 559.

Connecticut

I.(A)(1)-(14)	Private adoptions are illegal.
I.(B)	Another state's licensing agency must be approved by Connecticut D.C.Y.S. licensing division before entering to practice or place a child.
I.(C)(2)(b)	Unless waiver is accepted by court.
I.(C)(3)(b)	Illegal in state.
I.(C)(3)(c)	Stepparent may be waived.
I.(C)(4)	No.
II.	Independent adoptions are illegal in Connecticut. A recent Attorney General's opinion on outgoing independent adoptions indicates Connecticut Compact Office should not be involved in independent adoptions to your state—no Connecticut public or private agencies are to assist with any independent placements. If relative placement falls under Connecticut relative adoption relationship, Connecticut ICPC will assist in outgoing and incoming requests.

Vol. 21, Chapter 778, pg. 243.

Delaware

Private adoptions are not legal within state.

| I.(C)(5)(b)(1) | Child must have been in home one year before a petition can be filed. |

I.(C)(5)(c)(1)	Child must have been in home six to twelve months prior to the petition being filed. Once petition is filed, judge can act on it anytime.

Vol. 8, Title 13, Chapter 9, Section 1-29, pg. 63.

Florida

I.(A)(10)(a)-(b)	Only when the court finds the consent was obtained by fraud or duress.
I.(A)(6)(b)	Florida statute allows the prospective adoptive parent to pay for actual prenatal care and living expense of the birth mother, as well as actual living and medical expense of such mother for a reasonable time, not to exceed thirty days after the birth of the child.
	All of the items listed under (6)(b) could be construed to be living expenses or medical expenses. Attorney fees are limited to five hundred dollars, unless higher fee is approved by the court.
I.(C)(2)(a)-(b)	Not addressed in statute.

Vol. 16, Title 19, Chapter 8, Section 1-9, pg. 401.

Georgia

Vol. 16, Title 19, Chapter 8, Section 1-19, pg. 401.

Hawaii

I.(A)(4) & (5)	Law spells out that "proper person not forbidden by law" may place or receive an individual for adoption (usually a doctor or minister or attorney).
I.(A)(6)	Law is silent regarding compensation to birth mother.
I.(A)(10)(b)-(e)	After child has been placed for adoption unless approved by the court.
I.(A)(13)(b) & (c)	Unless expressly excused by the court.

I.(C)(2)(b)	Unless expressly excused by the court.
I.(C)(5)	As early as the same day decree granted if under unusual circumstances and attorney prepares and files final document with the court.
II.(A)(1)-(4)	As agency workload permits.

Vol. 7, Title 31, Chapter 578, pg. 401.

Idaho

I.(A)(9)(b)	No time limit following birth.
I.(A)(13)	By agencies.
I.(B)(5)	Work through Idaho-licensed agencies.
II.(A)(1)	Depends on availability of staff.

Vol. 3, Title 16, Chapter 15, pg. 350. Also: Vol. 4, Title 18, Chapter 15, pg. 92.

Illinois

I.(A)(6)(b)	Clothing and travel are not specified in statutes. "Other" expenses include those related to the adoption.
I.(A)(7)(a)	Father only.
I.(A)(10)(b)	Unless good cause shown for waiver.

Vol. Domestic Relations, Chapter 40, Section 1501-1529, pg. 385.

Indiana

I.(A)(6)(a)	If approved by court.
I.(A)(6)(b)	Clothing—if approved by court.
I.(A)(7)(c)	State law makes no specification as to when a consent may be taken after the birth of the child.
I.(A)(8)	Adoption Code requires consent of putative father; if paternity established, legal father must consent. Juvenile Code requires consent of alleged or adjudicated

	father when a petition is filed to voluntarily terminate parental rights.
I.(A)(10)(e)	Consent may not be withdrawn after adoption is finalized.
I.(A)(11)	Consent can be revoked prior to finalization if the court finds the person seeking the withdrawal is acting in the best interest of the adoptee and the court so orders.
I.(A)(14)	Prior agency approval in an in-state adoption may be waived by the court.
I.(B)(3)	Unless placement is made through the ICPC.
I.(C)(1)	Effective September 1, 1987, non-residents may file a petition in a state court if they are petitioning to adopt a hard-to-place child.
I.(C)(2)(a & b)	Law makes no specification regarding personal appearance.
I.(C)(4)(a)	Interlocutory decrees used only in Title IV-E Adoption Assistance cases in order to initiate adoption assistance payments.
I.(C)(5)(a)-(c)	After a period of supervision by a licensed private agency or county welfare department, length of supervision is at discretion of court.
II.(A)(1)-(4)	Public welfare departments will assist if they have sufficient staff and time, otherwise will refer to licensed private agency.
II.(A)(2)	State Department of Public Welfare regulation does not allow birth parents to be sending agent, must be a county welfare department or licensed child-placing agency or court-appointed guardian. Therefore, birth parents do not complete 100As.

II.(B)(1)   State ICPC will forward 100A and other materials prior to birth but will not sign 100A.

Vol. Family Law, Title 31, Article 3, pg. 151.

Iowa

I.(A)(4) & (5)   Only legal guardian appointed by court at termination of parental rights proceeding.

I.(A)(10)(b)   Ninety-six hours without cause after signing release of custody.

I.(A)(13)   The court has already terminated parental rights. The guardian gives consent to adopt.

II.(A)(2)   Direct placements are prohibited. Must be a termination of parental rights and guardian appointed.

II.(B)(2)   Only in public agency placements.

Vol. 39, Chapter 600, Section 1-25, pg. 611.

Kansas

I.(C)(2)(a) & (b)   Judge's discretion.

II.(A)(7) $55 an hour for No. 4, if no other agency resources found.

Vol. 4, Title 59, Article 21, pg. 588.

Kentucky

I.(A)(1)(2)   Independent adoptions require the approval, prior to placement, of Kentucky Commission of Social Services. To receive a favorable home evaluation with attachments and recording of interviews, both parents, unless absolutely impossible, are required.

I.(A)(4)(iii)-(vii) May participate as intermediaries.

I.(A)(5)	Although the birthparent may allow an intermediary to physically place the child, it is always considered that the person making the placement is only the person having the legal right to do so, i.e., the birth parents.
I.(A)(7)	Child selling or buying is prohibited by law.
I.(A)(6)(b)	Attorneys accepting fees for placements where birth mother is compensated may be operating like an unlicensed agency; issue being examined.
I.(A)(7)(b)(vii)	Birth parents retain parental rights until they are terminated in a Circuit Court action—may be done as part of finalization procedure.
I.(A)(8)	Unless father is unknown or files a disclaimer.
I.(A)(10)	All sections of #10 are subject to judicial decree.
I.(A)(11)	All sections of #11 are subject to judicial decree.
I.(A)(13)	Consents need not occur in court, but they may not be binding. Terminations of parental rights, which are binding, occur only in Circuit Court.
I.(B)(1)	Permission is sometimes granted to agencies in bordering states.
I.(B)(5)	In all adoption cases, the final hearing may be set after the report of the guardian ad litem, if any, and the report of the Department of Social Services required by statute, is filed. After adoption petition is filed, the department is granted 180 days to file a report in the case of the department placements and Kentucky-licensed agency placements, if petition was filed immediately after placements. In all other adoptions, the depart-

ment is allowed (by code) ninety days to file the report to the court.

I.(C)   By policy, after placement, supervisory visits are provided in agency placements monthly until adoption is finalized, or more often when there is need. In special-needs placements, intensive after placement services are provided daily or weekly, if needed.

II.(A)(5)   Not addressed in Kentucky statutes.

II.(A)(6)   Prohibited by administrative regulation. The state public agency is charged by statute to investigate all independent adoptive placements.

II.(B)(1)   Provided in-state requirements have been met.

Vol. 9, Section 199, pg. 106.

Louisiana

I.(A)(8)   If both are legal parents, consent to the adoption must be secured by each.

I.(C)(1)   While adoptive parents may have multiple residents, if adoptive parents or birth mothers are not domiciled in Louisiana they cannot file in Louisiana.

I.(C)(4)(d)   Interlocutory decree is not necessary in public agency adoptions.

II.(A)(4)   Local public agencies will conduct an assessment of prospective adoptive parents under "special" circumstances, i.e., financial inability of parents to have service provided privately.

Vol. 3, Title 9, Section 421, pg. 173.

Maine

I.(C)(2)   Varies.

I.(C)(5)(c)(1)   Usually six to twelve months.

II.(A)(7)   May, if new law passes this session.
Vol. IDA, Title 19, Chapter 9, Section 531-538, pg. 449.

Maryland

I.(C)(5)(a)-(c)   In no less than fifteen days after child's
                              birth, regardless of type of placement.

II.(A)(1) & (2)   If requested.

II.(A)(4)   If ordered by the court.

II.(B)(2)   If private agency.
Vol. Family Law, Chapter 5, Section 307, pg. 88.

Massachusetts

                              Note: Independent adoptions are not sta-
                              tutorily legal, but "identified" adoptions
                              are—decisions are based on a case-by-
                              case analysis. Consult Massachusetts De-
                              partment of Social Services.

I.(C)(5)(a)   Although court can waive this.
Vol. 33, Chapter 210, pg. 348.

Michigan

I.(A)(2)   Only if legal in sending state and to be
                              finalized in the sending state. A Michi-
                              gan-licensed, private, child-placing agency
                              must complete the home study and agree
                              to provide post-placement supervision
                              prior to the adoptive placement.

I.(A)(9)   Only for relatives within the fourth de-
                              gree of consanguinity.

II.(A)(3)   Only in relative adoptions.

II.(A)(4)   Only in relative adoptions.

II.(A)(6)   Licensed private agencies may accept pa-
                              rental relinquishment and place child for
                              adoption in agency-selected home.

II.(B)(2)   Only for relative adoptions.

Vol. 20, Chapter 555.24, Section 27.3178, pg. 199.

Minnesota

I.(A)(1)	Independent placement means a proposed or actual non-agency placement of a child by a parent or unlicensed third party with persons not related to the child within the third degree of consanguinity. Court may, however, waive agency placement requirements if it is in the child's best interest to do so.
I.(A)(1)-(3)	Consideration given in extended relative and personal family friend situations when pre-adoption counseling is provided.
I.(C)(3a)(3b)(3c)(3d)	Court may waive the requirement of an investigation and report to court.

Vol. 17, Chapter 259.21, pg. 249. Other child-placing regulations appear in Chapters 245, 257, and 260. Also see Minnesota Statutes, Vol. 5.

Mississippi

I.(C)(3)(a)	Investigations may be waived at court's discretion.
II.(A)(1)-(5)	Independent/Relative placements are usually handled by licensed private agencies. When a request is received by the local welfare department, the local agency can complete the adoptive study if ordered to do so by the Chancery Court. If an attorney calls the ICPC office to ask that an adoptive home study be done on his clients, the attorney is referred to a private licensed child-placing agency. If an independent placement is made prior to interstate involvement, and the receiving state requests an interview with the biological parents, that request will be sent

to the local welfare department if the placing agent is not known.

NOTE: Mississippi has a law which provides for licensure of social workers.

Vol. 20, Title 93, Chapter 17, Section 1-31, pg. 453.

Missouri

I.(A)(10)(a)-(e)   Not addressed in statutes.

Vol. 24, Title XXX, Section 453, pg. 419.

Montana

I.(A)(1)-(3)   Parent.

I.(A)(6)(B)   Not defined, determined by judge.

I.(A)(7)   Not defined.

I.(A)(10)(a)   Must get court order to revoke.

I.(B)   No.

Vol. 6, Title 40, Chapter 8, pg. 777.

Nebraska

I.(A)(6)(a)   Not specified.

I.(A)(8)   If married.

I.(C)(4)   No.

Vol. 3, Article I, Chapter 43, pg. 1212.

Nevada

I.(A)(15)   Consents signed out of state must be witnessed by a state or county social worker.

Vol. 2A, Chapter 170, Section B, pg. 445.

New Hampshire

I.(A)(1)

Vol. 16, Chapter 127, pg. 4977.

New Mexico

I.(A)(10)(a)	Immediately.
I.(A)(10)(b)	If Indian Child Welfare Act: may revoke up to two years.
I.(C)(5)(a)-(c)	Ninety days if child is under one year. If child is older, then 120 days.

Vol. 7, Chapter 40, pg. 89.

New York

I.(A)(15)	New York has two types of consent: (1) Extrajudicial consents can be revoked within forty-five days of execution—they are not accepted by many New York courts; (2) consents executed before a court are irrevocable.
I.(B)(1)(4)	In cases where children are being placed through ICPC into New York, the state does not require licensed child-placing agencies in ICPC states to obtain a New York license.

Vol. 52 A, McKinney's Consolidated Laws of New York, Section 374 of the Social Services Law and Vol. 14, McKinney's Consolidated Laws of New York, Section 15-b of the Domestic Relations Law.

North Carolina

I.(C)(5)(a)(2)	Time starts after interlocutory decree.
I.(C)(5)(c)(2)	Time starts at date of placement for adoption.

Vol. 2A, Part II, Chapter 48.

North Dakota

New statutory law also provides for Open Adoptions, whereby the birth parents are allowed to select the adoptive parents for their child. (See House Bill 1242.)

Vol. 3A, Title 14, Chapter 15, pg. 199.

Ohio

I.(A)(6)(a) & (b)	All expenses related to adoptions are subject to approval by the Ohio Probate Court.
I.(A)(11)	Subject to court approval.
I.(A)(13)(a)-(c)	Discretion of Ohio Probate Court.
I.(C)(2)(a)-(b)	Discretion of Ohio Probate Court.
I.(C)(3)(c)	Discretion of Ohio Probate Court.
II.(B)(1)	ICPC-100A is not sent until child is born. Background information on birth parents is sent.

Title 31, Chapter 3107, Section 1-19, pg. 92.

Oklahoma

I.(A)(7)(c)	Only under ICWA.
I.(A)(13)(a)	If parent is over sixteen years of age.
I.(A)(13)(b)	If parent if below sixteen years of age.
I.(A)(14)	Court may order agency investigation.
I.(C)(3)(c)	Stepparent adoption excluded.
I.(C)(4)	May be waived by court.
I.(C)(6)	Yes under policy but no under law.

Title 10, Chapter 2A, Section 60.1-.23, pg. 151.

Oregon

I.(A)(4)	Attorneys can assist birth parents in independent adoptions but not act as intermediaries.
I.(A)(6)(a) & (b)	Disclosure statement required of all moneys paid or estimated to be paid by the petitioner for fees, costs, and expenses related to the adoption including all legal, medical, living and travel expenses.
I.(A)(7)(c)	No limit.
I.(A)(10)(a)	Final decree.

I.(C)(1)	Birth/legal parent or one of the petitioners must have six months' residence.
I.(C)(2)(b)	Usually—up to the judge.
I.(C)(3)(a)-(d)	Agency may waive in certain circumstances.
II.(A)(1)-(4)	Subject to local public agency decision/workload.

Vol. 1, Chapter 109, Section 305, pg. 1169.

Pennsylvania

I.(A)(6)(b)	Adoption law states all fees must be disclosed in report of intermediary; court is free to take exception to excessive amounts.
I.(A)(8)	Both parents, if known, must give consent, or be terminated by court action.
I.(A)(10)(a)	Termination of parental rights and/or entry of final decree.
I.(A)(11)	A consent to an adoption may only be revoked prior to the earlier of either the entry of a decree of termination of parental rights or the entry of a decree of adoption.
I.(B)(4)	If finalization is to occur in Pennsylvania, home study and supervision must be done by a licensed Pennsylvania agency.
I.(C)(4)	Not used in Pennsylvania.
II.(A)(1)	Not a mandated service. Discretion of agency.
II.(A)(2)	Not a mandated service. Discretion of agency, intermediary assists birth parents.
II.(A)(3) & (4)	Not a mandated service. Sometimes will if requested.
II.(A)(7)	If services provided a fee is charged. Amount unknown—varies county to county.

Vol. 1, Title 1, Section 1-7, pg. 1.

Rhode Island

I.(A)(7)(a)
But note that a parent cannot voluntarily terminate right to consent until fifteen days after birth.

I.(A)(8)
Unless parental rights have been terminated.

I.(A)(10)(a)-(e)
Not addressed in statute.

Vol. 3A, Title 15, Chapter 7, Section 1-10, pg. 79.

South Carolina

I.(A)(11)
Requires a court order.

Vol. 8A, Title 20, Chapter 7, Section 1650-1890, pg. 465.

South Dakota

I.(A)(7)
Birth parents must legally relinquish parental rights via court action.

I.(A)(10)
Parental rights are terminated in court. On a voluntary termination, there is a thirty-day appeal period. Appeal must be based on procedural error or parent's claim of duress/coercion—not simply one's change of mind.

The adoptive family must have an approved home study prior to the placement of a child. State law specifies who may provide home study services. They may only be done by (1) licensed child-placing agency, (2) licensed social worker with two years of adoption experience, or (3) by the South Dakota Department.

I.(B)(1)-(5)
An agency must provide verification of licensure in the home state. In addition, any social worker employed by an out-of-state agency must be licensed by the South Dakota Board of Social Work Ex-

aminers in order to practice in South Dakota.

Vol. 9A, Title 25, Chapter 6, Section 1-20, pg. 89 and
Vol. 9A, Title 26, Chapter 4, Section 15.

Tennessee

I.(A)(6)(a)	Law not specific.
I.(A)(6)(b)	Not to exceed thirty days after birth.
I.(A)(12)	Law not specific.
I.(B)(a)(5)	Only with prior authorization by this office. Proof of licensure is required.
II.(A)(1)-(4)	Not required but advisable if help needed or if requested by court or attorney.

Vol. 6A, Title 36, Chapter 1, Section 101-140, pg. 182.

Texas

I.(A)(4)(ii)-(vii)	Placements may only be made lawfully as these individuals are managing conservators.
I.(A)(6)(a)	Compensation may not be allowed to birth mother except for medical or legal fees. These may be paid directly or indirectly.
I.(A)(9a)(9b)(9c)	See Texas Family Code for definition of consent.
I.(A)(11)	Court may waive.
I.(A)(12)(a)-(d)	An affidavit of relinquishment of parental rights which designates as managing conservator of the child the Texas Department of Human Services or an agency authorized by TDHS to place children for adoption is irrevocable. Any other affidavit of relinquishment is revocable unless it expressly provides that it is irrevocable for a stated period of time not to exceed sixty days after the date of its

	execution. See Texas Family Code, Section 15.03 and 16.05.
II.(A)(2)	Experienced DHS staff may provide this service but not all staff are familiar with ICPC policy on private adoptions.
I.(B)(1)(2)(3)(4)	Texas law is silent on this.
I.(C)(2b)	Unless the court allows one of the parents, due to hardship, to not appear.
I.(C)(5a1)	Court may waive this requirement.
II.(B)(1)	ICPC-100A is not sent until child is born. Background information on birth parents is sent.

Vol. 2, Family, Chapter 16, Section 1-12, pg. 506.

Utah

| I.(A)(8) | Father must register if illegitimate birth. |
| I.(A)(13)(a) | If independent. |

Vol. 9A, Title 78, Chapter 30, Section 1–15, pg. 352.

Vermont

Vol. Family Law, Chapter 15, pg. 437.

Virginia

I.(A)(6)	Virginia law does not specifically address the issue of compensation to the birth mother. The law does require that the report to court include information about fees paid by the adoptive parents.
I.(A)(10)(a)-(e)	Consent may be revoked any time prior to the issuance of the final order of adoption upon proof of fraud or duress.
I.(C)(1)	Non-residents may file petition in the Circuit Court where the agency which placed the child is located.
I.(C)(3)(c)	The court *may* issue a final order of adoption without requiring an investiga-

tion in stepparent adoptions when the following conditions exist:

1. One of the birth parents is deceased.

2. The non-petitioning parent consents in writing to the adoption.

3. The mother swears the identity of the putative father is unknown.

4. When a single person who has adopted later marries and desires his/her spouse to adopt.

I.(C)(4)(c)   Interlocutory orders may be omitted in the following:

1. Agency placements.

2. If child has resided in home of petitioner continuously for at least three years prior to the filing of the petition.

3. If child was legally adopted according to laws of foreign country and if child has lived with petitioners for one year or if child has lived with petitioners for six months and an agency has provided supervision.

4. If child was placed from a foreign country and has lived with petitioners for six months and supervision has been provided.

II.(A)(1)-(3)   If parent(s) request; No. 3 (above) is a local agency decision.

II.(A)(7)   Not yet.

II.(B)(2)   Mother must request service.

Vol. Domestic Relations, Chapter 12, Section 101-117, pg. 320.

Washington

I.(A)(4) & (5)   Licensed physicians and lawyers are exempt from the state licensing law. They may arrange and make placements.

254

I.(A)(6)   Not specified; reasonable fee for service may be charged.

I.(A)(11)   Within one year after court approval.

I.(C)(3)(c)   Only if petitioner seeks to adopt child of petitioner's spouse.

Title 26, Chapter 33, Section 10-901, pg. 491.

West Virginia

Vol. 14, Chapter 48, Article 4, Section 1-15, pg. 429.

Wisconsin

I.(A)(4) & (5)   A casual intermediary is allowed. However, persons making repeated placements must seek licensure. Placement is authorized only by the court so an intermediary or any other person may not aid in physical placement without consent of court.

I.(A)(6)(in general) It is a Class E felony for an individual to place or agree to place his or her child for adoption for anything exceeding the actual cost of hospital and medical expenses of the mother and the child incurred in connection with the child's birth, and of legal and other services rendered in connection with the adoption.

(A)(6)(a)   Amount is reported (itemized) to court which decides appropriateness of payment in kind.

I.(A)(7)   A full termination of parental rights is required.

I.(A)(9)   Notice of hearing is sent to a child aged twelve years or older and the minor to be adopted shall attend the adoption hearing if fourteen years or older unless court orders otherwise. The wishes of the child of any age is one of the factors the court shall consider in determining the

	best interests of the child in a termination of parental rights hearing.
I.(A)(10)(a)-(e)	Full termination of parental rights required. Termination of parental rights appeal must be filed within twenty days of termination of parental rights order.
I.(A)(13)	Full due process termination of parental rights required *before* child is placed.
I.(B)	Arrangements for service within Wisconsin must be made with a licensed Wisconsin agency.
I.(B)(4)	Full due process termination of parental rights required for all types of adoptions.
II.(A)(2)	Either local public agency, hired to do home study, if any, or attorney hired by mother or prospective adoptive parents helps file 100A. In fact, attorneys often do this because agencies are not available to assist in placements out of Wisconsin.
II.(A)(3)	A full Wisconsin termination of parental rights is required, so the attorney for mother or a guardian appointed by court has to help make legal arrangements for termination of parental rights *and* collect social and medical information. Wisconsin law ultimately requires that the *court* see to it that social and medical/genetic information is collected.
II.(A)(4)	Only Milwaukee County Department does public adoptions in Wisconsin (except that state staff do special-needs placements). Studies must be done by Milwaukee County D.S.S. or a *private* agency.
II.(B)(1) & (2)	Will send information in advance, if available, otherwise after birth of child. A private agency will usually be asked to assist.
II.(C)(1)(c)(5) & (C)(2)	Usually will be an agency. Because of

the termination of parental rights requirement, an agency will be appointed guardian and will initiate 100A.

Vol. 6, Chapter 48, Subchapter XIX, Section 81-975, pg. 749.

Wyoming

Vol. 3, Title 1, Chapter 22, Section 101-115, pg. 298.

Resources for Adoptive Parents

The following list is a resource for people who are considering adoption or who would like to have contact with a parent support group. Because the United States has a mobile and changing society, there may be changes in address, membership, purposes, or programs offered. When you write for information, be sure to enclose a self-addressed, stamped envelope.

ADOPTIVE PARENTS COMMITTEE, INC.
210 Fifth Avenue
New York, NY 10010
This organization has the facts on U.S. adoption agencies including fees and the availability of children. It can also help with independent adoptions and identify organizations that facilitate adoption of foreign children.

AID TO THE ADOPTION OF SPECIAL CHILDREN (AASK)
Box 11212
Oakland, CA 94611
This nonprofit foundation was established to help older, minority, and handicapped children find permanent homes. It can give you information and provides supportive services such as financial aid, counseling, and legal material. AASK has a number of local chapters.

BETHANY CHRISTIAN SERVICES
901 Eastern Avenue, NE
Grand Rapids, MI 49503
Adoption services is only one of the many kinds of family services offered by this organization. Bethany has a number of branch offices across the country.

CHRISTIAN CHILDRENS' SERVICES OF CALIFORNIA
P.O. Box 345
Norwalk, CA 90651-0345
This organization provides adoption and counseling programs.

COUNCIL OF ADOPTIVE PARENTS (CAP)
67 Wood Haven Drive
Rochester, NY 14625
This organization is involved in many different aspects of adoption including conferences on the older child and on racial identity.

EVANGELICAL CHILD AND FAMILY AGENCY
1530 North Main Street
Wheaton, IL 60187
This agency places both babies and hard-to-place children in evangelical Christian homes. They also have a foster-care program. Placements are made only within a fifty-mile or so radius of Chicago.

HOLT ADOPTION PROGRAM
P.O. Box 2880
Eugene, OR 97402
This organization is mostly concerned with the adoption of children from Asian countries.

INTERNATIONAL CONCERNS COMMITTEE FOR CHILDREN
911 Cypress Drive
Boulder, CO 80303
This organization is especially concerned with foreign and special-needs children. It provides counseling and agency information. There are branches in Newton, Maine, and in Allentown, Pennsylvania.

NATIONAL COMMITTEE FOR ADOPTION (NCFA)
2025 M Street N.W.
Washington, D.C. 20036
This organization lobbies Congress on behalf of adoption agencies, is active in public information programs regarding adoption, and serves as a clearinghouse for adoption information. It also publishes the *Adoption Factbook: United States Data, Issues, Regulation, and Resources*, which is the most complete and reliable source of adoption

statistical and other information, as the federal government no longer maintains statistics and other hard data regarding adoption.

NORTH AMERICAN COUNCIL ON ADOPTABLE CHILDREN
1340 Connecticut Avenue, NW, Suite 229
Washington, D.C. 20036

This organization concentrates on special-needs children. It can provide the names of parent groups in your area and can put you in touch with local adoption agencies.

ORGANIZATION OF FOSTER FAMILIES FOR EQUALITY AND REFORM (OFFER)
239 Vincent Drive
East Meadow, NY 11554

This organization is concerned with all aspects of foster care and is working to support legislation and policy that will keep foster care from becoming a dead end for children.

ORGANIZATION FOR A UNITED RESPONSE (OURS)
3307 Highway 100 N., Suite 203
Minneapolis, MN 55422

This is a national support group that reports which agencies are taking applications for foreign and U.S. adoptions, what kinds of children are available, and the costs and requirements. It can also provide a list of parent support groups.

PARENTS FOR LOVING ADOPTIONS NOW (PLAN)
P.O. Box 667
McMinnville, OR 97128

PLAN is involved with multiracial and international adoptions and the needs of special children. It accepts adoption applications.

PERMANENT FAMILIES FOR CHILDREN
Child Welfare League of America, Inc.
67 Irving Place
New York, NY 10003

This organization can provide the names of adoption agencies in your area. It publishes *Waiting Children*, which features the pictures and biographies of special-needs children.

SOUTH AMERICAN MISSIONARY EVANGELISM (S.A.M.E.)
P.O. Box 2344
Bismark, ND 58502
This organization provides domestic and foreign adoption services, though it focuses on placing abandoned children of Brazil and Colombia.

SOUTH BAY ADOPTION SUPPORT GROUP
21405 Roaring Water Way
Los Gatos, CA 95030
This organization, as its name implies, is a support group run by and for adopting families in California's San Francisco Bay Area. In addition to support group sessions, this group publishes a monthly newsletter and provides leads to prospective birth mothers and adoption attorneys and counselors, as well as how-to advice.

APPENDIX C

Suggested Reading

These books will offer extra information on several aspects of the adoption experience. Books written from a Christian perspective are so noted.

Arms, Suzanne. *To Love and Let Go*. New York: Avon Books, 1983.

Case histories of birth mothers, with a strong advocacy of open adoption.

Dobson, James C. *Hide and Seek*. Old Tappan, N.J.: Revell, 1974.

Not specifically concerned with adoption, but written from a Christian perspective with a very good section on self-esteem of children.

Feingold, Ben F. *Why Your Child Is Hyperactive*. New York: Random House, 1974.

An informative book on hyperactivity in children, written by a medical doctor.

Martin, Cynthia D. *Beating the Adoption Game*. San Diego: Oak Tree Publications, 1980.

Discussion of all aspects of adoption, pointing out some of the abuses and red tape encountered by people wishing to adopt.

Phillips, Carolyn. *Our Family Got a Stepparent*. Ventura, Calif.: Regal, 1979.

A book for children explaining the problems and feelings that can be expected when a new parent is introduced into the family.

Wender, Paul H., and Estelle Wender. *The Hyperactive Child*. New York: Crown, 1978.

An excellent book on the problem of hyperactivity written by two experts in the field.

Wheeler, Bonnie. *Challenged Parenting*. Ventura, Calif.: Regal, 1982.

> Explained by subtitle: A practical handbook for parents of children with handicaps. Written from Christian perspective.

Wishard, Laurie, and William Wishard. *Adoption, the Grafted Tree*. New York: Avon Books, 1979.

> Practical, psychological, and legal information about all aspects of the adoption process.

APPENDIX D

Read-Aloud Section for Children

WHO AM I?

My name is Rebecca and I am twelve years old. I live in a white, two-story house with my mom and dad and my big brother, Mark. We have twenty-one pets—two dogs, two cats, and seventeen goldfish.

Mark is a pretty nice brother most of the time. We play checkers and Monopoly together. He is teaching me how to throw a football the right way. He helps me with my homework when everyone else is too busy. But sometimes Mark teases me, and sometimes he gets grouchy. When he gets angry, he calls me names. Then I don't like him so much.

Mom says that Mark and I are just like any other brother and sister. I guess that is true in most ways, but in one way we are different. Mark and I are adopted.

Ever since I can remember I have known about being adopted. Here is how it happened in our family. When Mom and Dad got married, they wanted to have children. They waited and they waited. For seven years they waited, but no baby was born to them. But Mom and Dad didn't give up. They knew that there were people who had children they could not take care of, so my parents decided they would adopt some of those kids.

My brother, Mark, was first. Because he was two years old when he came into the family, he can't remember anything about it. Mom and Dad liked Mark so much that they decided they wanted another child. So they applied one more time at the adoption agency. Then they started waiting again. They waited for two years. At last they got the phone call they had been waiting for. The agency had a baby ready for them—a baby girl. That baby was me!

When Mom and Dad brought me home, Grandpa was waiting in the driveway with his movie camera. He took pictures of me sleeping in the car, of Mom trying to feed me while I was sleeping, of everyone holding me while I was sleeping. I sure was a lazy kid!

I love to look at those pictures. Mark was very funny. He kept petting my head as if I were a little kitten. You would never believe how tiny I was!

One time I asked Mom if she and Dad were disappointed that they had to adopt babies instead of having some born to them. She seemed surprised that I asked. She said, "Disappointed? We are glad! Why, if we had been able to have babies, we would never have gotten you and Mark."

In a lot of ways Mom and Dad and Mark and I are alike, but we are all different, too. My hair is darker than anyone else's, and it is curly. Mom is the only one with blue eyes, and Mark is the only one with freckles. I am pretty good in music—I can play the piano and the flute. My brother is awful in music, but he is a really good football player.

Mom and Dad say that they are not musical or athletic. But they want Mark and me to grow in our own ways and to develop the talents God gave us. That is why they encourage us so much. They bought me a piano so that I can take lessons. They never miss any of Mark's games. Mom says our birth parents must have been very talented to have made children like us.

Most of the time I don't even think about being adopted. Sometimes, though, things happen that put questions in my mind. Then I feel bothered till I get some answers.

One thing that made me start wondering was a school project that our class is doing. We have been tracing our roots, finding out all about our great-grandparents and what countries our ancestors came from and all that. I don't know any of that stuff about me. I don't even know about the woman I was born to.

I talked to my family about the project. My mom said

she didn't know very much about my birth parents either, except that the woman was part Spanish. I guess that is where I got my dark hair.

Then my dad said, "When you were adopted into our family, you became a part of us. Our ancestors are your ancestors."

"Yeah," Mark said. "Just like Mom and Dad's parents are our grandparents."

That makes a lot of sense to me. I know my grandma and grandpa really well. They live only two miles away from us. And no one could ever love me more than they do. They have time for me when everyone else is too busy to be bothered. They tell me stories about when they were young, and they like it when I ask them questions.

One day I asked my grandpa if he thought Mom and Dad could really understand what it felt like to be adopted. You know what he said? He said, "Rebecca, every one of us in this family is adopted—you and Mark, your mom and dad, Grandma and me—all of us."

I could hardly believe it! Dad looks just like the pictures in our family album of Grandpa when he was younger. Could it be true that my dad was adopted?

Grandpa must have seen the surprised look on my face, because he started to laugh. He said, "I guess I should explain what I mean. We were not all adopted by the parents who raised us. We were all adopted by God. Remember when you asked Jesus into your heart? That's when you were adopted into God's family. Since each one of us has done that, all of us are God's adopted children."

So adoption was all God's idea in the first place. We made our family the same way he made his. I like that.

Another time when I was wondering about things, Grandma told Mark and me some stories from the Bible about children who were a little bit like us. They were not raised by the people they were born to, either. One of them was Samuel. From the time he was a little boy he lived in the temple with Eli the priest. Eli took care of him and taught him about God.

Joseph was another one. He was kidnapped by his own brothers and taken away to Egypt to live as a slave. Can you imagine that? My brother would never treat me like that! Not even when he's angry with me. But in the end it all worked out well for Joseph and his family, because Joseph was able to save them all from starving to death during a famine.

Mark's favorite story is the one about Moses. Moses' own family loved him a lot, and they wanted to keep him with them. But they could not because of the cruel Egyptian king. After he was adopted by the king's own daughter, however, Moses was raised to be a prince in the royal palace of Egypt. Many years later he was able to get all his people out of that country.

Esther is my favorite. She was the Jewish girl who was raised by her cousin and who became queen of Persia. Even though it meant risking her own life, she went before the king and begged him to spare the lives of her people, the Jews, which he did. If it had not been for Esther, they all would have been killed.

All these stories really happened. You can find them in the Bible and read them for yourself if you want to. The exciting thing about these Bible people is that God put each one of them in just the right place for a special reason. One time I asked Mark if he thought that God had put us with our mom and dad for a very special reason, too. He just shrugged his shoulders and said, "Who knows?" I guess he doesn't think about things like that as much as I do.

But I could not stop wondering about it. I asked my parents what they thought. Dad said, "God does everything for a special reason, Rebecca. He put you in our family because that's exactly where he wants you."

"But why?" I asked.

"Because this is where you belong," he said. "Because God made you to be our daughter."

WHO ARE MY REAL PARENTS?

I know a little girl named Jenny who lives two houses away from me. She just started kindergarten. My friend Linda and I walk with her to school every morning.

Jenny is adopted too, but she doesn't look anything like her parents. Her mother has blond, curly hair; her father has red hair. Both of them have blue eyes. But Jenny's hair is straight and black, and her dark brown eyes are almond-shaped. That's because Jenny is half Korean. Her parents adopted her from an orphanage in Korea.

One day after Linda and I dropped Jenny off at the kindergarten room at school, Linda said, "Poor Jenny! I would hate to be adopted like her. Just think, she will never know who her parents are."

I said, "That's silly, Linda! She lives with her parents."

"That is not what I mean," Linda said. "I mean that she will never know her *real* parents. You know, the ones she was born to."

I knew exactly what Linda meant, and I decided it would be best to drop the subject right there. I have heard all that stuff about "real parents" before. Kids are always asking me, "Don't you even know your real parents?" And I will admit that I have done a lot of thinking and wondering about that myself.

It used to be that whenever I talked about the people I was born to, I would call them my "real parents." I would say things like "I wonder what my real mother looked like?" or "Were my real parents German or English or Italian or what?"

My mom and dad always tried to answer my questions the best they could. But my dad would always end up by saying, "Rebecca, we are your real parents. We took you as our daughter when you were just a tiny baby. After you were with us for almost a year, we were finally able to go to court and sign the papers that made your adoption final. We will never forget that day because that was when the judge finally declared you legally our child. That is how you came into our family. But to us it is no different than if you had been born to Mom and me."

I know that whole story. I have heard it lots of times. But sometimes I wonder, is it really the same as if I had been born to them? There are times when my parents do things that seem very unfair to me. They make me eat broccoli and spinach and other foods I hate when it would be just as easy to cook things I like, such as pizza or spaghetti. I have to go to bed when I am not the least bit tired. I have to do homework and practice the piano when all of my friends are playing and watching television. And that's another thing: I don't get to watch nearly as much television as other kids do. The thing is, my friends' parents let them do a lot of things that my mom and dad won't let me do.

Last year I loved horses more than anything else in the whole world. One night before dinner I asked my dad very nicely if he would please get me a horse of my own. He said no. I tried to explain how important it was to me and that I would take care of the horse and would even help find a place to keep it. But my dad just said, "Now, Rebecca, we have been through all this before. We cannot afford a horse." Then he went right back to reading his newspaper. He wouldn't even talk about it with me.

All of a sudden I got really mad and I yelled, "I wish I lived with my real parents! I'll bet that they would get me a horse! They'd care about the things that are really important to me!"

"You sure are dumb, Rebecca!" my brother Mark said. "You are living with your real parents right now. What do you think Mom and Dad are?" I could tell from his voice and the way he was looking at me that he was pretty disgusted.

Mom and Dad didn't say anything. I could not think of anything to say either, which is pretty unusual for me. So we all just stood there and looked at each other. I was feeling pretty bad about yelling at my dad like that. I was also embarrassed and confused. Finally I ran to my room, where I could be alone. I needed time to think things over.

Just what are real parents anyway? Are they the ones who make a child, or are they the ones who raise him? If someone's parents look really different from them like Jenny's parents do, can they still be real parents?

While I was wondering about all this, I suddenly remembered something I had read in *The Velveteen Rabbit*, about what it means to be real. I went to my bookcase, found the book, and looked up that part so that I could read it again.

The Velveteen Rabbit is about a stuffed toy rabbit whose greatest wish is to be real. The problem is, he doesn't really understand what being real means. So the rabbit asks the wise old toy horse who lives in the playroom with him just what "real" is. This is what the horse said:

"Real isn't how you are made. It's a thing that happens to you. When a child loves you for a long, long time, not just to play with, but REALLY loves you, then you become real.

"It doesn't happen all at once. You become. It takes a long time. That's why it doesn't often happen to people who break easily, or have sharp edges, or who have to be carefully kept."[1]

I think that horse really knew what he was talking about, don't you? What he said is just as true for parents as it is for toys. Parents who are not able to keep their children are the kind of people who break easily. It takes a lot of time and a lot of work to become real parents. It takes a lot of love, too. And do you know what? That sounds a lot like my own mom and dad.

Mom and Dad are the ones who did all of the no-fun stuff for me like changing my diapers and feeding me in the middle of the night and taking care of me when I was sick. They are the ones who have always helped and encouraged me. They are the ones who took me to Sunday school and church and helped me to understand about being God's child.

Mom and Dad are the ones who put up with me when I am grumpy and comfort me when I am sad. They listen to me when I need to talk. They answer me when I ask them questions. They leave me alone when I need to be left alone. They are always there when I need them. They love me just

---

[1]Margery Williams, *The Velveteen Rabbit* (New York: Avon, 1975). Used by permission.

because I am me. Doesn't that sound like real parents to you? It does to me.

It was silly for me to think that my birth parents could love me more than my mom and dad do. When I really think about it, I know that they never could.

I am glad that those first parents gave me life. Without them I would not even be alive. But they are not my real parents. My real parents are my mom and dad, the ones who love me and care for me every day. No matter whatever happens or how old I get, they will always be my real parents.

I wonder if Jenny is too young to understand about real parents? Someday I will tell her.

WHY WAS I GIVEN UP?

My mom and dad don't often talk about Mark's and my adoption with people outside our family. They say it is up to us to decide who we want to tell and when. Mark doesn't tell anyone. He says that it is nobody else's business. Although I don't see any reason to talk about it all the time like some kids do, I really don't care if people know.

One night when my friend Linda was sleeping over at my house, she told me that she was born in Germany. Her dad was in the army over there. Then she asked me where I was born. I said I didn't know because I was adopted. At first she didn't believe me.

"You look too much like the rest of your family to be adopted," she said.

I said, "Maybe so, but I was adopted just the same."

Then Linda asked, "How come the woman you were born to didn't keep you herself?"

I said I didn't know, which is the truth.

Actually, I've wondered that same thing myself lots of times. It is quite obvious that my birth mother didn't want me, or else she would not have given me up. But it seems as if she would have to have had a pretty good reason for not wanting me, and I surely do wish I knew what her reason was.

All the next day I thought about Linda's question. I could not get it out of my mind. When I came home from school, my mom was in the kitchen making brownies. I poured myself a glass of milk, sat down at the table, and asked, "Mom, do you know why I was given up for adoption?"

She said she did not know why.

"Maybe my birth mother was really poor," I suggested. "Maybe she could not afford to buy food and clothes and toys for me."

"That's possible," Mom said. "Still, there are many, many poor families who manage to do a very good job of raising their children. No matter how hard times get, Dad and I would never consider giving up you or your brother. We would all stick together, share whatever we had, and get by the best way we could."

"She may be dead," I suggested. "She could have died when I was born."

Mom shook her head. "No," she said. "I am sure that's not it. She is the one who signed the adoption papers, remember."

I waited a long time before I told Mom my other idea. I didn't even like to think about it myself. But finally I came right out and said it. "Maybe I wasn't cute enough for her." Even though it sounded terrible, I had to admit that it was a good possibility. If you could see me, you would know what I mean. I am not at all pretty. I am really tall and skinny—like a "bean pole," Aunt Betty says. I have bigger feet than anyone I know, and that includes my mom. To make things worse, my teeth stick out so much that I'm going to have to get braces on them next year.

When I said that, my mother stopped her work and turned around to look at me. "Rebecca," she asked, "how can you even think such a thing? You were the cutest baby I have ever seen in my whole life. Don't you remember all those darling pictures in your baby book?"

I remembered. I also remembered that many of them were pictures of me crying. That brings to my mind another possibility. Aunt Betty is always talking about what a fussy baby I was. She says that even when I was tiny, I would not eat my vegetables. As fast as my mom could spoon them into my mouth, I would spit them back out.

"I'll bet she didn't want me because I was such a bad baby," I said slowly, "always crying and making trouble for everyone."

Just then the timer on the stove started to buzz. The brownies were done. Mom took them out of the oven and cut them into neat little squares. She put the biggest and crunchiest one on a plate and brought it to me. Then she pulled up a chair and sat down beside me.

"Rebecca," Mom said, "your birth mother's decision to allow you to be adopted had nothing at all to do with what kind of a baby you were. That decision was made before you were born. She didn't have a chance to get to know you. In fact, it is very likely that she never even saw you. If she didn't know you, and probably didn't even see you, how could she possibly be disappointed with you for any reason at all? Anyway, Rebecca, you were a wonderful baby, wonderful in every way. And you have grown into a wonderful young lady. Your father and I are very proud of you, and we love you very much. We would not trade you for anyone else in the whole world!"

For a while I didn't say anything. I kept busy munching my hot brownie. Maybe my mother was right. If what she said was true, it really could not have been my fault that I was given up. What a relief that was!

After I finished the last crumbs of my brownie and my last swallow of milk, I said, "But, Mom, if the reason wasn't me, then what could it have been?"

"I know more about Mark's birth mother than I know about yours," Mom said. "Mark was older when we got him. His caseworker told us a lot about him. His birth mother tried to keep him, but she was too young to be a good mother. She was only fifteen years old, you see, and she was still in high school. She just could not earn enough money to support herself and a tiny baby, too. So she decided it would be better for everyone if she allowed him to be adopted into a family that could raise him properly. It is very possible, Rebecca, that your birth mother was in the same situation."

"Well, I wish I knew!" I said.

"So do I," Mom said. "I am sorry now that I didn't get more information from your caseworker when I had the chance. It is just that you were so little that I never stopped to think that the time would come when you would want to know things like this.

"But even though we don't know your birth mother's actual reason for giving you up, we can be certain of one thing. She must have agreed with Dad and me that it is important for you to grow up in a family with two parents who really love you and can give you a good home. Whatever her reason may have been, she surely knew that she was unable to give you the kind of home that she knew you needed. That is why she arranged for you to be adopted by a family who could. It was important to her to know that you would be happy and well cared for."

"Do you think it was hard for her to give me up?" I asked.

"I am sure of it," Mom said. "It was probably the hardest thing she ever had to do in her whole life. It must have been a very, very sad time for her. But do you know what? God used her terribly sad situation to answer your father's and my greatest prayer. He brought you into our family."

I guess my birth mother did the best thing she could do for me. I am really glad that she didn't decide to keep me when she knew that she could not take good care of me. And I surely am glad that God had a home for me to go to: a home where I am greatly wanted and loved, a home where I really belong.

Sometimes it is fun to imagine what I will be like when I am grown up. If I close my eyes I can almost see it. I will meet a really nice man who I can love forever. And he will love me, too, of course. He will be a Christian so that we can pray together and ask God to guide our lives, just like my mom and dad. We will get married and have children, or maybe we will adopt them. I am not sure about that.

But there is one thing I am sure about. I am sure that I will never, ever get myself into a sad situation as my birth mother did. I never want to have to make the decision to give up my baby.

AM I REALLY SO SPECIAL?

From the time I can first remember, people have been telling me how special I am. They still tell me that. I think they probably say the same thing to all adopted kids.

Some people say that our whole family is special and that is why God put us together in a special way. That probably sounds good to them, but I am not so sure I like it. I don't think I want to be that special. You know what it sounds like to me? It sounds like they are saying I am different from other kids, and I don't want to be different.

Lots of people say that adopted kids are "chosen" kids. Since the word "chosen" means "picked out," I always thought that was exactly what had happened—that my mom and dad had actually picked me out. I imagined that they went downtown to a big building with lots of rooms filled with baby cribs. In each crib was a tiny, newborn baby. There were babies of all kinds there: baby boys and baby girls, black babies and white babies, Indian babies and oriental babies, little ones and big ones, noisy ones and quiet ones. People could walk through all the different rooms and search through the babies until they found one that they wanted to adopt.

I imagined that my parents searched and searched, but they just couldn't find a baby that was exactly right for them. Then, tucked into a little crib over in a corner, they saw me. I was just what they wanted! So they checked me out and took me home with them.

Now doesn't that sound to you like the way a child would be chosen? Well, it isn't. But I didn't find that out until a couple of years ago. The truth is that my parents did not really choose me at all. Oh, they did choose to adopt a baby, all right, but not me. I just happened to be the one they got.

To tell the truth, it was sort of a relief to find out that I was not chosen the way I had always imagined. Being a chosen child isn't easy, you know. I always felt that I had to be exactly what my mom and dad wanted me to be. What I wanted didn't matter at all.

Even worse, I was always afraid of what might happen to me. I admit that there are many times when I disappoint my parents. I am not even close to being a perfect kid. What if my parents decided that they were sorry that they had chosen me? They just might make up their minds to take me back and choose someone else, someone they liked better.

There is another thing, too. Although I have always loved the stories about those special Bible people that my grandmother told me about—you know, Samuel and Joseph and Moses and Esther—they worried me, too. Those people were special, and they were chosen just as I was supposed to be. The problem is, every one of them did wonderful things with their lives. But what about me? I don't think that I will ever be as important as they were. I hope people don't expect me to be. If they do, I'm afraid that they are going to be awfully disappointed.

For a long time I have worried and wondered about this. Finally I decided to do what I should have done in the first place: talk it over with my mom and dad.

"People are always saying that I'm special," I said, "but I'm not sure I really understand what they mean. Do you think I am special?"

"Of course we do, Rebecca," said Dad. "You are very special. You are special to our family, and you are special to God. But there is something that you must understand. Every child in the whole entire world is special. There may be people who are not loved by a single person on earth, but even they are special to God. That is why God sent his Son, Jesus, to earth, so that everyone would have a chance to become one of God's children. And for everyone who loves

God and becomes his child through Jesus, God has a special place in his plan."

That is just what I needed to hear. Although I don't want to be any more special than other kids, I surely don't want to be any less special, either.

"But what about being 'chosen'?" I asked. "I know that you and Mom didn't really choose me, but people still call me a 'chosen child.'"

"And they are right," Dad said. "It is true that Mom and I were unable to choose a specific child to adopt. We could not do that, but God could. So we depended on him to do the choosing for us. And we are so glad and thankful that you are the one he chose."

"Do you mean that God chose me the same way he chose Moses and Esther and Samuel and Joseph?" I asked doubtfully.

"He sure did," Dad said. "Exactly the same way. God chose you to love him and to do the job he has for you to do. Of course that doesn't mean that he will give you the same kind of a job that he gave them. God doesn't give history-changing jobs like theirs to very many people, you know. He may have chosen you to be a teacher or a lawyer or a missionary, or maybe he chose you to be a veterinarian or a secretary. Maybe he wants you to be a homemaker like your mom. You see, Rebecca, the particular job that God gives you to do isn't what is really important. The important thing is whether or not you are ready and willing to do whatever it is that God wants you to do."

I like the way my dad explains things. Maybe being "special" and "chosen" are not so bad after all. In fact, I have noticed a funny thing. Lots of times I hear kids say that they wish they were adopted too. They say that then they would know for sure that their parents really wanted them. Maybe instead of only telling us adopted kids how special we are, people should be saying it to all kids. Maybe then everyone could feel special and chosen.

I am a chosen child. God chose me, and he made me a part of just the right family. I am also a very special person—

special to my family and special to God. This is just the way I like it!

WHERE DO I GO FROM HERE?

"If I were adopted, I'd want to find the people I was born to," Linda told me one day.

"Why?" I asked.

"So that I could see who they are and what they look like," she said.

I didn't say anything.

"Why don't you try to find your birth mother?" Linda asked. "That would be so exciting!"

I couldn't think of anything else to say, so I said, "If I ever did find her, I wouldn't know what to say."

In some ways I think Linda is right. Finding my birth mother does sound pretty exciting. Linda is not the only one who has suggested it to me, either. Some of my other friends have said the same thing. Even my Aunt Betty talked to me about it once.

When I asked my brother if he ever wanted to search for his birth parents, he said, "No way! Mom and Dad are the only parents I care about. I am happy with things just the way they are. Why would I want to cause any problems?"

I should have known Mark would say that. He is never curious about anything.

"Even if I did know my birth parents, it wouldn't change the way I feel about Mom and Dad," I explained to him. "They would still be my real parents, and they will always be the ones I love. Nothing will ever change that."

"But how would they know that?" Mark asked. "I mean, if you are really happy with them, why would you want to find some other parents?"

That is a good question, and I really don't know the answer to it. I guess it's just that I am curious. It seems as if I am always wondering about things: Does my birth mother look like me, skinny with sticking-out teeth, or is she beautiful? Was she awful in math when she was a kid? Does she play the piano or the flute as I do? I suppose questions like these don't seem very important to other people, but they are things that I just can't help wondering.

But there is another thing. If I ever did find out who my birth mother is and where she lives, I don't have the slightest idea what I would do about it. I mean, it would be pretty awful just to walk up and knock on her door. She probably would not even let me in. Why should she? After all, I am a complete stranger to her.

Of course, I would not actually have to go and see her. I could just write her a letter and tell her that I am happy with my family and that I am glad that she didn't keep me if she couldn't give me a good home. But then, what good would that do me? None of my questions would be answered. I would end up just as curious as ever.

"Would your mom and dad be mad if you wanted to find your first mother?" Linda asked me.

I said I didn't know. I had never asked them.

"Well, why don't you ask them?" Linda said.

And I said, "I just might do that."

But the truth is, I was afraid to ask them. What if they thought I didn't love them anymore? Or what if they felt that I didn't think they were good enough parents to me? I for sure did not want to hurt their feelings. I would not do that for anything in the world. So instead of coming right out and saying anything to my mom and dad, I just hinted around.

One time I said, "I saw a lady at the store today who sort of looked like me. I wonder if she could be related to me—maybe an aunt or something."

Another time I said to my mom, "It isn't fair for you to make me eat broccoli. It's not my fault that I hate it. My taste buds probably take after my birth parents. If I ever meet them, I am going to ask if they like broccoli, and I will bet they say no!"

I guess my mom got the idea, because she finally said, "Rebecca, I can understand your curiosity about your birth parents, about who they were and what they were like. If you have any questions you want to ask me about them, go ahead and ask. I don't mind at all. If I know the answers I will tell you. Unfortunately, though, I don't know very much. I wish I did, but I just don't."

"There are lots of times when I have questions, Mom," I said. "But I'm afraid that my questions will make you and Dad feel bad, and I don't want to do that."

"Your questions won't make us feel bad, Rebecca," Mom said. "You have a right to be curious. I certainly would be curious if I were you. I just wish that I had more information to give you."

I wish she did, too. I would really like to know what those other people were like.

When I was little I had some very strange ideas. I was sure that my birth parents were something really special— rich or famous or very important. I even thought that I might be a long lost princess or the child of some rich movie stars. I thought that I never was really given up in the first place, but that I had been kidnapped when I was a baby and given to the adoption agency. Now that I am older I know how silly that was. I suppose that if I ever do meet those people I will be disappointed at how ordinary they are.

I have seen television programs about people who actually did find their birth parents. In those shows the people always end up living happily-ever-after. But of course, those stories are just make-believe and that is the way most make-believe stories end. In real life, though, I don't think it would work out like that very often.

Mark read a story in the newspaper about a girl in college who spent years searching for her birth mother. Finally she found her. The girl was really excited, and she made a lot of plans for all the happy times she and her birth mother would have together. But things didn't work out at all the way she had planned. The woman was married by this time, you see, and she had three little children. When the girl called her on the phone, the woman got really angry, because she didn't want her husband and children to find out about that other daughter. She said that if the girl came around, it would ruin her whole life and that it was cruel and unfair for the girl ever to have searched her out in the first place. The woman told the girl never to call her again and never, ever to try to see her.

In the end the girl was very sad and very hurt. She said she wished that she had never started that search in the first place. Mark says it served her right for not being satisfied with things the way they were. I feel sorry for her anyway. I know how curious kids can get.

Probably my birth mother has a happy new life by now, too. She probably has a husband and children whom she can love and who will love her back. I hope so. If that is true, she certainly would not want me coming back and messing things up for her. It would not be fair for me to do that. When she gave me up, she gave me up for good.

Since God knows everything way before it happens, how could he possibly make mistakes? He couldn't! And since he doesn't make mistakes, then he must have put me where I belong, and that's right here with my mom and my dad and my brother. If I am already where I belong, then why would I need to know those other people from way back in my beginning?

There are still things that I wonder about, but it is only because I am curious. I don't want to find a new mother. I like my old one just fine. And I don't ever want to take the chance of making her think that she has not been a good enough mother to me, because she has.

I guess what I am saying is that I have got the very best parents right now. Why would I want to find any others?

WHAT DO OTHER KIDS SAY?

Last summer the Johnson family moved into our neighborhood. Pretty soon they started coming to our church. They have two kids: Michelle, who is one year older than I, and Jeff, who is one year younger than I. I did not know them very well, but I knew that they were adopted. They talked about it all the time.

One morning at breakfast Mom told Mark and me that

Mrs. Johnson was worried about Michelle and Jeff. Mom said Mrs. Johnson told her that they were having some kind of problems. Mrs. Johnson said it was probably because her kids were adopted.

"So what if they are adopted?" I asked. "What does that have to do with anything?"

"Mrs. Johnson seems to think that adopted children have a lot more problems than other children do," Mom explained. "She is hoping that you two can help Michelle and Jeff."

"Us?" said Mark. "What can we do?" He was talking with his mouth full again, but Mom didn't scold him.

"Once a week Michelle and Jeff have been meeting with Dr. Reed, the counselor at church," Mom said. "He has been trying to help them to understand and work out their problems. Dr. Reed thinks that if they had a chance to share their concerns with other adopted children, it might help them. At his suggestion Mrs. Johnson has invited you two— and also Steven Taylor—to meet with her children in Dr. Reed's office."

Mark didn't want to go until Mom told him that if he went, he wouldn't have to do any of his Saturday jobs. Then he suddenly decided that it wasn't such a bad idea after all.

The very next week we all got together. Dr. Reed was there, but he didn't talk much. Mark was the oldest one of the kids, and Michelle was next oldest. Steven is the same age as me, so Jeff was the youngest. Dr. Reed had the room set up with chairs for all of us, and Mrs. Johnson brought a bunch of popcorn and soda pop for everyone.

Dr. Reed started us off by asking if we thought adopted kids had more problems than other kids. Mark said no. Michelle and Jeff said yes. Steven said, "Everyone has problems. The thing is, adopted kids just have one more thing to think about." I agreed with Steven.

"It's more than that!" Michelle said in an angry voice. "Sometimes I feel like I am not even wanted at home. I don't really belong. Sometimes I feel like I am living with a houseful of strangers!"

I couldn't understand that at all. My family never seems like strangers to me.

"How can you feel that you are not wanted?" Mark asked her. "Your parents didn't have to adopt you, you know."

"But that doesn't mean they love me as much as they would if I had been born to them," Michelle said.

"I think I know what you mean," said Steven. "My little sister was born to my parents, and sometimes I can't help wondering if they love her more than they love me."

"I just wish I could know for positive sure that my parents do love me and accept me just as much as they would if I had been born their child," Michelle said.

I asked Michelle why she didn't just ask them.

She said, "Oh, I couldn't do that!"

I asked her why not. "That's what I would do. My mom says it's O.K. to wonder about things. She says she would wonder, too, if she were me."

"I always wonder about things," said Jeff. "The thing I wonder about the most is my birth parents. Sometimes I wonder if they ever think about me and wonder how I am."

"Well," I said, "even if you do ask your parents, you probably won't get all the answers you want because they won't know all the answers."

Then Michelle said, "One of the things I wonder about is why I was given up in the first place. I think it was probably because I'm ugly."

I couldn't believe Michelle was saying that. She's really a pretty girl. If only I looked like her! So I asked, "Why do you think you're ugly, Michelle?"

She said, "Because a girl at school told me so. She said, 'No wonder your birth mother gave you up. You were too ugly to keep!'"

"What do you care what she says?" Mark asked. "What does she know about it? I'll bet she was just teasing you."

"Probably so," Michelle said. "Kids are always teasing me about being adopted. One time a boy in my class said, 'I'll bet you had to be adopted because when you were born you were so ugly that your mother died of fright as soon as she saw you.' Lots of other kids have said that it is obvious that I wasn't good enough for my birth mother or she would have kept me."

"The same thing happens to me sometimes," said Jeff. "One time one of my friends got really mad at me, and he said that I was ugly and stupid and no wonder I was adopted."

"How come everyone knows that you are adopted?" Mark asked Michelle and Jeff. "You must talk about it all the time."

"So what if we talk about it?" said Jeff.

"So you are just giving the other kids something else to tease you about," Mark said.

"Everyone gets teased about something," Steven said. "If it's not about being adopted, then it's about having freckles or being dumb in math or being fat."

"Or about sticking-out teeth," I said. "The boys in my class call me 'beaver mouth.' I hate it!"

"Well, I would rather be teased about that kind of stuff than about being adopted," Michelle said.

"Then don't talk so much about being adopted. Then they will tease you about other stuff," said Mark. He was starting to sound sort of disgusted, the way he sometimes does with me.

"Adopted kids have lots of other problems, too," Michelle said, "like not feeling loved as much as kids who are born to their parents. Or feeling as if you are not as good as other kids. Or not getting along with your parents all that well."

"What is so special about those problems?" Mark asked. "Lots of my friends who are not even adopted say those very same things. You probably just think that they are special problems for adopted kids because you are adopted and those are the problems you are having."

"When things bother me, I talk them over with my mom and dad," I said. "Sometimes they can't help me, but most of the time they can."

"Not me!" Michelle said. "My parents are the ones who cause a lot of my problems. It seems as if they want to control my whole life. What I can't understand is, Why do they have to worry all the time? What is wrong with me that they can't just leave me alone?"

"If you think Michelle talks a lot about being adopted, you should hear our mom," said Jeff. "She talks about it all the time, to everyone. I just wish she didn't have to always make such a big deal out of it."

"Maybe she doesn't know it bothers you," I said. "You should tell her."

"But that might hurt her feelings," Jeff said. "I don't want to hurt her feelings."

"You could say it in a nice way," I suggested. "Not when you are angry or upset, just sometime when you are sitting around together. It really isn't fair to be angry with her about something that you have not told her bothers you."

"At least your mother is not afraid to talk about your being adopted," Steven said. "I know a boy whose parents never even told him. They just pretended he had been born to them. Then one day his cousin told him the truth. He was so surprised that he didn't believe it at first. Then he was really, really angry."

"I'd be angry, too!" Jeff said. "That's just like lying. Kids don't like parents who lie to them."

"If parents would lie about something as important as that, how could their kids believe anything they say?" Steven questioned.

"I guess since I am adopted I am glad that I know the truth," Michelle said. "But what I really wish is that I wasn't an adopted kid in the first place."

"Maybe that is why you are sometimes so mean to Mom and Dad," Jeff said to Michelle.

"Well, being adopted really upsets me!" said Michelle. I believe her. She surely did sound upset to me.

"If you were not adopted, where would you be now?" Mark asked Michelle.

That seemed like a pretty good question. I was wondering the same thing.

"You might not have a family at all," Mark told her. "Or at least you might not have one that loves you and can give you all the things you need."

"I think adopted kids should be glad they are adopted," Steven said. "Being adopted proves that your parents really wanted you. You didn't just happen to fall into your family, you know. They had to work hard to get you."

"I think that the most important thing is to be able to talk your problems over with your parents," Mark said. "Even if they can't give you answers, they can at least listen to you and find out what is bothering you. It will make them feel good to know that you want their opinion. Maybe if you talked to your mom more, she would not worry so much about you. That would solve one of your problems right there."

Then Mark said, "That's what families are for, you know: to listen to and help each other whenever they can."

Sometimes Mark surely is smart. You know what? I am really glad that he is my brother. And I am really glad that I am part of my family. In fact, I am glad I am part of both of my families—my mom and dad's family, and God's family. What more could I ask?